Sacrifice of the Innocent

jonathan r walton

Copyright © 2016 Jonathan R Walton

All rights reserved.

ISBN: 0-9794055-4-8
ISBN-13: **978-0-9794055-4-9**

ACKNOWLEDGMENTS

Special thanks to Philip Spence for helping me finish these books and staying on top of me to keep writing and promoting. Thanks to Jennifer O'Neal Pavlu for another great cover design. They get better as we go along. Thanks to my family for encouraging me to pursue my dreams. And to Hudson and Graham for always praying that daddy's books will sell.

1

The fiery Mustang blew through the red light at the intersection of Jamestown and Fourth Streets. It narrowly missed the seventy-year-old grandmother inching forward as her light turned green. Her heart was just recovering from its first erratic beat when the metallic silver Toyota Camry flew by. At least the Camry had alerted her of its passing. However, the earsplitting *booommmmpppp booommmmpppp* caused more panic than the passing of the first car. The petite, elderly woman loudly cursed and picked up her cell phone.

The Mustang jerked left onto a side street, almost slamming into a large cobalt dumpster positioned deep against the second building. The driver whipped to the right, attempting to avoid ramming it. The front end successfully dodged the bulky obstacle, but the driver overcorrected. The back end slid hard to the left, hitting the corner of the dumpster slightly behind the driver's side passenger door. The back windshield shattered, and the car momentarily stopped.

The driver frantically looked in the rearview mirror in time to see his silver pursuer push around the corner. He slammed his foot to the floor. The tires spun on the concrete for a second, leaving a burnt rubbery stench. He quickly gained traction and rocketed away.

He glanced in the mirror again. The chase car was directly behind him. He could almost make out the driver. He was vaguely familiar, as was the pursuit car.

However, it wasn't the nearness of the vehicle or the driver's identity that alarmed him most. It was the blue and red flashing lights approaching from behind. The nightmarish black Dodge Charger was vengefully unwelcoming. It could ruin everything. He yanked the wheel to the left, pushing through a small yard. The heavy car left its undeniable ruts through the plush greenery.

Back on the main drag, he looked between the buildings blurring by. Two more patrol cars where racing down the immediate side street to the right. He looked left. There appeared to be nothing there.

Water splashed above the hood of car, flooding the windshield and temporarily blinding him. The second car hit the same deep lake that had formed, its tributaries the ditches to either side, cresting from four days of rain. The police car maneuvered through the overflowing street, expertly maintaining control. Two more units passed simultaneously, only seconds behind him.

The driver of the Mustang noticed the two cruisers that had

joined the fracas. He cursed. He couldn't be taken. He couldn't be forced to answer. He'd never be forgiven. They'd kill him. Slowly and painfully. They'd punish him for the betrayal. He knew the rules.

Tears streaked down his cheeks. He cursed again. Ahead of him, a policeman scurried across the road, dragging a line behind him. The driver knew what was coming. The spikes were designed to shred the rubber from his rims. He anxiously searched.

There. Sixty feet ahead. A small opening between the hardware store and the billiard hall. He angled toward it, whipping the car hard at the last moment. The alley was just wide enough for his crimson dash to fit through. He looked back. The original pursuer made the turn, as did two of the three flashing units.

The alleyway opened, revealing an abandoned stockyard directly across the road. He couldn't turn left or right, police cruisers were moving toward him from both directions. His only choice was to ram the iron gate blocking the entrance to the empty shipyard.

The car burst through, sparks spattering from the passing of metal on metal. As he tore through, he realized his mistake. The yard was nothing more than a sandy enclosure. It had been built in the midst of a rocky, clayish canyon. He'd broken through the only entrance. He was trapped, dirt walls looming over him on every side. He checked the rearview mirror. It was too late; the yard was filling with unwanted blue and red. The Camry pulled behind him, and the driver's door immediately opened.

He floored it again, shooting forward. What do you do when you can't be taken? Where do you go when there's nowhere to run?

The only answer lay before him. Fifty yards. Beside the yellowish metal building. An old bulldozer powerfully stood its ground.

Not operated in months.

Parked.

Dusty.

Abandoned.

Waiting on someone to awaken it, to make it useful again. Sort of like him. This was the one chance he'd been given in the past ten years. No matter what, he couldn't fail them. They didn't afford anyone that luxury. He couldn't go back to the isolation. He could never go back.

He aimed his car toward the solid bucket of the iron mammoth before him. The two-foot blades extended like rusty talons at windshield level.

" Unum de multis. Nos es unus of plures. One of many," he muttered. "We are one of many."

The deafening crash caused visible reverberations in the ambiance of the industrial gorge. The talons ripped through the car. Dark smoke, half exhaust and half whirling dust, billowed from the wreckage.

The driver of the Camry darted toward the collision. A small caliber firearm clutched tightly in his right hand. Four cruisers surrounded him. The officers lunged from their vehicles, taking cover behind the rear tires and engine blocks of their units.

"Driver. Get on the ground. Drop your weapon and get down now. Driver… Drop your weapon."

The man stopped and turned toward them. His eyes were crazed, panic-stricken. Tears discolored his sandy cheeks.

Confusion.

Paranoia.

Not an altered state, merely unsure of what to do next. Things hadn't gone as planned.

"Get on the ground. Do not lift your weapon. Put it down. Place your weapon down. Now."

He dropped it at his feet.

"Driver. Move to your right. Take ten steps to your right and get on the ground."

Dazed, he awkwardly inched to his right. He'd taken five steps when someone pounced on him from behind. He hadn't seen the officer coming. Three more were on him before he could physically respond. Without hesitation, his arms were forcibly pulled behind his back.

"Sir, stop resisting. I'm going to use the taser. Stop resisting."

His body tensed, and he lay motionless. The cool steel of the handcuffs bit harshly against his skin. The tightness of the locks unmercilessly pinched his wrists. The image of the Mustang slamming into the bulldozer wouldn't leave his mind. It wasn't supposed to happen like this.

They violently sat him up. The floodgates opened, and his eyes gushed. "Noooo… noooo. He can't die. He can't… They've got my son… He's the only one who knows how to find my son."

2

The incarcerated man sat in an aluminum folding chair. He'd been blankly staring into the reflective partition for over an hour. He'd watched enough CSI to know it wasn't a mirror. It was a two-way glass. Someone on the other side was studying him. They were carefully observing his behavior. Would he panic? Get angry? Lose his composure?

The temperature had risen to between blistering hot and uncomfortably stiff. It wasn't high blood pressure. He'd forced himself to remain calm, breathing in his nose and out his mouth.

No. It wasn't a psychological trigger. It was physiological. They had turned up the heat. They were waging a mental war to see if he'd break.

He couldn't. There was too much at stake. He had to find his son. If he had to kill every one of them to leave this crummy police station, he wouldn't hesitate.

He wasn't a troublemaker. Truthfully, he'd never broken the law. Not once. Not even in adolescence. He'd lived a good life. He was considered an average man. He'd done better than many, but not as good as some. He was actively involved in his local church. A few days ago he never would've imagined being a criminal. He couldn't have imagined hurting anyone.

That had changed. He'd kill in a heartbeat. He'd murder in cold blood. He'd watch the life fade from someone's eyes. He'd be content knowing he was the reason they were sent to hell early. He'd even smile as he purchased their one-way ticket. He'd do anything to bring his son home. Anything!

On the other side of the glass, Homicide Detective Archer Madsen examined the arrest report. Two other men and a woman sat in the room as well. The first man was Todd Collins, the arresting officer. The second was Lieutenant Bradley Smith, the day shift commander of the unit on duty. The female was Dr. Regan Rees, a certified psychologist.

"We know who he is yet, lieutenant?"

"Not yet. The lead detective will be joining him shortly. He wanted to let him sit a couple hours first. It's been about that long."

"Who's the lead?"

"Conrad. His number was pulled."

Archer rolled his eyes. "You sure you want him working this one. This is the biggest case we've seen in a while, and he tends to attract attention."

"It wasn't my call Arch. The boss phoned as soon as he heard about the crash this morning. Told me to get Conrad on it immediately. Don't know why."

"Election year. His family has a lot of pull."

The lieutenant chuckled, "Well, I was trying not to think of that. Just do us all a favor and try to keep that to yourself please. For once don't speak your mind."

"I'll see what I can do."

The door on the other side opened, and a tall officer walked into the room and stood beside the suspect. He was casually handsome, with a cocky, boyish charm. He pulled up a cushioned chair and sat directly across from the detainee. He slid a small, squared bottle of water across the table. The suspect unscrupulously examined the detective before slowly fumbling with the lid. He finally got it opened and chugged the cool liquid down his parched throat.

"Thank you," he stated, as he placed the empty plastic container back down on the table.

"You're welcome… I need you're help."

"No. I need yours. I've got to get out of here. They're gonna kill my son."

"Sir. Please. One step at a time. We'll get there quickly, but I need to ask a few questions to know what I'm dealing with… ok?"

The man across the table sullenly nodded. "Please, we're wasting time. I don't have much left."

"Okay. Just focus, and we can get the prelims over quickly."

He looked across the table, maintaining eye contact. "What's your name sir?"

He was forcefully agitated, his voice growing slightly aggressive. "Seriously, you've had me in here for two hours, and you don't know my name yet. What kind of detective are you? We're wasting time."

"Sir. I'm gonna ask you to calm down… The car you were driving is registered to a private company. I've contacted them, but no one has answered. Officers are on their way to the corporate office. You have no identification on you or in your car. You've offered me no information. So it's been a slow process. If you want to speed things up, then help me out here."

"I can't. I don't even understand it myself. I only had one lead. The only link I'd been able to find, and y'all killed him."

"We didn't kill anybody. You were there. You watched him drive straight into that bucket. He wanted to die."

"I had it under control. You should have stayed out of it."

"Sir… you and your buddy turned our main road into a NASCAR track. You could have killed someone. Ultimately, you did. You were moving in excess of one hundred miles per hour down city streets. You both almost clipped a terrified old woman who was just trying to cross the road. Did you really think no one would notice?"

"I had one chance. I had to take it."

"Sir, just give me your name. I'll try to help you, but I need your name."

Dr. Regan Rees furiously scribbled into a miniscule, fine-lined notepad. Detective Madsen curiously observed. She looked over her wire rimmed glasses every few seconds.

The arresting officer seemed agitated. "Lieutenant, may I go in for a few minutes. I arrested him. He rode here in my car. He kept begging me to help him find his kid. Maybe he'll open up to me."

"Give it a shot Todd. Conrad is going nowhere fast."

Todd stood up and walked from the room. He nodded in Archer's direction as he passed. "Still coming for supper Arch? She's looking forward to seeing you."

Archer nodded and casually sat down in the corner.

The door to the room opened and the officer entered. The man in the chair lunged forward, flipping the desk over onto the detective that had been interviewing him. Todd stepped through, settling into a defensive stance against the man charging him. The man grabbed the handcuffs from the officer's gun belt, just as the officer connected with a right hand blow to the side of the face. The man staggered backward, but swung the cuffs hard against Todd's forehead as he fell. He crashed to the floor with a thud. Conrad moved from underneath the overturned table and scrambled to his feet. The assailant was already to the door. He caught it just before it closed and pushed his way into the hallway, shutting the door behind him. Conrad hit the door a half second behind him but was locked in the room.

The suspect had taken two steps when he heard the distinct click of a gun's hammer being drawn back. He slowly turned and found himself staring down the large barrel of a 357 Magnum.

"I'm begging you. Just twitch. I'm gonna plaster you all over this hallway."

"Please. I have to get out of here. You don't understand."

"I understand fine. That man you just hit is a good friend of mine. You better hope he's okay. If not, they'll be picking up pieces of you for the next two months."

The man cried. "I don't wanna hurt nobody. I don't. Please. Let me go."

The Lieutenant stepped into the hallway with a shotgun. The man started to run. Without hesitating, the lieutenant pulled the trigger. The gun kicked in his hands, and the man buckled. He was lifted from the ground to land four feet back. He helplessly gasped for air. Archer pounced and cuffed him.

The Lieutenant immediately got on the radio. "We need two buses now. Got two men down in here."

He opened the door and entered the interrogation room. "Is this how you handle interrogations Conrad? No wonder you were suspended. I want you upstairs and in my office. Now!"

A few minutes later, the man lay on a stretcher with an oxygen mask over his face. He was still struggling to catch his breath. The paramedic moved to the Lieutenant.

"He's gonna be fine. The beanbag hit him squarely in the

chest. A little closer to him than you had to be, but he'll live."

The Lieutenant nodded. "Glad to hear it. Take him to the ER. Detective Madsen is going to ride with you to make sure this doesn't happen again."

He looked at Arch. "Get as much from him as you can, and keep him contained."

"Will do... Sir, the girl in the room, can you have her escorted to the hospital as well?"

"I can take care of myself detective," she responded, as she moved from behind him.

He warmly studied her. "I meant nothing by that statement. I just think you could help me."

"Mind if I tag along then. I'm interested to see how this turns out."

"Lieutenant?" Archer shrugged.

The Lieutenant moved close to her and whispered. "You sure about this?"

She nodded.

"Okay... Arch, you're responsible for her. Keep her safe."

The woman groaned, "Uncle Brad, I told you I can take care of myself."

With that they climbed into the back of the ambulance and rode away.

3

The man awakened and abruptly sat up. His arms were positioned tightly downward. Both wrists were handcuffed to the rails on either side of the bed. He screamed. "Let me out of here. Please. Let me out."

Down the hallway, Archer stood looking out of a fifth floor window. He turned when he heard the tapping of her heels on the concrete floor. The shoes accentuated her legs nicely.

She was an extremely beautiful woman. Her dress demonstrated professionalism but with the slightest hint of allurement. Her long black hair hung tightly down her thin back. Her olive skin sparkled in the iridescent lighting.

He'd been attracted to her the moment he'd walked into the interview room earlier, only to have his heart dashed when he discovered that she was the Lieutenant's niece. He'd sworn never to date a woman he had to work with. It certainly wasn't responsible to date the family of a supervisor.

She confidently moved beside him. "So, Detective. Why'd you want me to tag along? Was it my charming personality or seductive good looks?"

If he were a few years younger, he'd have been embarrassed. As it were, he'd been through too much to be uncomfortable over a few words.

He smiled, "Sorry to disappoint you doctor. Both may be true. However, I was more interested in your observations of our suspect. I want to know what you think about him."

"Why do you think I have an opinion? And what makes you think my opinion matters?"

He smiled again. "I saw the way you were intently watching him. His movements. His words. His mannerisms. You know what you're looking for. My guess is you have some sort of degree in Human Behavior or Body Language interpretation. Which is it?"

She laughed. "Both. I just happened to be visiting and thought it would be interesting to show my uncle how it works. I find he doesn't have a respect for it… and you Detective, do you respect the science?"

"I honestly have no experience with it, but I'm interested enough to give it a chance."

"Fair enough. I have one request first. You interview him before I give my interpretation."

"Deal," he said, and shook her extended hand.

Ten minutes later Archer stood over the man handcuffed to the bed. The officer outside the door had told them that the man had been loudly screaming for the last few minutes. Archer moved his chair closer.

"Hello. I'm Detective Archer Madsen. I've got some good news for you."

"Yeah… what's that?"

"The man you hit with the handcuffs earlier is going to be okay. He's got a headache, but he'll be fine."

"I don't care about him. He can die for all I care."

"You know… you talk tough, but you're bluffing. You haven't wanted to hurt anyone through this whole ordeal. You could have been much more aggressive. I don't think you want to hurt anyone unnecessarily. But you're desperate. I want to know why."

"You aren't even gonna ask my name? Seems like all the other one was interested in was by the book interviews. I don't have that kind of time."

"Seems to me you've got all the time in the world, because you aren't going anywhere… I've got to be honest with you. You seem to be wasting more time than anyone. If you want more to get done, let me do my job. There's a certain way things have to happen. There's a little leeway, but for the most part, there are guidelines and protocols that must be followed. I'll try to work around what I can, but ultimately, I work for people who expect some by the book results. I'm sorry if you feel that's a waste of time, but that's the way it has to be."

"But he's running out of time."

"I'm tired of your babbling. I'm the one chance you've got. Wake up and smell what you've been shoveling. You tried it your way, and you've been arrested twice. Then placed in a hospital. So don't lecture me about wasting time. If you want me to listen to what you have to say, you have to give me the information I need. That's my deal. It's more than fair. You attacked a cop. I oughta just lock you up and throw away the key."

The man slightly relaxed, slinking lower into the bed. He thoughtfully shook his head.

"If I cooperate, will you really listen to me? I just want someone to find my boy."

Archer nodded. "I give you my word, and I don't take that lightly."

"Okay… my name is Max… Max Stanley."

"Okay Max. As I said earlier, I'm Detective Archer Madsen. Glad to make your acquaintance. Would be better under different circumstances, but we'll take what we can get. Right?"

Max uncomfortably shrugged, "I guess so."

"Okay Max, who was the man you were racing with down my streets?"

He defiantly shifted, "We weren't racing. I was chasing him. It wasn't supposed to happen like that. I needed him alive."

"Okay. Why were you chasing him?"

"He knows what took my son. He knows where it's keeping him."

"Okay. What was his name?"

"I dunno. It's a long story. After I found him, I tried to follow him without being noticed. I guess I wasn't careful enough. He recognized I was following him and tried to run. That's when you guys came flying in to save the day."

"So, you don't know his name?"

"No! I don't know his name! I've told you that already! I don't know anything about him, other than he had information about my son, and I needed that info."

"Okay… Do you live in this area?"

His face was again seared with hot tears. "Yes, we do. My wife, my son, and me. He's only eight. We've got to find him."

"Tell me about that? What happened? Who has him?"

"I dunno. I wish I did. I'd kill them all."

"Where's your wife? Do you have a way I can contact her for you?"

"She's home with her father. He's been with her since my son went missing. He came down to be with her during this time… until… until Carson comes home."

He called out a phone number and Archer wrote it down. "You mind if I give her a call. I need to verify your story. If you're telling me the truth, I'm going to do everything I can to get you out of this. I'll help you find him. If you're lying to me,

I'll do everything in my power to make sure you don't get out for a long time. You understand?"

"I'm not lying. I just want my son."

"How long has he been missing?"

"He's been missing two days. I've been trying to find him."

Archer stood up. "Give me ten minutes. I'm gonna verify your story."

Detective Madsen walked into the part of the room divided by the curtain. Dr. Rees had been watching from the slit in the white material. Archer lightly placed his hand on her elbow and escorted her into the hallway.

"First impressions? From listening. From observing earlier. What do you see?"

"I'd like to question him myself now. Hopefully get his wife in the same room. Observe them together."

"My thoughts exactly. Whatever is going on, we need to start moving on it. He said his son has been missing for two days. The window for finding him alive has already closed. If he's telling the truth, why didn't he come to the police for help sooner? He's put our backs against the wall."

"He didn't come because he's afraid. It's written all over him. He's terrified."

"Anyone with a missing child would be. That hasn't stopped countless people from involving law enforcement. Why is he different?"

"He's not just afraid because his son's missing. He's afraid of who has his son. He's taking them seriously."

"What do you mean?"

"Did you notice the way he responded when you asked why they were racing?"

"I gather personal information and compare. I assimilate the facts. I'd appreciate your interpretation of his words and behavior."

She smiled. "I understand. Did you notice the words he used?"

"Yes. He said he wasn't racing. He was chasing the man that had information about who has his son."

"Close. But this bothers me. He didn't say 'who' had his son. He said 'he knows 'what' took him. He knows where 'it's' keeping him'."

"Merely semantics."

"I don't think so. He hunched his shoulders when he answered. He retracted, drawing himself away from you. He didn't want to answer. He had been engaging you, but after that question, he didn't make eye contact again. His eyes slightly widened, indicating extreme vulnerability. He feels controlled by whoever has his son."

"Okay. We've got to get his wife in here. I'll have an officer pick her up. We need recent photos. We're going to find this boy."

He thought for a couple of seconds, and then faced her

again. "Meet me back here in 30 minutes. I want you to help me interview the couple. You comfortable with that?"

"I'm more than comfortable. I want to. I believe I can help you."

Thirty minutes later, she waited in the hallway for the ruggedly attractive detective. Her credentials spoke for themselves. She had more degrees than she cared to admit and had been involved in more research than seemed feasible. Most of her studies had been in the field of human behavior. The FBI had used her twice as a witness for the prosecution. Of course, she wasn't a vain person and kept her professional accolades private. It didn't matter that the locals didn't know her qualifications. If anything, she was over competent.

He coolly meandered toward her. Her lips turned up at the corners. She felt warm inside. If she were honest, she was maddeningly attracted to him. It wasn't just his physical presence. It was the tough guy persona that accompanied it. He walked into the room, and the atmosphere changed. He had an air about him. Not arrogance, she hated that. No, he was more self-assured. Like he couldn't be stopped. She found that hopelessly appealing.

He moved beside her. "His wife should be here any time. Would you mind escorting her in when she does? I'm going to have a quick chat with Max."

Before she could answer, he moved into the room with the suspect, who was still handcuffed to the bed. Archer firmly glared at him.

"Max. Your wife is almost here. I'm going to interview you

together. I'm going to keep my word and try to help you find your son. That ok?"

Max nodded a silent agreement. Archer moved to the side of the bed and placed a small skeleton key in the handcuff connected to his right wrist.

"Against my better judgment, I'm going to let you save face in front of her. She's going through enough. She's missing her son. She doesn't need to see her husband in chains."

Max nodded again. "Thank you."

"Don't thank me just yet. You make one move to get away, and I won't hesitate to drop you. She'll probably get protective and try to help you. I'll have to arrest her as well. Then, I'll throw more charges at her than you can count. You better make sure that doesn't happen. Are we clear?"

"Crystal."

"Then this should be easy," Archer said, as he removed the second handcuff.

The door opened behind him, and Dr. Rees moved inside, followed by a slightly overweight woman and a nicely dressed elderly gentleman.

"Archer, this is Mrs. Stanley… and her father… Morgan LeDiv."

Archer squared his shoulders, "Mr. LeDiv. I hope you're here in a familial manner, not a professional one."

His smug smirk made Archer want to smear it across his face.

"A little of both detective. We're here at your request first."

"All due respect. I didn't request you. I'm here because your son-in-law reported that his son has been missing for two days. There's no need for legal counsel. I just want to make sure the child gets home safely."

"We'll answer your questions, but I'm already working on getting him home."

"Well, getting people home is something you're definitely good at."

"Look Detective. I'm going to ignore your blatant disrespect for my occupation. I won't apologize for being extremely good at my job. In order for our great legal system to work, someone has to defend the accused. It's part of the process that affords this country her freedom. So, I'm not going to justify your offensive behavior with an explanation. I'm working to get the boy home."

Max interrupted, "Please. I'm glad all of you are here. I want to do anything. Get anyone involved. Bring the whole department up here. I just want you to work together to bring him back to us."

Mrs. Stanley took her husband's hand. "Oh, honey. Are you okay? They told me you were involved in a car accident. That you'd been arrested."

"I'm fine… Jessica… please work with him. He's gonna help us find Carson."

Archer pushed two chairs toward the standing guests. "Please, sit down."

He pulled two more chairs from the corner, and he and Regan sat. He removed his voice recorder and placed it at the foot of the bed.

"Tell me exactly what happened. From the beginning. Please, try not to leave out any details. I need everything. No matter how small."

Jessica Stanley spoke low, "We woke up yesterday, and my son was gone. Max woke up around four in a panic. He'd been having a nightmare that someone was taking my boy..."

Her eyes were foggy, but she held back the river of tears behind them.

"Turns out the dream was true. Carson had been sleeping with us in the bed. He was right there. He was in my arms...

Oh, God...

I'm a horrible mother...

My son was in my bed...

Whoever took him...

I was a foot away...

I didn't do anything to stop them...

I didn't know...

I'm his mother...

I'm supposed to protect him...

I didn't do anything to stop it."

She clamped down hard on her husband's hand. "I'm so sorry."

Regan interjected, "Mrs. Stanley... Jessica... It's not your fault. You can't blame yourself. Please, tell us about your son. What's his name? How old is he? What's he like? Anything will help us build a profile."

She hesitated, and then lifted her head and mumbled a few incoherent words. Regan tapped Jessica's arm a couple of times, and then tenderly brushed her elbow.

Archer didn't miss much. She was good. Extremely good. The distracting questions, the nonverbal reassurances, the gentle expressions. She was establishing trust. Whatever else he thought of her, Dr. Regan Rees knew how to handle an interviewee.

Jessica looked at Regan and slightly smiled. "His name is Carson... He's only eight. He likes Superman and Scooby Doo... He's always been a mama's boy..." Her voice trailed off again, and she squeezed tightly on her husband's hand.

"Sorry," Max interrupted, "This is difficult for both of us."

"It's okay," Regan quickly replied, "take your time. We're here for you. Just move at your own pace."

Archer stood up. "Max... Mrs. Stanley... Is there anything that sticks out in your mind from the days leading up to the kidnapping? Anything at all? Anyone suspicious? Anything happen that got your attention in the moment that you may have forgotten afterward? No matter how trivial it may seem, I need to know about it."

Max didn't hesitate. His eyes flooded. He couldn't contain his emotions.

"There are a few instances that stick out. I knew he would be taken. I was warned. I... I just didn't take it seriously."

"What happened Max?"

"I was in the check out line at Starbucks three days ago. A middle-aged woman was behind me. After I placed my order, she tapped me on the shoulder. I turned around, and she just stared at me. Then she calmly whispered, "It's coming for him. Protect him. It's coming soon...

...I was confused. I looked around, but no one else seemed to hear her. I was the only one that noticed.

The barista called for me to pick up my latte. I moved to the counter and claimed it. Then, I turned back to the woman who'd spoken to me, but she was gone. The door was just closing. I hurried outside, spilling my coffee as I ran. When I stepped onto the sidewalk, no one was there, and no vehicles were driving away. It's like she just vanished."

"What did she look like? Can you describe her?"

"I don't know. So much has happened since then. I remember... she had a tattoo on the left side of her neck. It was of some dragon or lizard. Her hair had a slightly reddish tint. It didn't look natural, like maybe it was dyed. That's all I remember. Sorry."

"That's exactly what she said? Nothing else?"

"No. That's it. Word for word. I can't get it out of my

mind."

Regan leaned toward him. "You only heard it once. You sure there's no mistake?"

"No. That was the message. Word for word. No mistakes. However, I never said I only heard it once. That's why I remember it so well."

"Wait, you heard it again?" Archer asked. "From someone else?"

"Yes. Less than three hours later I stopped at the drug store to pick up a couple of things for Jessica. I was on one of the Pharmacy isles. An employee was restocking the shelf from a box of toothpaste. It was an elderly gentleman, with small glasses resting on abnormally large ears. Slightly balding. His silver hair surrounded the sides of his head…

…I walked past him, and he grabbed my arm, whirling me around to face him. In a hushed tone, he said the same thing the woman had told me before. Word for word. There was no difference. I promise you. He said the exact same thing…

…He tried to walk away, but I grabbed him to ask some questions. He strangely glared at me. He said he hadn't told me anything. He hadn't even seen me walking by. He'd been busy unpacking his boxes. He picked up a phone on a pole beside him and paged for security to come to the pharmacy area. I left quickly, without incident.

I did come back an hour later once I'd calmed down. I wanted to see if the worker would talk to me again. He wasn't there. Another man was in his place. I asked when the first employee would be back. I described him the best I could. The man said he'd never seen or heard of him. He said he'd been the only one on the floor in that department all day...

...Then, as I was walking to my car, a kid came by on a skateboard. He pulled up a few feet away from me.

"Tonight's the night. Protect him well. It's coming for your boy tonight."

He jumped back on his board and flashed away. I tried to catch him, but he lost me in the alleyway. He too seemed to just disappear."

Jessica Stanley lurched forward, "C'mon baby. Please don't do this. We have to stick to the facts."

Max looked at Archer and Regan, "I promise I'm not crazy. This really happened. These are the facts."

"I believe you Max. It's okay." Archer rustled through a couple of pages in front of him, not looking at either of them. "What did you do after that Max? What happened next?"

"I went home and told Jessica. I didn't tell her I doubted myself. I just told her what all three of them told me. We panicked...

... Carson was supposed to go spend the night with a friend. We decided that wouldn't be wise. If someone were hunting him, we wanted him to be safe. We immediately called Jessica's father. He hired an off duty police officer to stay outside the house."

He hurtfully looked toward his wife. "We let him sleep in

our bed. He was in the middle of us."

She interrupted, the pain in her voice making it hard to hear her words. "He was so sweet. He didn't know anything was different. My little boy laughed until he fell asleep, overjoyed to be in our bed. We never let him do that. Not since he was a baby. We should have. I wish…"

She looked angrily away from them. Max took her in his arms and whispered in her ear. After a few seconds, he looked up.

"Sorry Detective. We took every precaution. We did. I placed my arm through…"

He looked down. "…I placed my arm through his shirt after he fell asleep. I thought if anyone tried to take him… I thought I'd wake up if I fell asleep… I thought I could protect him."

Neither interviewer spoke, allowing a few moments for the couple to grieve. Finally, Regan broke the silence.

"Mr. Stanley, earlier your wife mentioned that you were having a nightmare. Can you tell me about it?"

"Wasn't a nightmare. No… No nightmare…

It was real! It took my child."

He was visibly shaken. He flinched, his shoulders lowering, a visible sign of fear, like when a terrified puppy sticks its tail between its legs.

"Okay Max, tell me about it then." She gave Archer an attentive glance. "We need to know exactly what you saw."

He stammered forward. "We all slept together. Carson was between us. As I said, I put my arm through his shirt in case something tried to take him. I wasn't gonna let him go without a fight. I tried... I really did... I don't know why, but I tried to stay awake all night. I had my gun beside the bed. I was ready for it when it came....

...But somehow I fell asleep."

He sobbed, lowering his face into his cupped hands. "It's all my fault. I'm the father. His dad was supposed to keep him safe. I couldn't even stay awake. The last time I looked at the clock it was 2:17 in the morning. When I woke up it was 4:12. I couldn't stay awake for two more hours. Two hours. That's the difference between my son being with me or not. Two measly hours."

"The dream. I need to know about the dream."

He flashed a disturbed expression. "I already told you. It wasn't a dream. It happened."

Archer stepped toward him. "Max. We're listening. Tell us about it."

"I looked at Jessica. She was sleeping next to him. They both looked so peaceful. So beautiful. I was sitting up so I could better fight the drowsiness. I put my head against the head board for just a second. But that was all I needed. I fell asleep...

...That's when it happened. In a state of reverie it came to me. I tried to fight it. Look." He rolled his dark sleeve up his arm. The left forearm was severely bruised and swollen.

"Who did that to you?" Regan asked.

"It did. It came and stood beside me. I could see it, but I couldn't move. The room was dark. I thought that was peculiar, because we'd chosen to leave the lights on. It seemed less vulnerable. I panicked. I opened my eyes and immediately saw it. Standing there. Staring at me…

It looked like a man, but its eyes were acidic red. It was smiling, but not happily. It was sadistic. Like a clown, but not. A killer…"

"Like the classic movie… *IT,*" Archer said under his breath toward Regan. She ignored his comment and kept listening. If Max noticed, he didn't comment.

"I tried to move, but couldn't. I could hear it laughing. Standing over and mocking me. It moved closer and whispered. I could smell its sulfurous breath. It was hot. I thought my skin was melting from my face."

"Raiders of the Lost Ark," Archer mumbled again. "This is good. A Hollywood montage."

Regan shot him a solemn look. She quickly turned it toward Max, softening it as she did. "What did it say to you Max?"

He recoiled, as if he didn't want to remember.

"It's okay Max. It could be important. We need to know everything."

Max nodded his understanding. His eyes suddenly fluttered. He abruptly turned toward them. His eyes rolled back in his head.

"I've come for what's mine. I'm taking him from you. He was never yours. He belongs to me."

As he said the last word, his rigid demeanor changed. His eyes fluttered again. He slumped in his bed and cried.

"I think I surprised it. I lunged. Grabbed its head. I bit its ear in the struggle. I tasted it. The blood. It hit me hard. Then, I watched it slink into the darkness of the room. It had something in its arms. It was moving. It was screaming. It was Carson...

...Mom... Dad... Mom... Mom... Mom... Dad...

He screamed, calling us over and over again... But I couldn't get up... I really tried... But I couldn't move. I just couldn't."

He coughed, choking on the hot bile that had risen in his throat. He grabbed the small pink tray and vomited. He gagged a couple of times before throwing up again. After a couple of seconds he looked up, his eyes watering.

"I woke up, and then woke Jess up. We couldn't find him. He'd been taken...

...I went through everything. Looked for blood. There was nothing. It left nothing behind. Nothing except these bruises on my arm. Everything else was gone. There was no sign of him."

"Okay Max," Archer started. "Do you mind if we go and look over your house?"

"Sorry. I can't permit that," Mr. LeDiv spoke up.

"What?" Archer asked, "You've gotta be kidding!"

"I'm afraid not. Max is my client, and he's been arrested for reckless operation, assault on a police officer, illegal possession of a firearm, resisting arrest, and assault with a deadly weapon. Not to mention speeding, running a red light, four illegal lane changes, destruction of property, trespassing, and an expired inspection sticker. They threw the book at him. If there's a chance you could find something incriminating in the house. As his attorney, I'm afraid we can't risk it."

"Are you serious. For God's sake, there's a child missing, and you're worried about your win/loss record. I'm not concerned with the reasons he's incarcerated. At this point my only concern is making sure that the kid is safe…

…We're already two days into this. By most accounts, our chances of finding him alive are slim. Why aren't you worried about that?"

The attorney shifted his stance. "I'm looking out for my daughter. You wouldn't understand."

"Side bar. Please," Archer bellowed, walking to the corner with Mr. LeDiv behind him. Archer turned, his eyes hot.

"What's your problem?"

"I told you. I'm concerned about my daughter. You're right detective, and you know it. Chances are you'll never find him. If you do, it'll be a body, weeks from now. Decomposed and unrecognizable. Closed casket. She's got a hard road ahead of her. I have to accept that. I also know my daughter. She can't do it alone. She won't survive if she has to face this without her son and her husband. I can't let her lose them both. I have to protect her. You must understand."

"You're trying to bring him home?"

"What?"

"Earlier, you said you were working to bring him home. What are you doing? Do you have information you're not sharing? If so, Max's legal issues will be the least of your concern. I'll bury you under so many indictments your head will spin."

"Fine..." He shook his head. "I've been contacted with demands. I'm following through with them."

"You've been around the system long enough to know that's a mistake. You can't negotiate his safety. Not with these people."

"With all due respect. You've been aware of this kidnapping all of an hour. What could you possibly know about the people holding the child? I've been communicating with them since this began."

"I know they're serious. I know they've stricken severe fear into the father. I know he's convinced it's something almost otherworldly. They're well organized and highly manipulative. You can't just bargain with them for his release. I've seen the signs before. People this organized. They don't get caught, because they don't leave loose ends. They have no intention of letting the boy come home. You have to tell me everything you know."

"I'll send you a report within the hour. As for now, this

interview is over."

He stepped away from Archer and moved toward the door.

"Honey, it's time to go. Max, I highly recommend you stop talking to them if you want to see Carson again. I know what I'm doing. They've threatened us not to involve the police. As your attorney, "I'm advising you not to talk to them. As your father-in-law, I'm pleading with you not to."

Archer leapt toward him, "Please, Max. Don't take this nut job seriously. He's gonna get your son killed. Let me help you. Please. Just let me search the house."

Mr. LeDiv intentionally cleared his throat. "Detective, I'm afraid I'm the owner of the home. If you want to search the premises, you're going to have to go through me. I'm denying you access. So either give up the wild goose chase or go see a judge. Good luck getting a warrant."

Archer cursed. The attorney took his daughter by the hand and led her out of the door. She looked back toward her husband and waved. The look of concern and confusion on both of their faces was alarming. Yet, neither of them spoke against the advice they'd been given. As the door closed behind them, Max rolled onto his side, away from Archer and Regan.

"You heard my attorney. I'm afraid I'm gonna have to ask you to excuse yourself."

Archer pleaded, "Max?"

"Now!" Max replied. "I won't ask you again."

"Fine," Archer mumbled as he violently slapped the handcuffs back on each wrist.

"Don't say I didn't try. You're gonna have to live with your choice today. I'm not the one who'll have trouble sleeping at night if anything happens to your little boy."

He roughly double clicked the handcuffs and stormed out the door. Regan followed closely behind. She turned back. Max was crying. The cuffs didn't allow him to wipe away the tears, and they were rolling down his cheeks like rain.

4

Archer kicked the chair, sending it clanging across the concrete floor.

"I had him. I had him where I needed him. We had her. They were going to tell us. What's his problem?"

"Detective, I know it's not what you want to hear, but from an outsider's perspective, I understand his argument."

"Please. Detective is getting old. My friends call me Arch… And, what do you mean you understand his argument? There isn't one. There's a little boy out there. Alone. Afraid. Waiting on someone to bring him home. And we're sitting on our hands, because his parents, the only people who could help, are refusing to…

…And did you see her? Max was crying like Gisele when Tom Brady lost the Super Bowl… and she just sat there. Zero emotion. Guilt? Looks suspicious to me."

"Actually, that's not atypical. Parents rarely grieve at the same time. In cases of deep traumatic events, the mother and father usually grieve in stages. They don't realize they're doing so, but one remains strong while the other releases the angst. One holds things together, allowing the other to mourn. Usually, the male accepts the role as the stabilizer while the female grieves. From a psychological perspective it's predictable. The female usually gets angry because the male doesn't express enough emotion. She feels he doesn't care, and she doesn't understand why he's not as broken as she is. In the pain of the moment, she can't perceive that he's just trying to be strong for her. It's a vicious cycle that's tremendously difficult to break...

...In this case, it appears the man is the weakest link. She's probably the dominant in their relationship. He's a couple years younger. She obviously comes from a wealthy and reputable family. He seems less than confident. Sorry, but it all fits."

"It all fits," he scoffed. "And what's the deal with the way Max answered your question anyway? Don't tell me you're buying his act."

"What do you mean?"

"His Edward Norton."

"Edward Norton?"

"Primal Fear... Come on... Max spazzed out. He lost it for a second. Like something was speaking through him.

Seriously, I'm not buying it. This family needs serious help, and trusting LeDiv is their biggest mistake."

"Honestly, I'm not sure, but I don't think he's pretending. He's serious. He's desperate to get his son back... I'm having trouble doubting the wife as well. People suffer in different ways...

...However, I'd say that Mrs. Stanley agrees with you. She doesn't believe his story. I don't think she believes he's intentionally lying, but she doesn't believe he's telling the truth either. She seems to be getting through this the best she can under the circumstances. She's a fighter."

"I don't know. Doesn't seem like much of a fighter. Did you notice the way she wilted before her father? Something isn't right there."

"He's a powerful man. He's probably ruled over her as far back as she can remember. She married a weak man who allows her father to rule the roost. They've not delineated themselves as a family. Marriages rarely survive in those types of environments. You should know Arch; no husband likes to feel like less of a man around his spouse. Especially when it's to a father-in-law."

"Makes sense. We'd have had words a long time ago. I wouldn't fit in much there."

She grinned, "I can see that, but then again, you're not Max Stanley."

"You mean Max LeDiv? I'm pretty sure he took on her last name? If not, he should have. He was probably forced to sign a pre-nup."

She would have laughed, except for the ridged lines of disgust on his face. He was definitely a man who didn't like to be controlled. She had no doubt he'd have broken every bone in Mr. LeDiv's face if he would've been in Max's situation.

"What are we gonna do about this Arch? We can't just get a warrant to search the house. He's got too many friends in high places."

"I just don't get it. Saying he's worried about adding to Max's traffic violations is a joke. Whatever they're hiding, it has nothing to do with Max's joyride."

"I think you should stay on Max. He wants to get his son back. Deep down he knows you're more than capable of getting results. I'd play on that. Try to find out what he knows."

"Yeah. It's what I was thinking too."

"In the meantime, I'm going to have another talk with Mrs. Stanley, sans her father."

He thoughtfully studied her for a moment. "You know I can't let you do that. Your uncle will not approve. He's still my supervising officer."

"And here I thought you weren't the kind of man to let something like that get in your way."

He didn't smile. "Sorry, but if you think you can play head games with me, you're mistaken. Just because you carry a license to manipulate men doesn't make you different than any other woman I've dealt with. Ego is for younger, less experienced men. You can't control me by pulling the typical male's narcissistic strings."

"Understood," she slightly laughed. "Look Arch. I just want to help. My best way of doing so would be to talk with her away from the two men in her life. I think she'd be more open. I could find out what she's hiding."

"I've got no problem with it, but like I said, clear it with the Lieutenant first. I think we both know what his answer will be."

"I'm not some little school girl anymore. I'm a professional. I wish someone around here would treat me like one."

"A professional would understand that you can't get special treatment just because he's your uncle. He's still the one making the decisions. So everything goes through him."

She agitatedly glared for a moment, and then stormed out of the room. Archer watched her walk away. He shook his head and mumbled, before turning to walk back toward Max's room.

5

Archer sat in the lobby of the hospital. His phone vibrated in his pocket, awakening him from a light sleep. He checked his watch. It had been two hours since Regan had left. He flipped the phone open, placing it to his ear.

"Hello."

"Arch, I just off the phone with the Captain. He asked me to speak to you. Something about a run in you had with Mr. LeDiv."

"That didn't take long. What did he say?"

"He said to make sure you understand that you're to do whatever it takes to bring that kid home safely. Ruffle as many feathers as you need to. He isn't concerned with the bureaucrats. He's already spoken with the district attorney about getting a search warrant…

...The DA is obviously afraid of what could result, so he's not going to press the issue unless you find an extremely good reason. It appears you're on your own for now. I've shifted the guys around to cover us. This case is your only priority. We haven't had a missing child in this city in over thirty years. We aren't going to let it happen now."

"Thank you sir. I appreciate the support. Please pass that along to the Captain when you talk to him again."

"Will do. Also, how's Regan? I haven't heard from her."

"Strong-willed. Independent. A bit high strung."

He chuckled, "Looks like she's leaving an impression."

"Actually. She left me a couple of hours ago. She wanted to interview Mrs. Stanley without Mr. LeDiv around. He caused a scene while he was here. I told her it wasn't going to happen without your approval. She stormed out. Last I've seen of her."

He groaned. "Between us, she thinks I don't respect her career path. She doesn't know how closely I've followed her career. I spoke with the director of the FBI this morning. He told me she's been a tremendous help to them in the past. He said if she were interested in helping with some of my cases, I should jump at the chance. According to his records, she's an excellent profiler and interrogator. She's also been through field training in Quantico. So, as far as I'm concerned, she's officially your consultant on this case."

"Yes sir," he reluctantly sighed.

"Archer. One more thing. It doesn't sound like you'll have

to, but I'm trusting you to keep her safe. We don't know what we're dealing with yet. Don't let her out of your sight."

"So, you want me to find a missing kid while babysitting your niece. Is there anything else? Maybe I could mow your lawn or clean your house while I'm at it. Dinner and a movie?"

"Arch, just get the job done."

He flipped the phone closed. It's the only thing he knew how to do well. He couldn't fail, he'd never learned how. As far back as he could remember; it had never been an option.

. . .

Fifteen miles to the east, Regan pulled her black Lincoln Navigator into a parking space on the far side of the busy street. It hadn't taken her long to spot the limo carrying Mr. LeDiv and his daughter. She waited, carefully observing through the bustle of traffic that flowed like a line of ants scuttling in both directions. She wasn't interested in making a move yet.

Timing is everything. The key to any investigation is patience. The truth usually rises to the surface. Most often, reality is not how its been envisioned. Deception, disloyalty, and self-preservation have diluted it by the creation of smoke and mirrors that take time to sort through. Too many investigators let impulse override intelligence. Instinct is an influential piece to the analysis of every case, but unbridled it is destructive. There's a moment when events seem to align, creating the optimal chance for the truth to reveal itself. Regan knew that soon Mr. LeDiv would have to leave his daughter's side, and when he did, she'd be waiting.

The limo was illegally parked along the curb of one of the cities finest eateries. It was a jacket and black tie only establishment. The lunch menu's most inexpensive items topped one hundred dollars, and that was for a salad. This wasn't the kind of place she'd normally hang out. It wasn't because of the food. It wasn't because she couldn't afford it. She just couldn't stand the hypocritical and conceited clientele.

The door opened, and a powerfully built hoodlum wearing black stepped from the front passenger seat. You clean him up, dress him in the nicest Armani suit, but you still can't remove the pimp strut from his gait. Except for the tattoos around his neck, he looked the part of a wealthy man's chauffeur. However, the semi-automatic weapon outlined under his jacket gave him away. He was nothing more than an overpaid, rich man's gangster. A bodyguard for hire. Someone who didn't mind getting his hands dirty if needed.

He strutted to the rear of the limo and opened the door. Mr. LeDiv stepped out. He was brawny himself, having played professional football with the Miami Dolphins in his younger years. He still worked out like an athlete. His massive chest and arms cut an imposing figure. Many of his cases were helped because his appearance and body language demanded instant respect. He had an air of superiority and always spoke deliberately and without hesitation. There was no softness in him, and no toleration for weakness. He was built for success, and demanded it from his associates. Fear, mercy, and compassion were all signs of weakness. Show them, and he'd destroy you. There's a reason he had flourished in such a cutthroat business.

He unworriedly scanned the structures around him. Sensing

no threat, he looked back into the car and talked to someone, before closing the door and moving away. His thug stayed two feet to his left and slightly behind, hand always an inch from the decorative pearl handle just inside his jacket flap. Why did he feel the need for such protection? Usually, it's the prosecution that needs bodyguards, not someone with a high propensity for helping the guilty walk.

She sighed. After he had stepped into the building, she opened her door and approached the limo. She was two feet from the door when it opened in front of her. She leaned over the side and peered in. Mrs. Stanley's expression gave her chills.

"What's wrong? Is everything okay?"

"It's happening now, and your going to blow it. If they see you, it's over. They'll walk away and kill him. Please, you have to disappear. They could have seen you already."

"Who? Mrs. Stanley, who are you talking about? What's happening?"

"The kidnappers. They called right after we left Max at the hospital. They said they knew we'd been talking to the police. If they heard we were doing it again, they'd kill my little boy. If we just pay the money and move on with our lives, he'll be okay. They'll let him live…

…They were nervous. They wanted to meet now. They told us to come here with the payment. If we make the payment, there'll be no problems. We'll have Max within the next two days. You've to get out of here. Please."

"Why two days? Why not just give him to you at the exchange?"

"I don't know. We asked, but they wouldn't answer. They just told us that they were calling the shots. We could agree to their terms, or they would give him to us now as we requested. In five different pieces... Oh God, Please. You have to go... Now!"

"I'll leave Mrs. Stanley, but I need to ask you a couple of questions first. Answer them, and I'll be on my way."

The fear beneath the exterior of her pseudo composure was obvious. She was undeniably anxious and exhausted.

"Jessica, It's obvious that you aren't comfortable with this. I can see that. It's what I do... You aren't sure they're really going to keep their end of the bargain. You don't want to just trust that hardened criminals are going to abide by your father's code of honor... You shouldn't have to blindly throw your faith into that plan. We want to help you. Just let us do our job."

"But... but my father knows what he's doing. He'll get Carson home. He's gonna save my child. He always wins. He always has."

"This isn't a courtroom Jessica. He's not duping a judge forced to abide by written edicts. He's gambling your son's life on his ego. If you're so comfortable with it, then why are you so nervous? Why the tension in your eyes? The stress around your lips? The way you have your head lowered? It's because deep down inside, where it matters most, you know that just giving them money doesn't guarantee Carson's safety."

Her lower lip trembled. "Ask your questions. Please, do it before my father returns. He doesn't want us talking to you."

"Why didn't you and Max come to the police instead of consulting your father? Seems strange. Most people would have immediately involved the authorities. Why'd you go through him?"

"Have you seen the police report from the last kidnapping case here? I don't remember how long ago, but it's been many years-"

"No. I don't know anything about kidnappings in this area. Why?"

"Look into it. It'll explain a few things. My family has been through this before. My brother was taken when I was a child. I was there. The case was never solved. My father has spent the rest of his life studying these types of traumatic events. That's why I called him. He knows what he's doing."

"But he's emotionally involved. That clouds a person's judgment. He isn't going to see this clearly. He's too close. We're your best shot."

"No. That's what they thought last time, but listening to the supposed professionals didn't get my brother back. My family was shattered because local law enforcement didn't know what they were doing. To make it worse, they never even developed suspects. Whoever did it is still out there, and my little brother's bones are still rotting in a field somewhere."

Regan studied her. "What happened to your mother? You talk about your dad and brother, but not her?"

She looked up, disgust written across her face. "She's dead to me. She-"

"Why?"

Jessica struggled to regain her composure. The rage left her eyes. "Car accident. It happened a long time ago."

"I'm sorry Jessica. I didn't know... Do you think the kidnappings are somehow connected? It's odd that two kidnappings have occurred within the same family."

Jessica bit her lower lip and twisted her feet, fidgeting with a spot in the carpet. "I don't know. It's been so many years. I guess it's possible. My family has more money than most in this god-forsaken city. Maybe that's made us a target."

Regan nodded. "Possibly... but that would indicate that the kidnappers are local. Have you ever thought about that?"

"Sure. They have to be. I've always suspected it was some poor, down-on-their-luck immigrants looking for quick cash-"

"Why? Do you remember anything from that night? Did they talk with an accent? Anything that made you feel that way?"

She ashamedly lowered her head. "I don't know. I was asked a million questions back then, but I don't remember. Sorry, I wish I could."

"Okay... It's okay... I have one more question Mrs. Stanley."

"Please hurry. He should be back any moment-"

"Earlier, when your husband mentioned knowing that Carson was going to be taken, you told him to stick to the facts. What did you mean by that?"

She looked concerned. Her lip started to bleed from the pressure being applied from her front teeth.

"I don't know what's wrong with Max. He isn't taking this well."

"Well, most people wouldn't. Under the circumstances-"

"No. It's not normal. He's scaring me. It's almost like he's delusional."

"What do you mean?"

"He doesn't want to accept the fact that Carson has been kidnapped. He's fabricating unbelievable stories. He actually believes something supernatural is happening…

…I'm trying to be supportive, but at the same time, he's wasting everyone's time with otherworldly tales. Carson's odds are dwindling, and Max is creating a fantasy that I'm terrified to feed. I don't want him to sink any deeper into it. He needs to embrace reality. Today we endure the pain; tomorrow we enjoy the bliss."

Regan looked concerned. "He believes something supernatural has occurred? You mean like alien abduction?"

"No. Nothing like that… It's worse."

Her eyes narrowed, and she visibly shuttered. "Sorry. He really freaks me out. He thinks its spiritual. Demons. Monsters. All the stories he keeps telling me are ludicrous.

Strangers giving him crystalline premonitions... He's lost it... He believes a dark force is behind the kidnapping."

"Like a cult?"

"No... Like Satan himself."

Regan's forehead tightened. "Did you see a dark figure in the room that night?"

"No, I didn't. Everything else was as he said. He told me about his three visitations. He was extremely paranoid, running around the house in a crazed stupor. It took me almost an hour to calm him down...

I did finally agree to let Carson sleep with us, but only because Max was acting so desperate. But I didn't witness anything suspicious. I woke up, and Carson was already missing. Max was hyperventilating. He was just sitting there against the headboard, staring into the darkness of the room."

Regan shifted toward the door, placing her index finger on the handle. She pulled it toward her, opening the door enough to fit one leg through. As her foot hit the pavement, she positioned her body back into the car.

"Last one. If Max is just fabricating these stories; if the stories are merely the result of the extreme emotion of losing a child; how can we explain the fact that he told you about the warnings before Carson was taken? There is no such thing as pre-fabrication."

Jessica gasped, quickly looking toward Regan. "There is such a thing as pre-meditation. Maybe-"

"Are you saying you believe your husband could be involved in this?"

"It's time for you to go," Jessica said, tipping her head toward where her father had entered. He was just making his way from the building.

"Jessica, you do realize that it sounds like you could be implicating Max in this?"

"Please... Go... Now... God... He'll know I talked to you... Just go!"

Regan opened the door and stepped outside. The warm sunlight smothered her face. The brightness was a welcome contrast to the dim interior of the limo. She started to move briskly toward her vehicle, but turned and walked directly into his path. The high-rent hooligan stepped closer toward him and placed his hand inside his loose jacket flap.

"Mr. LeDiv," she said, "What a pleasure to meet you here. I was just about to go in for dinner."

"I'm afraid you're a bit underdressed, Miss, er... What was it? Miss Easy? And I'm afraid this one's a little out of your price range."

"It's doctor. Doctor Rees. I don't know what sort of manipulation you have over your daughter, but it's sick. You're a demented old man. She shows severe signs of social awkwardness and refuses to talk to anyone because of you. I could really help if you'd quit manipulating her."

He snickered as he moved past her toward his car. His hired gun harshly bumped her shoulder as he passed, exaggerating his motion to put extra force into the movement. Mr. LeDiv turned to her as the goon opened his door.

"You have a good day now Miss Easy."

He reached into his jacket pocket and pulled out a roll of bills secured tightly in a platinum money clip. He tossed the clip at her feet, its metal clanging as it hit the pavement.

"Dinner's on me," he said in a spiteful tone. He closed the door. The car drove away, leaving her alone on the curve, fuming at his incessant arrogance.

6

Inside the car, Mr. LeDiv sat quietly beside his daughter. He swallowed hard. Finally, he closed his eyes and sat his head against the seat.

Jessica sat in anguish. The silence cascaded around her. Whatever had happened, he was refusing to tell her. He was mad. She'd heard how Regan had handled the situation. She recognized that Regan had covered for her by pretending she hadn't been able to get anything from the interview.

Somehow, that wasn't good enough. He knew. That was the only explanation. Somehow, he always knew. He could always tell. She'd never been able to get away with anything.

She tried to ignore the nagging questions in her mind, but after a while lost to the power of curiosity. "Please, you have to tell me what happened. I have to know."

He never opened his eyes. Just sat back as if sleeping.

She pleaded. "How can you be so cold? You know the pain of giving up on someone. You know what it feels like to wonder how it's going to happen. You know the thoughts that ravage a parent's mind. Will he die peacefully or painfully? Will it be quick? How will it happen? Blade? Bullet? Drowning?"

She whimpered under her breath. Her mind was tortured.

"Will there be a body to bury, or will he just disappear? Will I ever get to see him again? Hold him? One more time? There are too many questions. How can you expect me to do this without knowing something?"

He opened his eyes but didn't turn toward her. "You'll see him again. Soon. You have to hold it together. We have to do this the right way. Everything is going to be fine. We have to make sure we handle everything properly. You have to trust me. I know what I'm talking about...

...What did you tell the fine doctor? Does she know anything?"

"No. She doesn't. She's searching for a grain of sand in the desert. She's like a gnat, annoying but not dangerous."

"Did she ask about Max?

"No. Nothing about Max."

"Good. I imagine she was more interested in me. So, what did you tell her?"

"Exactly what you told me to daddy," she said, as she placed her head on his massive chest and cried.

7

Archer stood outside the Stanley's home. It was a white panel house, lined beautifully with black shutters. The typical model of suburbia. A white picket fence surrounded the plush twenty-acre, exquisitely landscaped plot. They were established six miles out of the city on the outskirts of seven hundred acres of protected national forest. It was isolated and quiet.

He'd found it with no problem and left his car on a side road just inside the wooded area. He'd jogged the two miles in less than twenty minutes. Not great time, but not horrible considering it had been years since his track days.

This wasn't what the lieutenant had in mind when he'd told him to do whatever it took. He was sure of that. But he needed answers, at least a starting point. He'd already taken pictures of the concrete driveway leading to the double garage. Nothing seemed out of the ordinary, but he'd study the pictures more in detail later.

He moved onto the porch, clicking more photographs. Several metallic wind chimes ominously bristled in the whispering wind. He hadn't noticed the chilly breeze until the high-pitched crash of the chimes startled him. He remembered Max's descriptive image of the intruder that had taken Carson. He was never one to embrace fear, but something felt horribly wrong. Either Max's terror of the paranormal had sparked his own imagination, or something sinister had happened here.

He carefully maneuvered around the house, snapping shots from every angle. Nothing was amiss. Every window was closed and locked, as was every door. There were no other entrances into the house. He even considered the fireplace, but the chimney was far too narrow for anyone to fit down. Even if someone had managed to slide into the house from above, there's no way he or she could have climbed back up with the boy.

It appeared that Max's story was either completely true, which he had a hard time believing, or Max was telling a complete lie. There's no way an intruder could have just faded into the background. He'd awakened immediately. He had then awakened his wife, but she hadn't seen or heard anything. No one exited the house. In the stillness of the night, they'd not heard anyone leaving. It didn't make sense.

Archer walked to the rear of the house and put on the black, leather gloves he'd brought to leave no prints at the scene. Last thing he needed was the brass breathing down his neck because he'd been careless. He examined the rear exterior again. There, almost to the furthest corner, he found what he was looking for, a way into the house.

A large branch was hovering less than a foot above a window. The tree had a large black streak down one side. Its bark was barely clinging to the trunk. Several of the branches were loosely hanging downward.

He'd seen this before when he was a child. Lightning had struck the big oak tree in his front yard. Within a few weeks it had wilted. The jolt of the electrical current was enough to completely crush life from the tree.

He moved to the low hanging branch. It would have to look like an accident, but that shouldn't be terribly difficult. If he'd had a small child playing in the yard, he would've removed that tree months ago. As it were, he was glad they'd chosen to ignore it.

He stood close to the base of the tree and jumped high into the air, grabbing the branch and allowing his weight to pull it lower. Surprisingly, the wooden limb held him. He remained there, hoping his weight would eventually topple it toward the window. After a few seconds, he rocked back and forth, praying it would give.

First, he heard a slight snap, followed by another. Then, a loud crack penetrated the still afternoon. The branch fell hard, crashing against the window, littering shards of glass both in and out of the house. He landed on his feet beside the tree. The window had shattered just enough for him to reach in and unlock it. He carefully slid it up and climbed into the room.

It was humid. Musty. The light eerily danced against the back wall of the living area. He could barely hear the soft tingling of the chimes outside. He removed his flashlight and illuminated his surroundings. He breathed a sigh of relief. Despite the warnings flashing through his mind, the room appeared empty.

He started his search there. There was a fifty-five inch plasma television mounted to the rear wall. A couple of Wii remotes had been left on the brown leather couch. A stack of newspapers had been collected on the coffee table to the right. He snapped several photos of the articles to peruse through later. Nothing seemed to be disturbed.

He moved down the hall and quickly searched the child's room. It was a typical boy's den, decorated with modern children's characters. He didn't recognize half of them. Things had changed since his days of watching GI Joe, Thundercats, and He-Man. The action cartoons had mostly been replaced by educational programs geared to challenge the mind. No wonder so many young boys were growing up without the benefit of masculinity. Balance had been lost. A young man was either extremely smart and incredibly weak or physically gifted and exceptionally dumb. It was the way of the world, and it aggravated him.

At first glance, nothing in the boy's room was disturbed. He continued to relentlessly snap pictures.

He finished in the boy's room and traveled the short distance to the master bedroom. The bed was unmade. The blanket was thrown across the floor. The sheets were disturbed. It looked like they hadn't been changed in a few weeks. Max and Jessica had definitely gotten up in a hurry.

He could tell which side of the bed Max slept in by the slant of the mattress. He closely examined the sheets on that side.

Max had said he'd bitten the ear of his assailant. He'd tasted the blood. A bite like that should have left physical evidence.

He lowered the small pack from his back and unzipped it, removing a clear strip of plastic the size of standard typing paper. He slowly removed the covering from one side, leaving a sticky residue on the now exposed portion. He placed it under the bed and pressed it down hard onto the floor. He then lifted it, sealed it in a plastic container, and marked it as trace evidence. He took a second plastic piece and completed the same procedure on Max's side of the bed.

After he was finished, he removed a small rectangle device and placed it on the end of his flashlight. The beam transformed to a shallower reddish hue.

He shined the light on the bed again, and then stooped onto the floor and ran it over the misplaced blanket. No trace evidence on either. Mr. and Mrs. Stanley had obviously not been intimate in quite a while.

He was about to investigate the crumpled sheets when he heard the sudden sound. The unmistakable grind of tires peeling on concrete. He moved to the window and peered outside. A black limo was barreling down the driveway.

He removed the plastic tip from the flashlight and placed it back in the bag with the plastic evidence holders. He quickly removed a sizeable transparent bag and roughly forced the sheets into it. He then sealed the entire bag in the backpack and zipped it again.

He hurried to the window and again peeped through the side of the blinds. The limo was pulling to a stop in front of the house. He quickly moved, trying to replace everything as it had been. He had planned on using the photos to replace it all exactly, but at times the best plans have to be altered.

He ran from the room, down the hallway, and into the living area. He shifted his body through the small window again. Once outside, he slid the window down and extended his hand back in to lock it. It wouldn't fasten.

He couldn't leave it unlatched. They'd know someone had been there. The sheets would probably give him away if anyone realized they were missing, but the unlocked, broken window would be a clear indicator. He stood on his tiptoes; angling the best he could to apply more torque against the lock.

He heard their voices on the other side of the living area, just outside the door. Jessica Stanley, Morgan LeDiv, and a third male voice he didn't recognize. The third didn't sound as educated as the others. It didn't have the sophisticated intonation that only comes through years of snobbish entitlement.

The creak of the loose board three steps from the door warned him that his time was closing. He heard the jingle of keys in the lock. The doorknob and the window lock turned simultaneously. The front door opened, just as he slid his hand out of the window and sprinted for the woods. He made the thirty-yard dash and dove into the tree line for cover. He ignored the throbbing of the thick briars ripping through his skin. He wheeled around.

No one was standing by the window. He was safe. He quickly stood and followed the path back to his car. This time, adrenaline propelling him, the two miles were covered in sixteen minutes. He removed the bag, placed it in the trunk, and slipped into the driver's seat. He sighed once, breathing heavily at the thought of almost being caught. He turned the key, pushed the pedal to the floor, and made his way back toward the city.

8

Three men had emerged from the restaurant shortly after LeDiv's limo had pulled away. Regan had chosen not to follow LeDiv. If the kidnappers were inside the building, perhaps she could follow them to where they were keeping the boy.

The first man was six feet tall, give or take a couple inches. He carried himself like someone who thought they had a solid build, but it was obvious he hadn't worked out in months. His once brawny chest and arms had been replaced by a much softer midsection. He wasn't fat, just slightly overweight but heading in the wrong direction. He wore a soft colored, linen suit that was slightly out of season. He was trying too hard. No one wears linen in the fall. That's reserved for spring and summer fashion. He wanted to look like a high profile, drug kingpin from Miami, but the look didn't work for him.

The second man wore a slim fit, black suit. He was trim and well put together. His muscles weren't bulging, but he undeniably had the body of an athlete. He walked with the swagger of someone who made a lasting impression.

The third man was dressed more casually. He wore a long sleeved, button up denim shirt tucked into a pair of worn Wrangler blue jeans. His cowboy boots were alligator or Iguana skin. His Stetson probably cost more than the rest of his wardrobe together. He wasn't dressed to impress, and didn't mind one bit.

How had he gained access to the restaurant? They were extremely selective in who they allowed to pass through the doors. Jeans were strictly prohibited, even from the more relaxed lunch atmosphere. This man either had powerful connections, or he was extremely influential.

Clothes tell a lot about people. It is inaccurate to assume that a person's clothes reveal their personality. However, they do greatly determine how others perceive an individual. It's ridiculous for a female to dress scantily, revealing her assets, and expect men not to think of her in a degrading manner. It absurd for a businessman to under-dress around high profile associates and expect them to take him seriously.

Clothing alters perception. Conservative clothing tends to cause others to focus more on a person's individuality, interests, and personality. One can find ways to be conservative and fashionable. A provocative appearance most often elicits obscene false impressions. Most men will feel more comfortable making unwanted sexual advances on a woman dressed to draw attention to her body. Most women feel more comfortable approaching a man dressed less sexually alluring. It makes them feel less vulnerable.

Regan had spent hours researching the topic. She was more qualified than most to make an assessment. The first one was a wannabe. He tried so hard to look the part of a hardened criminal to mask his inward insecurities about his physical toughness. He was probably hiding or overcompensating for a physical disability that wasn't obvious to most people until they got to know him. Probably asthma or diabetes.

The second man was a head turner, but lacked the apparent stigma of someone willing to kidnap a child. He was a pretty boy who preferred to not get his hands dirty. He was more interested in looking the part than being the part. He needed to feel tough, probably because he'd been abused on some level growing up. He got pleasure in others plights, but most often merely watched as others inflicted the pain. He liked power, but lacked the discipline and mental toughness to generate it. He thrived by looking the part and living in the wake of others who possessed it.

The third man was the one that alarmed her. Every fiber of her being screamed that she needed to avoid him. His self-assurance identified him as the schemer. He had the brains and brawn to pull off this feat. He had the look of a prowling cat carefully circling its adversary before the death pounce. He wasn't dressing for a role he wanted others to perceive. He was the opposite. He wanted others to mistake him for exactly as he was dressed, because inside he was something else completely. He was a killer.

The first one carried a duffel bag around his left shoulder. What was in the bag? It couldn't be money. Mr. LeDiv hadn't carried anything into the meeting. His henchman had been packing nothing but the illegal firearm. Whatever was in the bag had already been there at the time of the meeting.

It couldn't be a payoff. Unless... Mr. LeDiv was smart. He survived by outwitting his opponents. He probably had a third party deliver the money just before he arrived. Then, he closed the deal. If he was ever accused, no one could say they'd seen him making a drop. He was there, but he wasn't involved.

The three men moved toward a dark two-door sports car. As they approached, the one with the bag veered off and jogged across the street to a parked Harley Davidson Street Glide Base. The seven hundred eighty-five pound stylish hog fit the man waiting on it well. He was athletically built and wore typical biker's gear. The Don Johnson wannabe handed him the bag and jogged back toward the others. The man on the Harley started the four-stroke engine, and slowly merged into the afternoon traffic.

Regan tried to make the best choice. Which suspect vehicle would be most likely to lead her to the boy? She chose the motorcycle. It would be harder to tail, but from what she knew, you always follow the money.

As she inched her way into the stream of traffic moving the same direction as the Harley, the man in the cowboy hat placed a call on his cell phone.

An agitated, gravelly voice answered. "Hey. What's the word?"

"Everything went as planned. She followed him. He'll lose her before ten blocks in this traffic."

"Good. Don't lose her. We need to know if she knows

anything, and we need to minimize who she talks to. She's the wild card."

"Shouldn't I just silence her now?"

"Not now. It would bring too much heat. She's the lieutenant's niece. Just do a threat assessment. If it's high, you know what to do, but make it look like an accident."

The line fell silent. The man in the cowboy hat pulled in, six vehicles behind Regan. He wasn't worried. While she was busy harassing Jessica Stanley, he'd had one of his men place a tracker under her car. He looked at the small computer screen in his hand. The brilliant red dot was blinking brightly. This was too easy. Like stealing candy from a baby, right after you'd beat its mother into oblivion. He smiled. He couldn't wait 'til she pushed too far. He was going to take his time… greatly enjoy getting rid of her.

9

Regan slammed her fist into the ceiling. She'd made the wrong choice. It had been impossible to stay close to the Harley with the myriad of obstacles whizzing by in both lanes. He'd easily been able to weave in and out, leaving her sulking in his proverbial dust.

It hurt to give up, but she'd exited to the side of the road. Knowing a little boy's life was hanging in the balance made her want to do everything possible to find him, but she was coming up empty. Furthermore, she felt alone. The boy's family was refusing to help, and local law enforcement was going through the motions of the political death dance. Young Carson Stanley didn't have a chance.

She pressed the gas pedal and headed toward the police station. The only solution was to convince her uncle to throw more resources toward finding the kid. His other priorities needed to be relegated to the back burner until Carson Stanley was recovered.

Thirty minutes later, Regan walked into the glass doors of the police station. They opened, sliding sideways when she was six feet away. She barely noticed the low hum of the motor pulling the door open. It tugged hard against the glass panel's weight.

That's how she felt now. Small, insignificantly quiet, thrashing against gravity to save a kid she didn't even know.

She briskly made the short walk toward her uncle's office. Her heels clicked across the floor, slightly echoing down the hollow hallway. The dense wood door was snuggly closed. Animated voices could barely be distinguished from the other side. The words were audible, but lacked clarity. She listened carefully, but had no better luck making out the conversation.

Without hesitation, she noisily banged at the center of the russet stained entrance. The voices faded as footsteps approached.

"You better have a good reason for interrupting me," her uncle said as he turned the knob. The door opened, and she stepped in. He smiled and closed it behind him.

"We were just talking about you Regan."

She looked past her uncle and recognized Archer in the chair opposite his desk. "Detective Madsen," she muttered as she nodded toward him. He gave her a slight wave. The Lieutenant straightened his back and motioned toward the chair next to Archer.

"Please. Sit."

"I'm afraid I can't. I have information," she blurted out. "I was following Mr. LeDiv, and he went to drop money at The Classica. I waited outside and a few minutes later three men came out. One of them was clutching a duffel bag. He handed it off to someone waiting on a motorcycle. I tried to follow him, but he lost me in traffic around the intersection of Georgia and Main."

The Lieutenant vigorously shook his head and threw up his hands in disgust. "That's why I can't trust you. You can't go around pretending you're a legit investigator. You're not even part of this case."

"But I should be, and you know it. This is important. It's becoming-"

"Becoming what Regan? It's becoming personal. You're a woman searching for a missing child. I wouldn't expect anything less, but that's exactly what we can't afford. It can never become personal. That's what the perps count on…

…When a case grows personal, it gets messy. When it gets messy, you make mistakes. When you make mistakes, people get hurt. You must keep your head clear-"

"I tell you that I tracked the money to four men, and your response is that I'm too emotionally involved. Whatever… I'll open my own investigation."

"You know you can't do that. Any information you find has to be turned over to the local authorities. If people don't cooperate when we approach them because you've already questioned them, we'd have a problem. I'd have to arrest you for impeding a police investigation, and don't think I'd hesitate."

"I know you wouldn't. That's the shameful part. You always did put the job above your family. Why can't you just admit that I'm good at what I do? Why-"

"Because you found three men with a duffel bag? Why is that even pertinent?"

"I also interviewed Jessica Stanley again. She told me to search cold cases about kidnappings from this area. This has happened before, in her family."

"What? Are you serious-"

"Oh, so you're interested now."

He slightly calmed. "I'll have some of the men look into it, but I still don't understand why you think you found some important evidence. All you saw is a duffel bag, and you never saw it with Morgan."

"What if I told you that the first man reminded me of a poor man's Don Johnson, and I could pick him from a lineup? What if I told you the second man reminded me of a slightly younger Derek Jeter, and I could identify him too? What if I told you that I could find the third man within twenty-four hours just because of his boots?"

"I'd be slightly impressed."

She exaggeratingly exhaled air from her nostrils, using the sibilant sound to make a statement. "And, what if I told you I remember the license plate of the motorcycle?"

The lieutenant sprang forward. "Do you?"

"I don't know. I did. But I think I've forgotten it in all the emotions."

"Touché."

"It was personalized. SWGGER"

She mockingly looked toward Archer. "So detective, did you come up with anything useful in your spare time?"

Archer shook his head, "I can't share private details of this investigation with those not assigned to the case. Sorry."

She turned sharply toward her uncle. "What is this, the secret boy's club? You can't be serious. It's obvious that I can bring something to the table that you two can't."

"High levels of estrogen mixed with tiny amounts of testosterone," Archer quipped.

She wheeled around to face him. She was about to speak when the lieutenant interrupted. "Regan, I've been talking it over with Arch. I'm still not one hundred percent convinced, but I'm willing to sign off on this only because he's giving you a high vote of confidence."

He removed a file from his desk drawer and placed it in front of her. "I'm ready to officially invite you to be a consultant on this case… However, there are some conditions…

…This is the paperwork clearing you, as well as references

from two different sources with the Bureau. You're good to go as far as this office is concerned. You just need to remember that I've got full veto power at any time. If you cross me, don't follow directions, or play Lone Wolf Mcquade again; it's over for you."

She sheepishly grinned.

"Regan, this is serious. Archer is in charge. This is his only priority. Everything, and I mean everything, must go through him. Every decision. Every thought. Every concern. Don't move without consulting him, and never get out of his sight."

"But I don't need a ba-"

"This isn't a debate."

He grunted and then softened. "Look Regan, I'm torn. I'm trying not to view you as the little girl I've loved since she was born. It's difficult. I know you can take care of yourself, but something doesn't feel right…

…Unfortunately for you, I'm not only family; I'm your commanding officer. So take it or leave it. You can sign on the dotted line and move forward, or you can walk out and stay out of our way. That's your only options. Any other involvement, and I will lock you up until this is over."

She reluctantly took the pen and placed it on the line. She looked toward Archer, who appeared to be ignoring the conversation. She was aware that he'd heard every word.

Why not sign? She wasn't doing this for herself. She was doing it for a frightened child that had been cruelly ripped from his only security in the world. She gripped the pen more tightly and furiously scribbled her name.

Archer walked to where she was sitting and smirked. "Okay, now that you're officially on this case, in my spare time, I broke into the Stanley home."

The Lieutenant and Regan both whipped their heads toward him. "You did what?"

He relaxed into the soft chair. "Yeah. I broke into the house."

The Lieutenant's face was livid. "God Arch, she's not safe with you either. You're worse than she is. What were you thinking? No, wait… You weren't thinking."

"I was careful."

"Careful? Do you remember who owns that home? May I remind you that LeDiv is the best attorney we've seen in years? He'll be all over this. He has powerful connections. He's going to find out it was you, and when he does, I can't protect you."

"No worries. I was in and out with no problem. I wasn't seen. I covered the break in to look like an accident."

Regan ignored the urgency in her uncle's voice. "So, what did you find?"

"I'm not sure yet. I took the sheets from the bed Max was sleeping on when he fought the attacker. If he bit his ear, there should be physical evidence."

The lieutenant groaned, "This just goes from bad to worse."

"Anything else?" Regan cheerfully asked, ignoring him again.

"I took a million pictures of the exterior and interior of the house. Every inch of that house is covered. Jaxon, from the lab, is working on building a virtual tour of the home. Said he needed a few hours."

"He can do that?"

"I didn't know either. I asked him to print the pics. He said he'd do better. Modern technology. Efficient and amazing."

The Lieutenant calmed a little. "I understand why you two are pushing so hard. I get it. But we have to be smart too. Don't you think they'll notice the sheets are missing? How long after before they realize the 'accident' was manmade?"

"Hopefully long enough to keep that boy alive and bring him home. After that, hold me responsible. I'll deal with the repercussions."

Regan interrupted again, "Sorry to keep butting in, but you can deal with our reprimands later. We've got a case to work on…

…Arch, anything from the sheets yet?"

The Lieutenant nodded and walked from the room. Arch grinned at her.

"Not yet. The lab is looking through it. Shouldn't take long."

"So, what's our next move?"

"I'd say let's go back to the beginning. Where it all started."

"You mean, Max?"

"Yep. We've got to get Max to cooperate. Hopefully he'll help us. He wants to save his kid. There's no denying that, but something is off with him. We've got to figure it out. Let's go to the hospital first thing in the morning."

He removed his gun from the drawer and holstered it at his side. He had a feeling he'd need it soon.

10

The door squeaked open, allowing the pale moonlight to briefly cast an iridescent shadow across the floor. In the far corner, the object rested against the wall, the only item in the peculiarly empty room. The man who opened the door looked in and thoroughly studied the article.

It was a three-by-three steel cage, standing approximately two feet tall. The floor consisted of soft rubbery foam placed over the metal crossed beams. A single pillow was lying on the foam.

The kid was on his stomach, facing the wall. He appeared to be sleeping. Seems like all the kid did was sleep. They practically had to wake him up to give him his rations. It had been a while since he'd been around children, but he didn't remember his children sleeping this much.

Satisfied that all was well, he closed the door and moved away. Carson rolled over and longingly peered into the area the man had just vacated. Tears fell down his plump face.

He heard them walking toward the door every time they came. They terrified him, so he pretended to be sleeping. So far it had worked; they had left him alone. They occasionally brought him food and water, but he hadn't eaten. All he wanted was to be back with his mother. That was the only place he'd ever felt safe.

Sitting alone in the miniscule prison was difficult. He hardly had room to stretch his legs. He was getting cramped in the tight space. It felt like the walls were caving in, making it difficult to breath. He had cried for the first few hours, but after several veins had ruptured in his cheeks from the force of his bereavement, he'd given up and gone silent.

The air was cold, and he had no blanket. The water was stale. It tasted of cheap plastic. The food was Kid's Cuisine chicken nugget meals, the ones in the blue microwavable containers. His mother used to feed them to him when she was too busy to cook. He'd always enjoyed them, until now. They didn't taste as good from a cramped cell in a dark room.

He heard the man's voice on the other side of the door. "The kid sleeps too much. It's not healthy."

"Come on man, are you serious? We're doing this, and your worried about his sleeping habits. Really?"

He'd grown used to hearing their voices. They incessantly argued, bantering back and forth about insignificant details. This time, a new voice spoke. It was muffled, but vaguely familiar. It was somewhat soft, but rough and edgy. The fact that it sounded familiar made him strangely more relaxed.

However, the edginess made him revoltingly uneasy.

"You need to make sure he eats. He needs to be strong for the exchange."

"He won't be accepted if he's weak and hungry?"

"Of course he'll be accepted, but it won't be as good for our future if he isn't properly nourished. He needs to be in the best health as possible."

The man that always delivered his food spoke again, "How much longer do we have to hold him here?"

The edgy voice answered, "The exchange will be made Saturday night. Midnight. Under the harvest moon."

"It's only Wednesday. We can't speed this up? What are we waiting for?"

"It's routine. We have to stick to the plan. People get messed up when they grow impatient."

"But why does it have to be that way. Isn't he wanted? It shouldn't matter when or where. It doesn't make sense."

"You've got a lot to learn. You criticize the process while you reap the rewards. You should study your history before you so freely run your mouth."

"You're right. I'm sorry. I'm out of line. Please. Forgive me."

"We'll forget about this. Just make sure you keep him healthy. Keep him rested and full. When he's offered, we don't want them getting upset with us. If they're happy, we'll get a great reward. It will be worth it."

"I'm glad we don't have to do this too often. It's stressful. It hurts."

"Pain. Don't talk to me about pain. I know full well the weight it brings, but understanding the pain puts a premium on pleasure. There's no victory without a battle. There's no peace without a struggle. There's no gain without sacrifice. We live because we've learned that. We embrace it."

The footsteps moved toward the door again. He rolled back over and faced the wall. The aging door creaked open. He could feel the eyes staring toward him. After a few seconds the door closed and the footsteps meandered away.

The edgy voice created chills down his spin and lower back. "He doesn't know his purpose. Doesn't know why he's in the cage. Doesn't even know why he was born…

…He was made for this. His life will bring us such fruitfulness. We'll live in the abundance. Once the exchange is made, we'll be so greatly blessed. The benefactors of their benevolence. For him. Our lives will be changed, and we may never have to do this again."

The voices grew silent, and the footsteps stopped echoing across the floor. Carson placed his head on his arms and gently cried into the sullen stillness of the moon's eternal gaze.

11

Archer slammed his phone down, almost breaking it against the engrained wood of his coffee table. This was a nightmare. He shouldn't have waited. He should have ignored the fatigue and pushed through the night. He'd chosen to go home and get five hours of sleep. He could think more clearly. His senses would be more alert. He'd be better prepared. It had made sense. However, hindsight reveals the illogic nature of our decisions long after we've made them. What had taken place since he'd fallen asleep was preposterous.

He picked his phone up and dialed the number she'd given him the evening before. She answered on the third ring. She sounded like she'd been running a marathon.

"Hello. Arch, you're an early riser. You didn't strike me as one chasing the worm."

"Me? Nah. I like my sleep. Anyway, look who's exercising

before the sun's officially up."

"That obvious huh?"

He laughed, "I'd sound worse. It's been a while for me."

She smiled. "So what causes you to call this time of morning? We're not supposed to meet for two hours. What's up?"

"You haven't heard the wonderful news?"

She was too tired to detect the sarcasm. "What? Did they find Carson?"

"Not exactly. We aren't that lucky."

"Then what is it? Another break in the case?"

"Try another snag... Max is missing."

"Missing? He got away. I thought you had an officer posted at his door?"

"Well, he walked right past him. Apparently, Mr. LeDiv has some dreadfully influential connections. He woke up Judge Lawson in the middle of the night. The judge set bail. Mr. LeDiv posted his bail, and Max walked out a free man."

"He almost killed a police officer, not to mention the old lady. How is it that he just walked out of there?"

"The judge ruled that he wasn't a flight risk. As long as he agreed to stay in town, he could be released. So he's free, and we have no idea where he's hiding. I already placed a call to Mr. LeDiv, and he isn't talking. He was upset that I woke him up so early…

…I just don't get it. He still seems more interested in helping his son-in-law avoid legal trouble than bringing the boy home. It's almost like he trusts the kidnappers for some reason."

"You think he's involved? It's possible. Jessica stated that the kidnappers had heard that they'd been talking to the police. It sounded like someone had tipped them off, not that they'd observed it themselves.

I'd love for it to be true so I could wipe that smug grin off his grimy face, but I don't think the leading defense attorney in the state would be stupid enough to get involved in kidnapping, especially in his own family."

"Regan, I agree. It doesn't make sense. We've got to find Max. I'll pick you up in an hour. That enough time?"

"Make it thirty minutes. I'm done working out. Just need a quick shower. I'll be waiting."

"See you then," Archer said as he slammed the phone down.

12

Max paced the floor. There was something burning through the exterior of his emotions.

Resentment. Why had his father-in-law taken such an interest in getting him out at such a pivotal time? All resources should have been devoted to Carson. Any distraction was a waste of time. He hated himself for making stupid choices that had led to detracting the police and his attorney from bringing their child home. He'd been asking questions about the exchange since he'd been released. He'd gotten no answers.

Mr. LeDiv had picked him up from the hospital in the limo. They'd walked right past the guard placed at the door. He knew they considered him a risk to run. After all, he'd given them no reason not to. How had it come to this?

Mr. LeDiv had taken him to a posh hotel in the downtown district. Elegant and expensive, he'd never been able to afford such a place on his budget. Any other time, something like that would have mattered. Not tonight. He wasn't impressed with the porcelain décor across the foyer. He wasn't enchanted by the architecturally stimulating ceilings or the visually alluring lush carpet. The archaic chandeliers didn't register. He was focused, extremely thoughtful, about finding their young son.

Mr. LeDiv had opened the door to a large room on the bottom floor. It wasn't a standard hotel room. It wasn't even a luxury suite. It was more like an extremely stocked conference room with a bed. He was certain his entire house could easily fit in the area that he was now standing.

He saw her standing against the opposite wall. She turned, tossing her hair over her shoulder, allowing it to fall neatly to the side. He used to find that so gorgeous, but lately they'd been anything but attracted to one another. Life had a way of precluding the feelings of yesteryear. Fires that once sparkled were lucky to retain embers. Rivers that once cascaded vibrantly into oceans of bliss were blessed to trickle into dried up reservoirs of ruin.

She moved toward him, her once alluring walk replaced by the urgency of the hour or the stagnancy of midlife. Her gait was rapid and penetrating. He could see it coming. Her anger. Her hate. Her spite. Her pity. One of several emotions he'd grown accustomed to feeling from her. She said she cared for him, but he could feel the truth in her gaze. She hadn't loved him in a long time.

He'd never been able to measure up. They'd married young, a perfect couple. However, the reality of his inferiority had reared its ugly head not long into their honeymoon stage. He'd gone from fearless to fragile and couldn't measure up to the powerful figure her father commandeered. He always played second fiddle. He had wanted to be her everything, but it was increasingly apparent that he would always be the second most influential person in her life.

He adored her in every way. He still thought she was beautiful, charming, exceptionally brilliant, and charismatically enthralling. Her physical appearance hadn't changed much over the years. If he evaluated her honestly, she was more beautiful today then when he'd first met her. From the moment he'd laid eyes on her, his heart had melted, and he'd never recovered. Why she no longer affected him that way, he didn't understand.

Nothing else had changed either. Her wit and dry sense of humor, her love of life, her effortless charm; had all been refined. Like a fine wine, she'd only grown more mystifying with age. She was beautiful, the type of woman every man would dream of having. Her only fault wasn't her own. It was her family, that egocentric and selfish unit that devoured the world to feed itself. He'd tried to hide it, but he'd grown to hate them. Ultimately, that was the wedge that had been forcibly driven between them.

All that had temporarily changed when Carson was born. She'd immediately reprioritized. It seemed his prayers had been answered. He had become relevant again. At first he'd felt like nothing more than a sperm donor, but over a few months that had changed. They grew close again. He felt loved, needed, and even wanted. He'd missed those sentiments.

However, it was short lived. Carson had gotten sick after a few months. It was an unexplained childhood illness that almost claimed his life. As the father, he'd been powerless to do anything for him. No matter how much he tried. No matter how much research he compiled. No matter how many overtime hours he'd worked to stockpile money for treatment. It hadn't been enough. Carson continued to get worse.

As much as he hated it, they'd had to call the one person he'd sworn to never go to for help. His father-in-law had all to graciously been willing. However, as is usually the case with people who have large purses, even when they say there are no strings attached, the strings from the moneybags cut a wide path. There's no debt incurred like the one of feeling you owe someone the life of your only child.

They'd never recovered. He hadn't placed demands on them. It was hard to explain. To the casual observer it was nothing. However, there was a subtle blanket cast over the fire of their home that smothered the passion they'd been nurturing. Once again, daddy dearest was the savior, and Max was the rejected third wheel, riding in the backseat of his own marriage.

Now, he found himself in the same predicament. He was doing everything possible to bring Carson back. He had investigated, chased clues, hunted suspects, and ran from the police. He'd been so close. Within a few feet of getting answers.

Yet as always, he'd come up empty, and Daddy Millionaire had come to the rescue. He could pounce, causing devastation at any moment. Why wouldn't he just get it over with? Perhaps he enjoyed toying with people too much. He got pleasure from causing pain to the man that had stolen his daughter's heart.

She moved toward him, taking his hand in hers. "Oh Max… What were you thinking? You poor thing. You could have been killed."

Her pitiful tone turned his stomach. He wasn't a child. He'd been doing the best he could. Why couldn't she see that? Why couldn't she accept him for the man he was? Strength comes in various forms. He didn't need the power or wealth of Bill Gates or Donald Trump to be happy. That's not how he defined success.

She reached her slender arm toward him and attempted to touch his face. He moved away from her. "I'm fine Jess. Really, I am."

"But I've been worried sick. I'm so frightened. I hope you understand Max. I never want to lose you. No matter what happens, we'll get through this. Please, tell me we'll get through this."

"We always do Jess. You know that. We're survivors. We'll be fine."

"But I want to do more than that." She paused, thoughtfully looking toward him. "You okay honey? You don't seem yourself."

"Yeah," he muttered, "Try being me for a while. It sucks."

"What do you mean Max? I've lost a son too. You need to stop feeling sorry for yourself and realize that this isn't just happening to you. It's happening to us. Please Max. I know it hasn't been great between us lately, but I love you. I don't ever want that to go away."

"We haven't lost a son Jess. It sounds like you've given up. As much as the savior dad is putting into this, I thought you'd be confident he's coming home."

"You're right Max. That's not what I meant. Just please understand that I'm here with you baby. We're in this together. You aren't alone."

"No. You aren't alone Jess."

He took a deep breath, as his eyes seemingly grew a leak. "I'm incredibly alone."

She reached for him again. "Max, you're never alone. You've never been. Where's this coming from?"

"Jess. Listen to the way you talk to me. Like I'm a child. Like you don't respect what I'm trying to do. I'm a nuisance, distracting everyone's attention from Carson. I tried my best, and I haven't been able to help him. I'm useless."

"Max. Please."

"No. Stop Jessica. You know it's true. You think I don't realize that you think I'm crazy? The kid on the skateboard. The lady at the coffee shop. The man at the store. You think I don't see how you look at me when I tell those stories? At least the police were interested. But not you Jess… You told me to just stick to the facts, but those are the facts. It really happened."

She grunted. "I'm sorry Max. I'm trying to be supportive, but you're making this difficult. None of it makes sense. I know we have to emotionally cope in our own way. I get that. I'm just struggling to understand your way. That's all."

He turned away. "I'm not coping. This isn't a defensive mechanism Jess. It happened."

"You're so selfish!"

She slapped him. "Why just you Max? Have you asked yourself that? Why did they confront just you? Why didn't any one approach me? And Max… If there's a supernatural agenda at work, why the warning? Why not just take him?"

He rubbed his chin. His cheek still smarted from the blow. He'd thought of that already and had no answer.

"I dunno Jess. I wish I did, but just because I don't understand, that doesn't change what is."

"Dark figures in the night? Shadow people? The truth is that someone took our son, and it's terrified us. We have to accept that. The sooner we do, maybe the sooner we can learn the truth. Please Max, snap out of this. I need you to snap out of this."

He started to speak when the door opened again. Mr. LeDiv stepped into the room.

"It's all set. We can have him in three days. They're holding him 'til then to make sure the rest of the money is properly deposited overseas. Midnight. Under the harvest moon. The exchange will happen then. So, I'd suggest that we all just relax…

…Honey, I think we should leave Max alone for a while. It's been a long… and… uh… traumatic day for him. The young man could use some rest."

Jessica nodded and reluctantly walked to her father. Max cried as the door closed, leaving him once again alone to face the uncertainty.

13

Either perfect timing, or she'd been watching out of the window. She opened the door and stepped outside just as he pulled into the driveway. She was to the end of the stepping stone walkway as the car stopped beside it. She pulled the door open and slouched into the passenger seat. He calmly looked her over.

There was no denying her beauty. It was the kind of beauty that made her dangerous, the kind that turned heads and intimidated people. The kind that's most attractive because the person possessing it doesn't fully grasp how beautiful they are.

Her hair was long, but she'd tied it in a small knot over her left shoulder. Her cheeks were still burning from the early morning exercise. Her hair smelled like the fresh fragrance of floral shampoo. Her clothing wasn't revealing. She didn't need them to be. True seduction doesn't need dramatics.

She cast a glance in his direction, and the spell was broken. "We going somewhere, or you planning on staring at me all day?"

He cleared his throat. "I wasn't staring. I was just trying to figure out if you're really gonna wear those shoes."

"What's wrong with my shoes? They don't match or something?"

"They match fine, but they're heels. We're gonna be on our feet all day. You sure that's the right choice?"

"Yes. Just drive the car. I'm a big girl. I'm gonna be fine." She laughed, as she tossed her tied hair over the opposite shoulder.

He pulled out of the driveway. "Figured we'd head to the courthouse first. Something has been bothering me. I want to check it out."

"Yeah. What's that?"

"Why this family? And why now?"

"Explain."

"What made them a target? There are more wealthy families in the state, definitely in the country. The LeDiv's and Stanley's aren't popular names except in this area. That means they drew attention to themselves-"

"Or the kidnappers have to be local," she interrupted. "That makes sense. So why the courthouse?"

"We're going to review some old case files. They also keep a stockpile of old newspaper articles. I want to know if they were part of something that could've made them targets."

"Which one are you leaning toward?"

"I never lean. Creates uncertainty and carelessness. It leads to predetermining evidence instead of merely interpreting it. Too much is overlooked because you think one way, while the truth is hidden somewhere else. It's not fair to the victims or their families."

She nodded. "He tells me you're the best. My uncle I mean. He respects you. Says if anyone can get that boy back, it'll be you."

"I've gotten lucky a few times."

"I've done my homework. You're much too modest. You usually get who you're going after. The Kinsler Case, that was you wasn't it?"

"That was a long time ago."

"You see any similarities between that case and this one?"

"No. There aren't any. Different city. Different family. Different results."

"Is that the only kidnapping case you've ever worked?"

"Yes." He looked out the side window, subconsciously avoiding her.

"Why does it bother you to talk about it? After all these years, you haven't been able to let it go?"

"If I need a shrink, I'll schedule an appointment."

"Sorry. I shouldn't have brought it up. Just habit I guess. I was just trying to make conversation."

The silence lingered for a few seconds before he gently interrupted. "I'm sorry. I shouldn't have jumped down your throat about it. I suppose you're right. I never talked it out. Deep down it's still with me."

"Why didn't it work out the way you wanted?"

"The family took matters into their own hands. Against my advice, they tried to pay the ransom. They lost the money and the kid. I'll never forget it. The blank stare. The empty eyes. The cold response as I had to tell her mother."

"I'm sorry. No one should have to go through that."

"That wasn't the worst part. Someone tipped the parents off about a possible dump sight. The girl wasn't there, but I'll never forget the mother's screams when she found the girl's clothing.

Matted...

Muddied...

Stained...

...She lost it. Yelling maddeningly into the morning air. It took three officers to keep her out of the ditch. Her husband just fell to his knees. He was no good to her. He couldn't move. Couldn't speak. He was the one who had made the choice to move away from my advice. He looked at me. Our eyes locked, and he knew. He knew he was the reason. He knew he should've listened. To this day, she's never been found."

"It wasn't your fault. You should've felt vindicated. His decision should've absolved you from the guilt."

"Vindicated? I felt anything but. I broke a promise when I didn't get that kid home. I should've done more. I should've made him listen. I should've locked him up until the case was over. I was young and indecisive. My youthful arrogance cost a kid her life. I cost a family its future."

"You kept up with them after that? You didn't let it go."

"You can't just let that kind of thing go. It stays with you. It's worse than hell. You can't just move your way out by the power of positive thinking. It's too real."

"So… What happened to them?"

"The mother was committed to a mental hospital six months later. She lost her ability to cope with reality. The father turned into an alcoholic. Last I heard he was dying of cancer.

Desperate.

Forgotten.

Empty.

Alone.

One day that family was on top of the world. They had it all. In nine months their entire existence was reduced to a memory. That changes a man."

"But you caught the people responsible didn't you? I thought you found them?"

"I found them. Tracked them down by following the money. They were renting a single room in a crummy apartment. Living below their means. Trying to stay low profile."

"The report ended there. What became of them?"

He didn't answer. She waited a full sixty seconds, but he didn't respond.

"Arch. What happened to them? Did they go to trial?"

He coldly turned. "They didn't want to be taken in. End of story."

"End of story? What's that mean?"

"It means I walked away, and they didn't."

She swallowed hard. "You… You killed them?"

"I did what I had to."

"What you had to in that moment, or what you had to in order to live with yourself?"

"Is there a difference? I did what was needed."

She thought for a while, unsure of how to respond. Finally she tried to divert back to the present case.

"That's why you're worried about them paying the ransom?"

"It's the wrong choice. It's always the wrong choice. It just buys time. It doesn't change the end result. It never works the way the family thinks…

…I understand desperation, and in desperation people try things they wouldn't normally. In a case like this, you just feel like you have to do something to get your child back. However, the one thing you can do is usually the one thing that gets them killed."

"Is there a chance it could ever be the right choice? I mean is it an established certainty? Is there a chance you're handling this case differently because of the experience of the previous one?"

"I already told you, I don't lean. These things have to be by the book. You can't just follow your gut when lives hang in the balance. Instincts are good at getting you out of a jam, but they're sorry at keeping others alive."

"I understand, but I think sometimes you've got to follow your heart and see where it leads. Anyway, I just want to make sure we're on the same page Arch. I want to do everything we can to get this child home. If you're right, we're his only hope. That's hard to swallow. I don't want to leave a stone unturned."

He nodded, "I understand, but you've got to trust me. I trust you, or I wouldn't have requested your assistance. Just give me the same courtesy."

"One more question… Please?"

He looked into her eyes, trying to discern where this was going. "If we find these kidnappers, will they refuse to be taken in too?"

He turned away. "I'm not proud of what happened Dr. Rees, but I'd do it again under the same circumstances. One thing you better know for sure, if they make a move on us, I'll put them down. I won't hesitate."

The only sound for the next few minutes was the slight ticking of Regan's watch and the low hum of the tires across the pavement. She thoughtfully studied him as he drove in silence. Had he murdered those men, or had they drawn on him first? No one would ever know. The courts at that time wouldn't have been interested. Most people would have congratulated him for giving them what they deserved. She wasn't sure if he was capable of murder, but one thing was certain, Archer Madsen was a dangerous man.

14

Six hours later they'd hardly spoken. He'd given her the assignment of looking through newspaper clippings, magazine articles, and Internet reports. He wanted public records that could possibly frame the LeDiv and Stanley families in a negative light. In the mean time, he'd been scouring historical cases as far back as he could find. He found her sitting at a desk in a private study room, and opened the door.

"May I sit down?"

She warmly smiled, nodding for him to take a seat. "I'm sorry about earlier. Sometimes my assertive psychological brain gets the best of me."

"It is what it is. Let's just make sure this case doesn't turn out like that one… Did you find anything?"

"I've read just about every file from the past two years.

There's nothing. There's no mention of their wealth, influence, or power. There's nothing linking them to any entities worth large amounts of money. Maybe LeDiv is the real target because of his profession. Maybe he got someone off for murder, and one of the victim's families is seeking revenge.

"The only problem with that theory is that he wasn't the one contacted. The kidnappers directly contacted Max. If LeDiv were the target, he'd be the one sought out, especially by these people. They are too well organized. They wouldn't take anything for granted, and they sure wouldn't just assume the Stanley's would contact him. They would've involved him from the beginning."

"There's nothing else. None of them are linked to anything that suggests financial gain."

She studied him. "What about cases? Has Mr. LeDiv won any high profile cases that would have guaranteed large amounts of money? Any lawsuits or litigations involving clientele of questionable character?"

"A few months ago, he represented an oil company in a class action lawsuit. He easily got them out with minimal damage. He had key evidence ruled inadmissible, one piece after the next…

…I don't see how that could've caused any of this though. It wasn't highly publicized. The employees have moved on with an appeal to the Supreme Court. They wouldn't do anything to hinder the case before it makes it up the ladder."

She flipped through a couple of pages she'd printed. "Something doesn't make sense. Nothing happens by accident. The kidnappers targeted them for a reason. The less we find making them appealing to outsiders, the more likely it becomes that we're dealing with locals. I've looked through the files, and I can't find any local groups organized enough to pull this off...

...Mrs. Stanley told me this had happened in their family when she was a child. I don't know if there's a connection, but I've been curious."

He nodded. "It's interesting. The historical cases only go back thirty-two years. After that, there are no records. A courthouse fire destroyed them all. That's about the time that the LeDiv's would have lost their child...

...I found one other kidnapping case in the last half century for this area. The child's name was Matthew Grimm. I don't know if these two families are connected or not. In this part of the country anything is possible."

"I guess we'll be spending time at the library reading through the genealogy section," she joked.

"Actually, I've already got someone else on it. Between them and the lab, someone will turn over the right stone. We're going to refocus on Max. He's still the key to this. We've got to find him."

"Have you talked to Mr. LeDiv again? Or is he still refusing to help?"

"He's a closed book. He doesn't want to have anything to do with us. He sure isn't going to tell us where he's hidden Max. We're gonna have to find him on our own."

"I hope he doesn't live to regret it. I hope we can get the boy in spite of him."

Archer had been thinking the same thing. Mr. LeDiv was making a grave mistake. These kinds of mistakes never turned out positive. The writing was on the wall. He hoped she could live with the results, because their chances of finding the boy alive were slipping through their fingers with each passing minute. The boy was probably already gone. Another body. Another lifeless corpse. Another grieving mother. Another heart broken father. Another messed up family.

15

Max stirred from his sleep. He hadn't meant to, but he was worn out. He'd collapsed, half in fatigue and half in depression. Whatever the reason, he'd fallen asleep. He wanted to curse, to scream at himself. How could he sleep when his son was missing?

He reached into his pocket and felt through the loose change and crumbled dollar bills, removing the Nokia flip phone. He held down the speed dial.

A calming voice answered. "Hello… Max… You there? What's wrong?"

"Jess, I'm losing it. I can't keep it together. I'm trying, but I can't. I need you."

"Max. I'm doing everything I can to find Carson. I don't have time to coddle you right now. Please… Max, pull yourself together."

"I was together Jess. I almost had him. I would have found our son. I was so close. But the cops blew it…

…And that guy, he just ran his car into the bulldozer. It wasn't an accident. He wanted to die. He didn't hesitate. He never let off the gas. Who does that? Why?

"We've been through this a hundred times already."

"Jessica, listen to me. Something supernatural is happening. I saw the dark figure. It came into our bedroom. It carried our son away on his shoulders. I couldn't move. I couldn't respond. I could see him, but I was too paralyzed to help…

…I can't get it out of my head. I was there Jessica. I looked into its eyes. I felt its fury. There was so much hatred. I can only imagine what it's doing to Carson."

"And that's exactly what it is Max. It's your imagination. There's no other explanation. Dad has been in constant contact with the kidnappers. They provided us proof of life today. While you were off chasing phantoms and getting yourself arrested, we were trying to get to the bottom of this. We've collected money. We're gonna completely pay them soon. It's almost over. They've promised us my son will get to come home."

"Jess. The skater hero? The old Target employee? The coffee chugger? I imagined all of them?"

"I don't know. I just don't know anymore. I've been more than patient. I've waited on you to get this together. I thought you were finally gonna come around and help me. I thought we could finally be something. Now, all this has happened. I don't think we're getting past this Max. I don't think you're gonna let us."

"All I'm asking is that you believe me. Why won't you just do that? You used to trust me. Now, look at us. You hardly believe a word I say."

"Find proof Max. Make me believe you. I'll look for him my way. You look yours. Hopefully we'll meet in the middle. I don't care who finds him. I just want him found."

Max listened hard, as the *booooommmppppp boooommmmppppp booommmmpppppp* on the line sounded powerfully more rejecting than ever. Why was she doing this? He wasn't crazy. He knew what he'd seen. The creature had come into the room and stolen Carson. It had carried the terrified child out. Carson had been crying, not really screaming, but faintly aware that someone was taking him away from his mom and dad.

He could only imagine what must have been going through his young mind, and it repulsed him. A small child, ripped from the security of his own blanket and bed. Forced away from his parents.

Probably hungry.

Lonely.

Afraid.

The last thing he'd seen was his father. The one supposed to be strong, fierce, and protective. But Carson had seen him weak and unable to move. That wasn't fair, and at this moment, Max hated himself for it.

He sat, nervously rocking back and forth, trying to conjure tears that refused to surface. He stoically stared against the walls, discerning patterns in the shadows, praying they'd give a clue as to where Carson was being held. He needed a miracle, something to shatter the hopelessness that enveloped him. Something to restore the fragileness of his mind.

He stood up. He knew what he needed to do. The coffee shop. Target superstore. The kid on the skateboard. He'd revisit them. Interview people. Hopefully someone had seen something that could help him find his son. He walked into the open closet and stood below the top shelf. Moments later he reached above his head and removed an unmarked shoebox. Removing the lid, Max pulled a six-cylinder handgun from the box and placed it in his waistband. He rifled through the box and removed an old wallet. He flipped it open and looked in the mirror. The badge may have been old, but he was certain it would still pass as current to anyone who didn't know better.

He smiled. He wasn't gonna ask questions as the father of a kidnap victim. He was gonna ask as a detective. He knew he'd get much more cooperation that way. He smiled again, the corners of his mouth rising like crooked pointers.

It had been a long time since he'd worn the badge. He liked the feel of it. Memories flooded his mind. The power. The excitement. The brotherhood. Until the accident.

Because of what happened, he'd been forced to an early retirement and sworn to never don a badge again. He'd never felt the urge. Not until now.

Jessica Stanley shook her head. She looked across the table at the man she respected more than anyone else in her life.

"He's not doing so well daddy. You were right about him not being able to handle this."

Mr. LeDiv smiled and placed his hand over his daughters. "He's taking it hard. He's not from the same stock as us honey. Don't hold it against him. When you've been through hell, it makes it easier to deal when trouble comes. When you've never had to deal with anything, it's a lot harder to handle the pressures of life. He'll adapt."

"He thinks he's losing his mind."

"That's what I expected. We prepared our plan knowing he'd be little help. What has to happen is up to us now. He'll come around after it's all said and done. He'll be grateful that we acted without him. Trust me."

"I do trust you. I trust you more than anyone. So far, everything has gone like you said it would. I know you've dealt with this sort of thing before. I never have. So I have to rely on your instincts… Do you really think he'll be okay? I can't lose them both."

"Don't give up yet. Just hold on. I think everything will turn out okay. One day you and Max will look back on this and be thankful it happened. It will bring you closer together. That's how this works. You just have to trust the process honey. Right now it seems impossible. It feels the pain will never end, but I promise you that it'll be over soon."

She lowered her head and lightly sobbed. "It just hurts. I

feel like I've already had to sacrifice so much. I don't think I can take another loss."

He removed his hand from hers and placed it around her, drawing her into him. "It's okay. That was a long time ago, dear. It's been forgotten."

He snorted air through his nostrils. "I mean, most people don't even know about your brother. What happened to him was a tragedy."

"But I still feel it. It's strange, but I can't seem to let it go. It hurts so bad sometimes."

"Well, you know what they say about twins. There's a connection that remains after death. He passed on, you didn't. In some ways, maybe you're still holding on to that. You need to let it go. It's the only way you'll ever heal."

"You know, I never even told Max about it. He doesn't even know I had a brother."

"It's okay honey. It wouldn't have made a difference. It was a long time ago. There's no reason Max needed to know. Sometimes it's easier just to let things stay buried."

"I just need Max to be okay daddy. I can't get through life without him. You know I love him."

He smiled. "Of course you do sweetie. That's why I'm promising you that it's gonna be okay. He loves you too, and love is a powerful thing. It gets you through a lot of battles you couldn't get through any other way. It makes you do things you inwardly wish you didn't have to. It helps you overcome the hurt and terror of life. That's the power of love.

Sometimes you make difficult choices. You make sacrifices for those you truly care about. Do you understand?"

She reluctantly smiled back. "Yes sir. I understand."

"Good." He stood up and walked away, leaving her alone to contemplate her husband and son's fates.

16

Archer shook the man's hand that was standing in front of him. They exchanged pleasantries. Archer turned toward her.

"Ronin, this is Dr. Regan Rees. Dr. Rees meet Detective Ronin Stern."

He was an older man, nicely dressed but not overly done. His hair was grey, and his face showed the lines of years of hard work. He was tough and carried the quiet confidence of years of experience. The mutual respect between the two men was apparent. She guessed the elder man had been a teacher or superior officer to Archer at some point. He probably viewed the younger as a son he never had, taking the role of a father figure in his life. All in all, he reminded her of the consummate southern gentleman.

The older man smiled warmly. "Ex-Detective Stern. Just call

me Ronin… Well Arch, you sure pick 'em better now. She's much prettier 'n me."

It was obvious he'd caught her off guard. Archer laughed. "Much prettier than you Stern. There's no comparison."

He paused a couple of seconds, letting the awkward tension envelope her. Finally, he looked toward Ronin, still chuckling.

"So, what made you call me down here? You said you had something I'd be interested in."

"Sure do. You know I still keep up with things. It's in my blood."

"Once a detective, always a detective," Archer replied.

"Exactly. It's just natural. You know?"

Archer nodded. "Yes sir, now what you got for me?"

"It's about your case, the kidnapped kid."

"What do you know about that?"

"I know that things aren't always what they seem Arch. Don't know much more than that. I'm looking into it… I mean, if you want my help on this one?"

"We're talking off the record and below the radar? You know I can't let you do anything officially. You can't be seen on this one."

"I understand. I'm not talking official. I'm too old for that anyway. I just turned sixty-three two days ago… And I know Arch; things aren't like the used to be. They've changed since I was your F.T.O."

"Yes sir... They have. But I trust your judgment more than anyone I've ever worked with. If you tell me you can be invisible, I believe you."

The older man slightly smiled, "I got it Arch. I'm just here to help you."

"Okay ole man. Whatcha got then?"

"Not much yet. I'm digging into it a lot deeper, but did you know that Max Stanley was a cop when he met the young Jess LeDiv?"

"No. Are you serious? Why didn't anyone pick up on that before?"

"I guess they didn't find it pertinent."

"And you do? You think it's important."

"Not really. But what is important is why he's no longer a cop. I did some digging. There are bad skeletons in the closet Arch. The mental and emotional kind, almost impossible to deal with."

"Explain... please."

"He was an up and coming officer in Detroit back a few years ago. He was pursuing a male unsub suspected of raping a sixteen year-old girl in her parents' minivan. The unsub ran into what Max thought was an abandoned warehouse. Turns out, it wasn't. Some of the local kids used it almost every afternoon as a paintball war zone...

...Of course, they kept that fact extremely private. So this building looked like an empty graveyard from the outside, but the inside was a maze of barricades and dark corners. Max had stepped twenty feet inside when one of the teens jumped from behind a barricade with what looked like an automatic weapon aimed at him...

...He did what any of us would have. He pulled his weapon, aimed at center mass, and fired three times. It was textbook. Internal Affairs took all of two days to conclude the investigation. They found he wasn't at fault. They ruled that he needed to take a few weeks off and have a few sessions with the department shrink. The kid didn't make it. He died on scene."

"That's tragic. What happened from there?"

"Well, he visited the shrink for three months as requested. After the three months, she was supposed to clear him for active duty again, but she refused. She said he had severe issues that could be detrimental to his performance as a police officer."

"Like what?"

"I don't know all the details, but I know P.T.S.D. As well as performance anxiety, not of a sexual nature... He was afraid to pull his weapon again. You can see the danger that could pose to those around him in the law enforcement community. Despite the warning, a brotherhood of officers rallied around him, insisting that he be placed back on active duty. Of course, this couldn't happen without medical clearance, which he never obtained...

...Finally, he quit. He just up and walked out one day. Got up from his desk and never looked back... I talked to his old Captain. The Captain said it wore Max down. He was never the same after shooting the kid. He blamed himself no matter how much they tried to convince him otherwise. The rapist got away. It was all too much for him. The Captain was concerned that Max would kill himself or turn vigilante and start killing others...

...Max had always been known as a tough, independent cop, but this neutered him. Turned him soft. He lost his aggressive attitude. It's quite sad actually."

"It's extremely sad," Regan replied. "All that happened, and now this. It's too much for one person."

"Yeah. You want to know what's really bizarre? The child's name. The kid he shot was named Carson Smith."

Regan snapped her head around. "Carson. He named his son after the teenager he killed?"

"That is strange," Archer echoed. "Why would anyone do that? That's sort of twisted."

Regan looked at him. "We could be in trouble Arch. Maybe we're looking at this wrong. We need to dig into his past. We have to know everything about him."

"Okay. What aren't you saying?"

She looked unsure, nodding her head toward Ronin. Archer caught her glance. "It's okay. He's good. What aren't you telling me?"

"If he was delusional enough to name his son after his victim, that's not good. It means he's either carrying an extreme amount of guilt, or the Captain could have been right. Sometimes people become so delusional that they kill themselves. At other times, they substitute people for someone else in their minds. Like his own son is standing in for the other boy. The problem is that the person often gets trapped in his or her delusion. You can try, but you can't change the past."

"So, he could be involved in this somehow? Hiring someone to kidnap his child so he could play the hero. This time, he could save Carson instead of taking his life?"

"Exactly. But it's dangerous Arch, because the person is really mired in the murk of his or her own twisted mentality. As much as they try, they can't change what's happened. So, history just repeats itself... Arch, if I'm right. Carson is in trouble. Max could kill him, never realizing that he's done it again, until it's too late."

"That's an outlandish form of substitution don't you think? I mean come on. Have you seen the way he talks about his kid? He's a grieving father wholeheartedly searching to bring his son back home. There's no way he's part of this."

"Arch, you're leaning. You believe he's innocent, when the truth may point in a different direction. You don't know anything for sure. I think we need to examine all options."

"I know you're right, but I just can't get his expressions out of my head. They're genuine. He's concerned about his son. Those emotions are real. The fear isn't imagined. Whatever the truth is, he isn't pretending about those emotions."

"That may be true, but you have to consider that he could also be highly delusional. He could be responsible for his son's kidnapping and not even remember. He could be rooted so deeply in a savior complex that he can't see anything else. I've never seen it so profoundly before, but theoretically, it's possible."

Ronin sat down. "I think I've heard something like this before. I was reading scientific studies from some cases in New York. The crimes were a couple of years ago. The perpetrator modeled his victims to fit family members whose deaths he felt responsible for. In a way, he was reliving the guilt of not being able to save his own family. Killing others made him feel alive again. It wasn't an act of pleasure. It was merely an adherence to his emotions. He killed others so in some sick way he would have the power to save them if he choose to-"

Regan interrupted, "I remember that case. It created national headlines in psychological journals. The family members had been burned in an apartment fire. He was the only survivor...

...It was strange. He started killing people that reminded him of his family members. Exercising power over them helped him create credibility in his own mind. However, as I mentioned before, the person often gets stuck in the reality of the fantasy. The past can't be recreated; it can only be reenacted. Therefore, the suspect is destined to kill again. Killing is their only sense of living."

Archer appeared skeptical. "So, could something like this hypothetically be applied to kidnapping?"

"I doubt it. Not kidnapping only. That's my point. If he was delusional enough to have his own son kidnapped, you can believe he'd be delusional enough to kill him without realizing he'd recreated his original sin."

Archer thoughtfully studied her. "I just don't know. I'm not buying it… But, you're right Regan. We should cover every aspect."

He turned to Ronin. "Would you mind following up on this? Follow the old contacts. Track it down the rumor mill. Do what you do. I need answers fast. I want to know everything about it. I want to know the personal details of his life. His finances. His contacts, acquaintances, and friends. His favorite hangouts. I want it all."

Ronin sneered. "I'm not as young as I used to be. This might take me a few minutes."

"Make it happen Ronin. I'll look forward to hearing from you. You've got my number."

He looked at Regan. "Ready for some real police work. We need to interview his therapist. I need you for that call. One professional to another. They'll set it up in the interview room."

Ronin called out as they made their way toward the door. "You kids be careful… Arch… Watch your six. This one's gonna be dangerous. I can feel it."

"Will do Ro… You be careful too."

Ronin nodded as the door closed behind them. He'd had a dream about the boy last night. He'd learned to give them much credence. Many times they'd turned into reality. Sure, he'd heard rumors. He'd heard what the boy's father had been telling the authorities. Maybe that had influenced him. He wasn't sure, but his dream had been revealing. Scary actually.

A dark form had taken the child. Carried him into the night. He'd been carried into a field that was brimming with hooded figures. There was a dagger. An animal on an altar. Blood everywhere. Screaming.

He'd awakened to the boy's screams from inside a miniscule gloomy cage. After he sat up, he swore he'd still heard the shrill squeals echoing down the midnight street. He'd listened intently while the sounds promptly faded. Hopefully he'd have more luck tracking down the boy's father. He had a feeling they'd all need as much good fortune as they could get. This one was gonna be tough.

17

Max tried to remain composed. His head was swimming in the deep abyss of clouded perspective. The voices echoed through his head. Not audibly, but distinct nonetheless. They effortlessly drained him of the will to move forward. He wanted to pursue. To plan. To investigate. To annihilate anyone that kept him from finding his son.

He knew the truth. Kidnappers hadn't taken Carson for money. It didn't make sense. Too much about that raised red flags. His father-in-law hadn't become so influential by accumulating bad choices. However, he was wrong about this. Dead wrong.

At best, the lie about the money was a decoy to buy time for something far more sinister. At worst, Carson was already dead, and they'd decided to cash in since their prior endgame couldn't be completed. Either way, he was certain this hadn't started out as a way to make quick cash. There were too many easier ways. There were too many low profile but wealthy marks.

He hadn't been targeted. He'd kept a low profile. His only enemies were from a long time ago. Sure, they could have found him by now. He hadn't hidden that well. However, he figured after all these years he didn't have to. The boy's family had moved on, accepted fate. It was probably easier that way.

He walked into the records department. He wore a classic fit black suit, with a starched white-buttoned dress shirt. He casually meandered to the front desk and stood in front of the receptionist. She was a young, cute African-American who looked like she was there for her striking figure more than great work ethic. Not that pretty girls couldn't be diligent workers. Just that you can sometimes tell the types that men hire more to fulfill their own fantasies than for actual job performance. He smiled. Who was he to judge? If you're gonna have to look at someone all day every day, she might as well be worth looking at.

She smiled back, her face radiant in the otherwise cramped style of the room. Her expression seemed easy, the kind of girl he imagined the District Attorney would love to have working his front end.

He was banking on a couple of things in order to make progress. First of all, he was hoping she'd seen him in the office before. He'd been in a few times with Mr. LeDiv. If she recognized as much, he wouldn't seem out of place. He'd be able to access the records with little problem. Secondly, he was banking on the fact that he could get the information quickly enough to not be noticed by anyone else who knew he'd been a fugitive.

Law enforcement personnel frequented the records department daily. Any of them could recognize him from his fiasco yesterday. That unwanted attention would raise concerns. Those concerns would get him removed. He wasn't working for a law firm. He was gathering information to benefit his own standing. The legal system doesn't work that way.

"Can I help you sir?"

He smiled again. A few years ago his smile alone would have gained him access anywhere he wanted. A few pounds heavier and a few desperate years later, he needed to conjure more of the old charm.

"You've helped me already. Just lookin' at ya has brightened my day."

She laughed. A little awkwardly. Maybe he'd come on too strong.

He didn't return the humor. He held her gaze. That was the secret. He didn't want her to think he was joking. He didn't want her to feel that he was trying a cheesy line to get something from her either. Even if that were his purpose, the key was to make sure she didn't know it. He waited for the right moment; that little sparkle of curiosity in her eyes. She wasn't sure of his intentions, but she was interested enough to pay attention. He recognized it and leaned slightly toward her on the desk.

"Perhaps you can. I'm one of the many assistants to Mr.

LeDiv-"

He noticed the grimace. Slightly discernible, but definitely there. He was correct in his analysis. His father-in-law wasn't liked around the District Attorney's Office. He'd planned on that.

"Look. I know he's hated around here. You should work for him. He's hated worse over there. But it's a good paying job, and everyone else said I needed more experience. He was willing to take a chance on me when others wouldn't. So I'm stuck serving my time until someone else notices. I don't like it either."

She nodded, slightly relaxing. "I understand."

He placed his hand on top of hers. "Please, don't tell anyone I'm here. Don't mention that I came. I'm investigating off the records and don't want to start trouble. I just need to pull a few files and need a couple of hours in the most private spot on this floor. Think you can help me with that?"

He'd pulled it off. Her curiosity had turned to intrigue. He'd offered her the chance to rebel against the status quo. Even though it was a small part, she could assist someone working against the natural flow. He knew before she answered, she was going to help him.

"Right this way," she said, as she got up, leading him away. She pulled him to a door in the far back corner of a large open room. The room had several tables placed throughout. For now it was empty, but he'd been there several times when it had been nearly full of young lawyers studying case files, perusing records to find legal loop holes for their benefit. He needed to avoid that sort of crowd.

She opened the door and ushered him inside. It was a storage closet. There was a small table in the back with various chemicals and household cleaners pushed to one corner.

"It's where I come to study when I'm on lunch and want to avoid the inexperienced lawyers who hit on me all day. Sometimes I'm just not in the mood ya know."

He lightly grinned. "Got it. You don't have to worry about that from me," he said, as he pointed to the band on his finger. "Happily married for many years."

"Good for you. Don't get that too often in this profession. The ones who stay married usually don't describe it as happy. That's why they stay botherin' me."

She walked to the table and pushed the supplies further into the corner. She pulled a soft, swivel desk chair from under a rack of shelves and slid it toward the open spot on the table.

"Have a seat sir. I have a fifteen-minute break. Usually by now the vultures are pouring in, scouring the records. Give me a list of the files you need, and I'll pull them for you. Shouldn't take long. You can stay hidden."

He quickly jotted down the list and handed it to her. "Thanks. I owe you one. You ever get in trouble, just come down to the defense department and look me up."

"You're welcome, but I hope to stay out of that kind of trouble. If I need your help, it's probably already too late for what I want to do in life. You know, they don't take too kindly to criminal activity in law school. One day, I hope to be the first black female Supreme Court Justice. "

"I like your chances, but the offer stands. Hopefully, you'll never need to take me up on it. I appreciate what you're doing for me just the same."

She walked away, locking the door behind her as she stepped outside.

Twenty minutes later he was still waiting. He nervously looked at his watch, as if somehow staring at it would force his wait to be over. What if he'd read her wrong? What if she were merely playing him? What if she'd recognized him? She could have called the police. Maybe they were forming a line in the lobby, just waiting for him to come out.

But, he wasn't exactly wanted at this moment. He kept telling himself to calm down. He was out on bail. There was a difference. He was following all the rules. He wasn't a criminal until the court decided he was. Why was he so nervous?

His thoughts wouldn't let up. It had been twenty-five minutes. What if she'd called LeDiv? That was possible. The old man had connections everywhere. There seemed to be dreadfully few stones in the city he hadn't already turned over. If life were a mafia movie, he'd for sure be playing the part of Marlon Brando. He ran this town.

He looked at his watch again. Twenty-eight minutes. He stood up and paced toward the door. He was just about to reach for the knob when he saw it turn. The door opened, and she stepped inside.

"Sorry. It took a little longer than I thought."

She looked at him inquisitively. "The file you asked for on Mr. Max Stanley. You know that file was activated again yesterday. He was involved in a shooting a few years ago, but there had been nothing else in his records from then until now. That's what took me so long to find it. It was already pulled. Someone had it checked out early this morning."

"Any way of knowing who?"

"I knew you'd ask. So I did some quick digging. Garrison Reed of the Federal Bureau of Investigation logged it out. Any idea why the FBI would have interest in the same file you wanted?"

He panicked. His heart was pounding in his chest. Why would they want to investigate him? He wasn't guilty of anything other than trying to find his son. His ordeal had all started yesterday. How had they tracked it so fast? It didn't make sense.

Maybe it wasn't him. Maybe they were looking into the case of his son. But that didn't make sense either. They didn't know about his son. Local law enforcement could have tipped them off, but information was usually kept private in this area of the country. They didn't take kindly to outsiders sticking their nose where it didn't belong. He felt lucky the police department was investing as much into this case as they were. They never liked making a public spectacle. He highly doubted someone from inside the department would have invited the Feds in.

He also doubted that LeDiv would have called them. No. He was certain that weren't the case. LeDiv needed to be the hero. His way was always the only way he'd consider. He didn't believe in consulting others. If they disagreed or tried to present an alternate way, he'd shoot them down. He always knew best. Always. So, why was the FBI looking at his file?

He quickly looked at her, trying to conceal the emotion in his eyes. "Did this agent pull any other files, or only looked into the one on Max Stanley?"

"It's strange. The same agent was here most of the day yesterday. He pulled some of the same files that you're asking for now. A couple of them were still waiting to be filed back. I just haven't had time to get to them yet."

"Which ones"

"Well, he looked through all the files associated with Mr. Stanley and his wife. He also searched for any files concerning missing children in the area. A couple of the missing children were cross-referenced with the ones that you requested about child kidnappings."

He stared into the wall as if looking for a mystery to be revealed. "You okay," she asked.

"Sorry. Just thinking. If you don't mind, what else did he review? Do you know?"

She proudly giggled. "I sure do. There was a reason I ran over my fifteen minutes. I was investigating it. It seems that he spent the majority of his time researching every employee of the LeDiv Law Firm. He also investigated most of the parties they've represented over the last ten years."

"That information isn't protected?"

"The intricate details between the firm and its clients are. However, anything that comes out during the trial is considered public information and subject to the Freedom of Information Act. It's not protected by law."

"Listen. I need about an hour to stay here and go through these records. Can I hire you to do something important? Off the record. Nothing illegal. Just something I don't have time to do myself."

She looked into the shadows of the room. "I dunno. If the D.A. knows I've been moonlighting on the dark side-"

"It'll be our little secret. No one will know. Just like no one will ever know about this," he said, as he placed six one hundred dollar bills on the table.

She studied them thoughtfully. "Man, I hate you. What are you asking me to do?"

"Just pull the same records the Fed studied yesterday. Put them in this room. I'll be back in the morning to go through them... Does anyone but you ever come in here?"

"No, just me." She stared down at the floor, as if she expected it to open up and swallow her. "Do you mind telling me why you're so interested in what he was doing?"

"Long story. Honestly, it could lead nowhere. However, it could be what I need to break my case. Sorry, wish I could say more."

She picked up the money. "This says plenty. I'll have them out for you when we open tomorrow. Don't be late. Tomorrow is the early rush. I'll let you in at eight if you can make it by then. When you're done here, just lock the door behind you."

"One more question… Did you happen to see a file on a missing kid from the past week? I believe his name is Carson Stanley."

"No, but you're not the first one to ask me that. The Fed, he asked me the same question, and then spent a considerable amount of time checking to see if anything had been recorded. As far as the D.A.'s office is concerned, he hasn't been kidnapped."

She left him to search his and his wife's case file. His was amazingly skeletal. He was surprised to find that hers was exceptionally bulky. He slowly examined the pages, afraid of what he might find. Afraid of what the Fed had already found. He needed someone to talk to. He needed answers. He had nowhere to turn. After tomorrow he'd do it. He'd gather the facts. Then he'd contact Archer Madsen. It seemed to be the only way.

18

Regan stiffened, refusing to relax in the cushy chair from the Police Department interview room. She was facing a sixty-inch television screen on wheels. It was mounted three feet above a computer board intermittently blinking various shades of red, green, blue, and white. A three-inch eyeball sat on top of the screen, the camera sending her image across several thousand miles to another person she'd be communicating with shortly.

Within seconds the blue screen turned into live video feed. A vertically challenged, plump woman sat at a large oak desk. The décor behind her spoke volumes. She was extremely wealthy and dealt with only the most important clientele. Regan pegged her for early to mid fifties based on her appearance. Of course, a couple of surgeries in the right places could deceive anyone into that belief. Her eyes told another story.

That was how Regan sized people up. Most often, the eyes are the talebearers of the soul. It's rare for the eyes to keep secrets. They usually can't mask the warmth, pain, joy, surprise, fear, rage, bitterness, seduction, honesty, or myriad of other emotions lurking beneath a person's controlled exterior. The eyes are the telltale sign of a person's psyche.

Millions have been won or lost. Marriages marred or enhanced. Secrets protected or released. Victory assured or negated. The animal kingdom perceives threats or potential mates. All by the power of the eyes.

One holds a gaze too long; they're probably lying. One glares slightly too hard; there's probably dissention in the ranks. One looks away too swiftly; there's a truth they don't want discovered. The eyes widen merely a touch beyond the norm; there's a reason they're afraid.

The eyes give away a person's thoughts and innermost feelings. They are the gauge to one's moral fortitude. There's much to be said about the power of human expression. Regan had already learned enough about the woman she was now speaking to.

"Dr. Regan Rees. I've been looking forward to meeting you. I never would have guessed it would be under these circumstances. You're office tells me that you have some questions."

Regan caught the slightly condescending tone. She knew the game, and she didn't flinch. She wasn't sure if the woman was telling the truth or not. She'd probably done a quick Internet search and read enough of her profile to be dangerous.

"Just in case you're wondering Regan. I've had my eyes on you quiet a while. Graduated at the top of your class twelve years ago. Have established a lucrative business. Could be doing much better except you still take on the low-income clients who can't afford to pay. Much is to be said about your nobility. As you can tell, I gave that up a long time ago-"

"I'm not impressed Dr-"

"And I'm not finished yet. You were married once. Two years. That's all it lasted. You tell yourself it's because he was problematic and uncompassionate, but deep down, you know its because you were married to your work before you married him. He couldn't get over that…

…At one point you thought you wanted children, but you made the choice to pursue your career instead. Now, you've almost given up on every girl's dream of white picket fences, the man of your dreams, and miniature versions of the both of you playing in the yard. You think it's just about too late-"

"Enough mirroring yourself Dr. Lloyds. If you'd like to know my story, I'd be glad to meet you in person one day and share. Today's not that day, I'm afraid I'm a little preoccupied."

Dr. Gale Lloyd's smile faded. She tried to recover before anyone noticed. "I wish you would. I've had my eyes on you. If you want to shut down the small business and come partner with a real player, let me know. We'd love to have you."

"And if you'd like to compare testosterone levels with the boys, I'd be glad to leave the room… I mean I've got to be honest. I'm not up on the Who's Who of the psychology industry. Before today, I didn't even know you existed. So let's just cut the crap. I'm trying to help local authorities find a kidnapped child. I would appreciate the professional courtesy of your assistance... If... there's anything professional about you."

She forced a smile. The eyes again. She wasn't used to being talked to like she talked to everyone else. She was used to getting her way, used to everyone bowing down at her feet. Oh well, everyone's dreams have to be dashed at some point. Reality usually slaps you in the face, and when it does, it strikes with a vengeance.

Her voice was rigid, "How can I help you?"

"Well, I need information about a patient of yours. You saw him a few years back. I'm sure you'll remember. There was an accident with the police department. A kid was killed."

"You'd be surprised how many of those cases I get. I'm afraid you'll have to be more specific."

The sarcasm was dripping off the end of her words. Regan ignored it.

"Do most of those involve the son-in-law of Morgan LeDiv?"

Her eyes flinched upward. "Morgan LeDiv. I'm afraid I don't know the name. I still need you to be a little more specific."

Archer was standing just out of the camera's view. He shifted on his feet and took two steps sideways, entering the camera's line.

"Hello Dr. Lloyd. I'm Detective Archer Madsen. Dr. Rees is consulting with me as lead investigator on a kidnapping case. The person of interest today isn't a suspect at this point. He's the father of the missing child. However, we've seen enough red flags to warrant not ruling out his involvement. We're on a bit of a time crunch. So any help you can give would be greatly appreciated. Our department would owe you one. The person's name is Stanley. Max Stanley."

She smiled. "I appreciate your courtesy and candor detective. Max Stanley. I know the name well, and I do remember the many sessions I had with him. He was extremely distraught over killing that child. A paintball gun I believe. That was the difference between the kid living and dying. Such a pivotal decision to buy one of those things. Such a critical error on the kid's part to not recognize the danger and stay hidden."

She paused, looking directly into the camera, her eyes seemingly piercing into theirs on the other side of the screen.

"I'm assuming you have a warrant. Dr. Rees, you know we're bound by law to keep the sessions private. Unless you have a signed warrant from a Federal judge, I'm afraid there's not much I can do to accommodate you."

"I'm assuming you haven't had your secretary check your fax. The warrant was sent over an hour ago. I'm also assuming Federal Judge Randy Crenshaw's signature should be good enough."

There was that self-righteous look again. He could also see Regan's look of surprise as well. What? Because he was a cop, he couldn't run with the big dogs. He knew the law, probably better than they did.

"Detective, I'll have to look into the particulars of the warrant. I'm afraid I'm at one of my several satellite offices today. I'll contact my secretary later and get back with you when I've had time to review it. Good enough?"

"No. It isn't. Look Doctor Lloyd, I sort of understand patient/counselor privilege. I get it. But what I understand more is that a little boy is missing. We have no leads. No clues. Nothing to help us bring him safely back. It seems that everything we do have points erroneously back to the father. I don't know if we're going to clear him or convict him. Right now, I don't really care. I just care about the kid…

…I'm not sure what you can and can't say legally, but I know there has to be something you can give me that I can use to narrow my search. I'm not asking for particulars. We both know it could be hours before you look over that warrant and get back with me. The kid is living on borrowed time already, if he's even still alive. Do you really want that on your conscious because of some bureaucratic red tape? I don't."

She contemplated his words. After several seconds she shifted backward, the tenseness relaxing from the edges of her mouth and eyes.

"You're right. Some things take priority. What do you want to know?"

Archer motioned toward Regan, who took over again. "Thank you Dr. Lloyd. Please tell us anything you can without directly violating his privacy. Everything you say will stay in this room."

She nodded. "Max Stanley came to me a broken young man. He was truly distraught over killing that child. Before, he had the reputation as a choleric personality. A real go-getter. When he came to me, he was meek and timid; a broken shell of what had been described. He asked all the questions indicating he was depressed and taking it extremely hard-"

"What type of questions?" Archer asked.

"Questions like: Do you think I should have hollered my identification louder? Maybe he didn't hear me? Maybe I should have just let that one suspect go? He wasn't worth the price of a child? Do you think the boy will live again in another life? Do you believe in Heaven? How will the boy's family be able to cope with the fact that he's gone forever? Do you think God will forgive me for taking an innocent? You know, questions like that."

Regan scribbled furiously in her notepad. "Dr. Lloyd, I know you can't answer specifically, but did Mr. Stanley ever exhibit characteristics indicating that he could pose a threat to himself or others?"

"Well, as I already mentioned, he demonstrated early signs of severe depression. He started mixing his medications with alcoholic beverages almost every night. He started living as someone who wanted to die-"

"Suicide. Did he ever mention it?"

"No. Not once. I asked him several times. He told me that he wasn't considering it every time I asked. He never avoided the question. Never even deflected. I had no reason not to believe him…

…However, he wasn't afraid of dying either. I was pretty sure that he wanted to in fact. He wouldn't get away from dangerous situations. Even encouraged them."

"That's why you never released him back to the force. You didn't think he could handle it. You were afraid he'd get himself killed."

"I was afraid he wanted to. It wouldn't be suicide by cop. This would have been a new diagnosis. Cop's suicide by criminal. I didn't want that on my conscience."

"Did you ever think he was a hazard to those around him? Or were you just concerned with his own safety?"

"Honestly, I wasn't sure. That's another thing that bothered me. It seemed to be isolated, but one thing you learn quickly in our line of work is that there are no guarantees. Often, things aren't as they appear. Right when you think you've gotten it figured out, it takes a turn for the worst, and you realize you didn't really know anything."

"Did he ever exhibit antisocial behavior or P.T.S.D.?"

"Not antisocial behavior. Stress Disorders. He carried some of the signs, but not enough to consider it a cluster."

She looked thoughtfully away from the camera. "I was never sure, but he seemed to develop a coping mechanism toward the end of our therapy sessions that made me slightly uncomfortable. I noticed it in the last two sessions. After he quit the department, I lost the ability to force him to continue.

I never saw him again."

"What were the tendencies that bothered you?" Archer asked.

"I don't know. I labeled it as substitutions. He would talk to others like they were the kid he killed. My secretary noticed this while he was waiting outside in the lobby for one of his appointments. A child was there. He called him by the victim's name several times. The boy's mother was afraid and threatened to call security. I had to take him back early that day…

…I asked him about it. He told me he couldn't control it. It just happened. He didn't even realize it until after the fact. I tried to tell him that he couldn't just make others become the boy. It wouldn't bring the boy back, and it wouldn't help him cope with the loss any better. He needed to just deal with the guilt and move forward."

"How'd he respond to that?"

"Well, he responded okay during the session. The next week I found out that he was still doing it though. He tearfully admitted it, and again told me that he had no way of making himself stop. No matter how hard he tried, it just happened."

"Were you concerned for the kids in the community at that point? Did it seem he'd be able to take one of them?"

"I don't know. I honestly don't. It felt like he was on the verge of a psychotic break. Anything would have been possible at that point. His attitude was extremely narcissistic."

"He doesn't seem like the classic narcissist."

"Not the traditional signs. No. You're right. But very much so by my own terminology. He felt like he couldn't forgive himself. Like he was somehow responsible for righting all the wrongs created by this situation. Like he somehow had to do more than God and fix the emotional issues of everyone involved. It's impossible. Because he was unable to act like a god, he grew distraught."

"One more thing Dr. Lloyd. He's married to the daughter of an exceedingly wealthy defense attorney. They had a son shortly thereafter. Any guesses what he named his son?"

Her countenance fell. She looked like she was going to be sick. "Please, don't tell me he named his first son after the victim. That's demented."

"I've never heard of that doctor, have you?

"Yes. Only once."

"How'd that turn out?" Archer asked.

"Not good detective. The father ended up killing the child. That started a spree of him killing six others before the authorities were able to catch up to him. When they did, he went down fighting. Refused to be taken alive."

"So in your medical opinion, you'd say the prognosis looks pretty bleak."

"Looks deadly. Whatever happens from here, it can't be good. Look, I'll review the warrant and if everything is in order, I'll send all my files and personal notes first thing in the morning. I can't do better than that."

She looked directly into the camera again. "Dr. Rees, I have been a fan of yours for a few years. I meant what about said about partnering. If you're ever interested-"

"Maybe one day-"

"What I mean to say is that I trust your evaluation of my personal notes and files, but if you have any questions about the content or their interpretation, call me on my personal line... Call at any time."

"Will do. Thank you Dr. Lloyd."

With that, she pressed the exit button, the window on the screen closed, and the doctor was gone. The screen returned to its prior light blue state, before bleeping out all together.

19

Archer was deep in thought as he made the short journey from the interview room to the lab. The elevator dinged, and the door opened in front of him. He stepped through it with Regan at his side.

"What did you think of the interview?" he asked.

"Other than the fact that she's a-"

"Careful Regan. She helped out in the end. It's all about knowing how to get to people. You should know that, being your profession is notorious for mind games."

She smirked, as he rounded the corner and was met by a well-built man in his early forties. His blond hair and baby blue eyes made him the classic all-American male. He probably watched football and basketball on the weekends, while grilling steaks and potatoes on his Grill Master. She knew the type.

"Jaxon. How's it going bro?"

The blond man extended his hand and caught Archer's in a half high-five motion. "Not too bad man. I got that stuff you asked for," he said as he pulled a folder from behind his back. "Step into my office."

They walked into a glass room. Jaxon pressed a button, and the shades slowly lowered to the hum of mechanical springs. The room grew dark. Jaxon hit another button and a three-foot holographic image emerged in the center of the room.

"This is your first official tour of the LeDiv/Stanley home front. I've got everything from your walk up the driveway, to your rummaging through the inside of the house. I've been through this four times, hoping to pick up something that might save you time-"

"Did you?"

"Oh yeah. Toward the end. I didn't see it until the fourth time, but there's definitely something you'll want to see. Probably scare the pants off ya."

Archer shot him a look. "I know. I know," Jaxon responded to the glance. "You don't scare easy."

"If you don't mind Regan, we can look through the complete tape later. Go ahead Jaxon, get me to the part that will cause this fear."

Jaxon caused the image to move forward. The scenes kept changing. Moving from the driveway, to the perimeter of the house, to the backyard, and finally to the inside of the house. Jaxon moved the image to a certain point and then stopped it.

"Pay close attention. Top right of the screen."

They watched. The images scrolled around. Until, Jaxon hit the pause button. "You didn't look hard enough. I'm a little disappointed in you Arch."

Archer laughed. "Just show it to me again Jax."

The second time through, Jaxon paused the image. Look in the upper corner now Arch. In the glass reflection from the microwave."

Archer swore. Jaxon had been right. It was frightening. He hadn't been the only one in the room. Someone else's reflection was there, clearly outlined in the reflective surface of the microwave door. Someone had been lurking in the shadows. The face was visible, but not discernible.

"Jax, did you run the few prints through IAFIS?"

"Yes sir. Nothing. No partial matches even."

Regan looked confused. Jaxon smiled. "It's the international fingerprint database. Law enforcement agencies use it to find suspects based on fingerprint analysis."

"What about the sheets and dust from under the bed and around the room? Any evidence there?" Archer asked.

"Interestingly enough; yes. I'm not sure if it's the break in the case you've been hoping for, but it's undeniably interesting."

He removed a couple of pages from the folder and placed them on a small table in front of them. DNA evidence from the sheets indicates recent sexual activity. Quite a bit actually."

"But, I thought-" Regan started.

"Yes. Supposedly there wasn't much action between the unhappy couple. So, I ran the DNA through CODIS," he paused and casually smiled at Regan. "The DNA database… Anyway the female sample is undeniably the once beautiful Mrs. Jessica Stanley. The male sample comes back to a Tom Gleason. Ring a bell?"

"Afraid not. Should it?" Archer replied.

"Well, he's head of security for Morgan LeDiv, as well as LeDiv's personal bodyguard. Looks like he's been doing a little personal guarding of LeDiv's daughter's body as well."

Regan scowled, "So Mrs. Stanley was having an affair. Is that why they're trying to keep this under wraps? They're worried Max will find out and be upset. They don't want rumors that would darken the illustrious family name. There's got to be more to it then that. That's not enough to risk your child's life over."

Archer looked at her. "Unless, she's aware of Max's psychological issues. Not excusing her, but that could be why she turned to an outside romance. She felt trapped, and Gleason is a powerful figure. She's afraid if Max finds out, he'll kill her."

"Sure. Makes sense. It's happened before… Another scenario possibly exists, although highly unlikely."

"Yeah, what's that?"

"Perhaps she has something to do with the kidnapping. She's tired of Max. Tired of married life. Tired of a husband and kid messing up her game. She's got the perfect man that knows some powerful people. He could make them both disappear-"

Archer smiled. "And she could be playing her daddy to get as much ransom as possible for her and her new white knight to go riding off into the sunset. I like it."

Jaxon interrupted them. "Both plausible; but will the evidence support either. We'll have to wait and see. I'll be looking into it. In the meantime, has either of you heard of FERET?"

They both shook their heads indicating their negative response.

His face glowed. "It's fairly new. The FBI is engaging in using it as an upgrade from IAFIS. It's amazing. Intriguing. Supposed to work with the IPhone. Made to work in sync with the phone's camera system and connect wirelessly to the FBI and INTERPOL databases. It's state of the art and strictly scary because of its propensity to violate so many privacy laws. It's-"

"Jaxon," Archer urged, "the point."

"Ah, yes. The point. FERET is a facial recognition software. Highly developmental. But I just so happen to know some people who know some people, and-"

"Jackson now."

"Sorry Arch. It's just so exciting. What I'm trying to say is that I was able to run that partial face through the software. I got a match."

"So you know who was in the room with me?"

"Not exactly."

"I thought you got a match?"

"I did Arch, but the file is classified."

"What's that mean?"

"It means that the man in that room is either employed by the FBI, CIA, or some other agency above our pay grade. Not only does he work for them. He's so high up the hierarchy that he's untouchable. So untouchable, that the people I know, and the people they know can't even find out who he is…

…Sorry Arch, it's the best I could do. I hope you have some pull with the Bureau. If not, seems like you're staring down the rabbit hole."

Archer swore again. This case wasn't getting any easier. He wasn't feeling any younger. The stress was building. The muscles in his neck were tensing. His blood pressure was rising. It was starting to feel like the old days.

20

Regan shot up in the bed. Something had startled her from her sleep. She'd heard scuffling in the hallway. She reached onto the nightstand and fiddled through the familiar knickknacks, trying to find her wire rimmed glasses. Without them, the room was a blur. She could hardly see the door through the darkness.

She had been extremely tired when Archer had dropped her off, but she always slept the same. She kept the lights off and the air turned low. Now, she wished she wouldn't have made the first choice.

She finally found the soft frames and hurriedly sat them on her ears, immediately looking toward the door. She was certain she hadn't left the lights on in the hallway either. She never did. Her friends considered her part of the *Go Green* movement before it existed. That was the by-product of being raised by a single mother struggling to make ends meet. Every dollar counted, and energy conservation could save a few pennies. The habit had continued into adulthood, but it had never impacted her. The only reason it mattered now was because the light in the hallway was shining brightly under her bedroom door.

She wasn't paranoid by any means, but she'd grown accustomed to sleeping with her bedroom door locked. She'd gotten into that habit since living in university apartments in college. People would sneak in and try to steal other's possessions right under their noses. She was grateful now. The fact her door was locked should buy her a little more time if someone were still in the house.

She slowly made her way from the bed, contorting her face as the springs screeched inside the mattress. If someone were out there, they now knew that she was awake. The high-pitched whine of the metallic barriers had resonated like an alarm.

She slowly made her way toward the dresser. She opened the top drawer and removed a small can of pepper spray. She made her way toward the bed and removed her cell phone from its charger, holding the button until it flashed on. She entered his number from memory.

A groggy voice answered on the other end of the line. "Regan… Everything alright?"

"No. Someone is in my house. The noise awakened me. They left my hall light on. I never leave it on."

"Oh God. Hang up and dial 9-1-1. I'll be right there. It'll take me a few. Hang tight kiddo."

She hung up the phone. Instead of dialing the emergency number as she'd been instructed, she dialed another one. He answered on the second ring. He didn't sound like he'd been sleeping.

"Hello Regan. What's got you up at three in tha mornin'?"

The urgency in her voice caused his pulse to race. "Arch. Someone's in my house. I'm afraid to go check. I don't know if they're still here."

"I'll be right there. Don't worry. It won't take me long."

. . .

He lunged from the bed, already fully clothed. The smell of the cheap hotel room greeted him, as his senses were suddenly alert. He grabbed the strap hanging on the side post of the bed and flung it around his shoulder. The gun hit his rib cage as he swiftly grabbed the keys from the table. He opened the door and stepped into the damp air.

He saw it coming a mere fraction of a second before he felt it. His movement to avoid the blow was just enough to keep him from getting knocked completely unconscious, but not enough to keep him from becoming highly dazed. He took the brunt of the blow directly off the side of his temple.

He unsteadily leaned against the stucco wall of the hotel and tried to assess the situation. He saw two sets of legs moving toward him. He couldn't identify either as his attacker. It had happened too quickly.

He wasn't taking any chances. He reached for his gun and pulled it from the strap, leveling it toward the advancing duo.

His vision was starting to return. One of the two stopped a few feet away. The other kept coming, plowing into him at full speed, sprawling him backward. His gun bounced to the ground a few feet away. The man on top of him relentlessly pounded at his face, the brass knuckles ripping through his skin. He could feel the warmth of his blood leaking down his cheeks.

. . .

Regan moved toward the closet behind her. The closet or under the bed were the only two hiding spots in the room. She should have thought of that when she'd decided to rent the place for a couple of months. It wasn't exactly a fortress, but at the time, she hadn't known she'd need one either.

She saw the sudden shadow under the slit in the doorway. She scurried backward, her shoulders hitting the wooden slats of the closet door. She turned around and slowly slid it open. Her hand still clutched tightly to the pepper spray. She prayed it would work.

She looked again toward the door. The shadow was still, but something was off. Something bothered her. She didn't know what, until suddenly she did.

The lock was facing the wrong direction. It wasn't latched. It was wrong, all wrong. She always checked it, and then double-checked it. She had been tired, but she hadn't made a mistake tonight. That meant that someone had been in her room after she had fallen asleep. Someone had unlocked the door from the inside. She turned toward the window. The white fabric of the thin curtain was lightly flapping in the breeze.

She panicked, barely able to control her breathing. The doorknob turned. The shadow under the door moved. This was it. Someone was coming for her.

The door swung open, and a large figure stood in the open light of the hallway. He wore a face mask that reminded her of a creepy angel. It was completely white with cutouts for the eyes and mouth. He was dressed in all black except for the cherub covering.

She was barely visible in the shadows, half in and half out of the closet. She switched the safety off of the pepper spray and prepared to use it. The large masked intruder came for her. She waited until he was six feet away and then steadied herself, raising her arm toward him. Her finger was already beginning to apply pressure to the button that would spew the spiced liquid into his eyes.

Her arm never made it up. She felt the solid grip of someone from behind. He pulled her into his body, before shoving her hard through the half opened closet door. It ripped off the small hinges with her. They both landed three feet away.

She helplessly floundered on the floor in front of the first assailant. The one that had been hiding in the closet grabbed her by the hair and violently lifted her upward. She screamed, half from fear and half from pain. He turned her toward him and slapped her hard across the face. She fell back onto the bed. He positioned himself on top of her. He was dressed in the same frightening disguise as his cohort.

"Shut up. Shut up now if you want to live." His voice was garbled, obviously distorted by a voice modulator underneath the veil.

She believed he was serious. She lay quietly but squirmed underneath his body. He positioned himself directly over her waist, holding her arms down level with her head.

She wasn't the kind of girl to sleep in the nude, but she wasn't a conservative gown wearer either. She wished she had more covering her than the thigh length sheer t-shirt. She felt revoltingly exposed, and the two men cowering over her weren't hiding their enjoyment at the sight of her.

The first one removed a knife from his belt and held it tightly against her throat. He cut a narrow slit on the neck of her t-shirt, causing it to open slightly.

"Back off the case. Back off now. Forget the boy. Forget the kidnapping. Move back where you came from. Because next time we ain't gonna play so nicely. I'm gonna take my time with you."

He leaned forward and kissed her hard on the neck, before moving forcefully to her lips. She resisted at first, and then passionately returned his advance. The second suspect pulled on him from behind.

"Come on man. We gotta jet. We ain't supposed to handle the merchandise this time. Let's go."

The first one looked at her through his mask. He pursed his lips through the cut out.

"I pray you make a mistake. I hope you don't go home. Because I really wanna come back and finish what I started. Soon, I'll see you real soon."

The second man yanked him away and led him through the door. They shut and locked it. Their shadows disappeared down the corridor. Then the light flipped off. Everything was just as it had been when she'd fallen asleep.

Almost everything. She was lying on her back. Her face slightly swollen. Her clothing torn. Her pride insulted.

She was trembling. Fear of what might be coming, mingled with the realization of what could have happened left her uncharacteristically out of control. She wanted to cry, but the tears wouldn't come.

She stared at the door for a few seconds before she heard more footsteps echoing on the wood floor in the hall. She was too paralyzed to move. If they were coming back...

She heard him shout her name a second before the door was knocked off the hinges. She looked up and stared into the rugged and swollen eyes of Archer.

His shirt was ripped to ribbons. He was bleeding profusely from a gash on the side of his neck. His left eye was swollen halfway shut. His face looked like he'd been beaten with hammers. However, he was standing in her doorway, gun in hand, ready to save her from whatever was assaulting her. It hadn't mattered. He'd charged in without knowing what he was up against. That had to mean something.

He rushed forward. She held up her hand, slowing him down, urgently pointing toward the bathroom. She got up and moved toward it, with him a half step behind.

"Cotton swab. Hurry. Top shelf of the medicine cabinet."

He opened it and removed a swab from the package. She quickly grabbed it from his hand and moved it vigorously under her upper lip. She then flipped it around and moved the opposite end around her bottom lip. Opening the bottom drawer by the sink, she removed a plastic bag of pre-wrapped dental floss and emptied the floss into the drawer. She took the swab and sealed it tightly into the plastic package.

"You okay," he yelled. "What happened here?"

She nodded. "Scared out of my mind, but I'm fine."

"Did they hurt you? Did they-" He was unsure how to finish the question.

She answered it anyway. "No. They didn't. They said they would if they came back. If I didn't leave this case alone."

"What's with the swab? You collected evidence?"

She nodded. "He kissed me for intimidation. Figured I'd use it against him. Kissed him extra hard to make sure to swap as much spit as possible."

He laughed. She was one tough girl. "That's nasty, but effective I guess."

She was still shaking. However, his closeness brought an uncharacteristic calm.

"Yeah, if my DNA collection is what breaks this case, you're gonna owe me dinner."

"Done," he said, "and anywhere you want to go."

He calmly and amusedly looked her up and down. "As

much as I'm enjoying the view, and I am... You may want to consider putting something a little less comfortable on. Backup will be here any moment, and your uncle will never live it down if you aren't wearing something that at least resembles clothes."

She was embarrassed, as she scrambled for something to wear. She could hear the movement of men hurriedly rushing down the hall. Archer stepped to the doorway to stop them just as she threw on another t-shirt and favorite pair of jeans.

"It's okay Arch. Let 'em in."

"You okay honey," her uncle asked as he moved toward her. "You really okay?"

"I'm fine for now, but these people aren't playing around. They don't want us working this case."

"And after this episode, I'm afraid I'm gonna have to revoke your agreement with the department. I don't need you getting yourself killed."

Before she could say anything, he looked toward Arch. "I have officers checking over your place. Two men are dead. God Archer, did you beat them to death before you shot them? There's blood everywhere."

Archer just grunted and turned to face Regan. "You should listen to him. Forget this case and go home."

"Archer Madsen, if you think I'm going to be bullied by some thugs with a penchant for dramatics, you're sadly mistaken. I'm more determined to solve this case than ever. Obviously, we're on to something. We're making headway, or they wouldn't be after us."

"No. We're not Regan. You could have been killed tonight. It's only luck that you weren't. No one would have got to you in time. Don't you get it? They could have had their way with you and been gone if they'd wanted. Worse, they could have killed you when they were finished. We wouldn't have known until tomorrow. By then, they'd be long gone."

"Well, now we know to be more careful. I'm not walking away from this."

The Lieutenant looked blankly into the full-length mirror, not even noticing the reflection. "Regan. We'll talk about this tomorrow. Come home with me. I'll have a unit follow us and stay parked outside."

Regan looked at Archer, her eyebrows lifted inquisitively. "Arch, how did you get here so quickly? It didn't take you long."

He shrugged, avoiding eye contact as he turned to walk from the room. She briskly moved toward him.

"Arch, seriously, how'd you get here so fast?"

The Lieutenant grinned. "Save yourself the questions honey. He's not talking, but twenty bucks says he was sleeping at the roach motel down the road so he'd be close to you."

Archer walked out and closed the bedroom door behind him. The Lieutenant's guess had been correct. He was paying to stay at the inexpensive hotel. He wasn't about to let something happen to her. It hadn't taken him long to realize that something was off about this case. It was dangerous. They'd started in shallow waters against the pull of a docile current. They'd been slowly led into the raging depths of an un-chartered sea. Now, bloodthirsty sharks were viciously churning the waters around them, and he'd do everything in his power to keep her safe.

21

Max furiously waved for the cab to swing over and pick him up. Finally, after three unsuccessful attempts, the forth yellow chariot raced to the side of the road and opened the doors.

Max lumbered into the seat and threw himself against the padding. He was still afraid to be seen. He needed to stop being so paranoid. He'd draw more attention by acting abnormally.

The cabby looked at him through the rearview mirror. "Ya chill man?" the cabby asked with a slight Caribbean accent.

"I'm good. Just shut up and drive."

"Sho thang brudda. Just trynna make convo. Dat's all."

"If I wanted to talk, I'd find a confessional instead of a cab. I just need you to get me to the D.A.'s office."

The cabby turned his attention from the rearview mirror and pushed steadily forward. They'd been driving for five minutes when Max heard the sirens blaring as two marked patrol cruisers flew past him on the left side. Two more followed closely behind. He could also hear the distant blare of fire trucks maneuvering down the busy streets. Whatever was happening, it was big.

"Any way to avoid the mayhem and still get me there on time. I have an appointment at eight."

The cabby glanced at his watch. "For you. Ten minutes early. Nuttin' exta brudda."

He highly doubted the no extra charge part. Riding a cab through the city was highway robbery. They had their way with you, and then made you pay a king's ransom. Somebody was making a killin' from the city's largest transportation network.

Usually, he preferred the subway. However, today was different. He was on a time crunch. He didn't want to put her in a bind, but he desperately wanted to know what the Bureau was investigating. Six hundred dollars worth of want.

"Look a dat brudda! Looka like Beirut."

Max lowered his head to peer out of the semi-tinted window of the cab's backseat. He immediately noticed the tendrils of dense smoke towering above the buildings in front of them.

"I thought you were taking me away from the drama. I need to get to my appointment. This isn't a sightseeing tour."

"Dis da only way mon... Relax."

As the cab whipped around the corner, Max recognized the familiar industrial parkway. He suddenly panicked. It couldn't be.

"Step on it. Now."

The cabby punched the gas and sent them rocketing down the street. He slammed his brakes a mere thirty seconds later. The cab pulled sideways in front of a section of the road blocked by police cruisers and other emergency personnel.

Max dropped money through the narrow slit in the window. He swung the door open and lunged from the backseat.

"Keep the change," he said as he slowly made his way toward the inferno. "Oh God… No… No… No."

It was the District Attorney's Records Department building. Firefighters were frantically running back and forth like ants whose mound of dirt had just been disturbed. At least three trucks were propelling water into the flames through high-powered hoses. The water was yet to have more than a negligible effect. The fire was spreading too swiftly, lapping at the building with indescribable intensity. Max fell against a stone wall across the street, watching his only leads smolder to embers.

He picked up his phone and dialed the emergency hotline.

"9-1-1, what's your emergency?"

He didn't answer, finding it hard to formulate words. The voices were back again. Screaming at him. It was entirely his fault this was happening. Carson would be alive and safe if he weren't the father. All he could do was hurt and destroy. It's the only thing he'd ever been good at.

"Hello? If you have an emergency please state it. If not, please hang up and don't waste my time again."

"Hello. Wait. I need to speak with a Detective Madsen please. It's important."

"Sir. This is an emergency hotline. If you need to speak with one of the detectives, I can give you our main number to call."

"Lady. Does it sound like I'm calling to chat about the weather? This is an emergency. Just do what you have to, but get Detective Madsen on the phone."

After a few seconds the voice came back. "I've got him on the line sir. I'm patching you through now."

"Hello. This is Detective Madsen. How may I help you?"

Max's voice cracked. "Archer Madsen?"

"Yes, this is Detective Archer Madsen. Who am I speaking with?"

"Detective, it's Max Stanley... You may want to get over to the District Attorney's office and check it out."

"Max. We've been looking for you. Why don't you come on down to the precinct. We have some catching up to do."

"Archer, listen. This is important. I'm not coming in. I've gotta find my son. But you need to listen to me. The records at the D.A.'s office are being expunged right now. There's something there they want hidden."

"I heard it on the scanner. Fire at the public records building. Why should that be news to me? And who are you referring to Max?"

"Because I was there yesterday. A nice girl helped me find answers. She was pulling more charts for me to meet her this morning. Now the place is burning to the ground as we speak. Do you really think that's a coincidence?"

"Max, where are you? Let me meet you. I don't think you're involved in this like some of the others do, but I'm having a hard time proving it since you refuse to cooperate."

Max breathed deeply into the phone. "Not yet. Need more time. Sorry."

He pressed the button and ended the call.

. . .

Archer swore. "It was Max. He said something about the fire at the district attorney's office. He doesn't think it's an accident. I think he must be in the area. He said he was supposed to meet someone there this morning for information. He must have gotten there to find it on fire."

Regan's expression puzzled him. She stared into the distance, looking at, but not into the glass divider positioned between them and the nearest office. Her blank stare alarmed his keenest senses.

"Regan, what's wrong? What's happened?"

She caught his eye as she struggled to compose herself. "I just received a call from Dr. Lloyd's secretary. She won't be returning our calls or sending any files."

"What happened, the warrant not up to her standards?"

She looked abysmally into the shadowy interior of the desks around her. "Not that at all... Arch, she was found dead this morning in her bathtub. An apparent suicide. Her wrists were slit, and she'd taken an overdose of prescription pills.

The secretary says she helped Dr. Lloyd pull the files last night before they left the office. She was going to send them over first thing this morning. Now she's dead, and the files are missing."

Archer slammed his fist into the concrete panel nearest him. He'd been attacked and nearly killed. Regan could have easily been in the morgue this morning. The District Attorney's personal records building had been breached and destroyed. Dr. Lloyd, who'd graciously helped them yesterday, had apparently killed herself. The files associated with the case were conveniently gone. The only connection to all four was Max. He could proclaim his innocence all he wanted, unless he did something to prove otherwise, he was about to go down hard.

Archer was tired of playing games. He was tired of following protocol. He'd been punched in the mouth, tasted the blood, and knew only one way to retaliate. He was going to strike back with a vengeance.

22

Twenty-five minutes later, Archer stepped out of a police cruiser and walked toward the downed building. It was still smoldering, but most of the flames had been subdued. Regan walked beside him. Neither of them spoke, dispassionately taking in the unfolding scene.

He walked to a tall, thin woman Regan had noticed a couple of times around the precinct. She was slightly older, and carried herself with the swagger of an experienced professional. Archer stopped in front of her.

"Burnt flesh. Never could quite stomach the smell. Still gets to me. Only one victim, or are there more?"

The woman looked directly into his eyes. "I don't have the details yet. So far there's only one. Looks to be a young black girl. We're going to have to match dental records, but the D.A.'s office claims she has to be Monique Jones. She was the secretary for the records office."

"Well, I guess questioning her isn't an option."

The woman laughed. "Not sure she's got any pertinent information now, but you can give it a shot if you'd like."

Regan would have been repulsed by their sarcasm, but she'd witnessed it before. Some people deal with death by becoming rigid and cold, shutting down all form of emotion all together. Others turn to humor. Obviously, that was his way. She couldn't judge him for that. Good people do whatever it takes to cope.

"Melissa, do you know if anything was saved?"

"No Arch. I'm afraid the entire building is a loss. What the fire and smoke didn't destroy, the water and foam did."

Archer nodded and walked away, continuing around the perimeter of the building. He stopped on the west side and looked longingly into the few flames that still smoldered. He found it difficult to see through the sweltering heat waves rising from the rubble. The waves visibly danced in front of him, casting mirage like shadows. He gazed through the torrential obscurity and saw him sitting alone against a sidewall across the street.

Archer casually rounded the corner and made his way around the maze of police tape and camera equipment set up by the local media. Once on the outskirts of the crowd, he shifted back toward the right, angling slightly in the direction he'd noticed Max. He slowly peered around the corner, and there he was, still seated with his back pushed firmly against the wall. He approached and calmly sat down beside him. Max never looked in his direction, seemingly oblivious to the fact that someone had just approached him.

"Max. You okay?"

Max eyed the rising cloud like a spiritual revelation was about to come soaring from its midst. His voice was uneven when he answered.

"It's my fault you know. Got a Midas touch I guess."

"What do you mean Max? Did you set this fire?"

"Archer, one cop to another, do you believe I'm the man I'm being made to appear? I don't have anything to do with my boy's kidnapping. I didn't burn this building down. I didn't mean to get that man killed when I was chasing him. I didn't mean for any of this to happen. Why's it happening to me?"

"You're not responsible?" It was more a question than a statement.

Max continued staring into the mesmerizing thickness. "I got her killed. She was helping me. Very nice girl. Pretty. With big dreams. And I took them. Now her family will have to live knowing that she was never a smidgeon of what she could have become."

"Is that a confession?"

"Archer, read between the lines man. I'm waiting for your help because I've got nowhere else to turn. I don't trust my father-in-law. I don't trust my wife. She acts like she's married to him. I don't know where to turn. I don't know why I trust you, but I do."

Archer nodded. He wasn't sure if a vote of confidence from a known psycho should boost his ego or not. He ignored the comment and followed up with a question.

"Why were you coming back here today? Why didn't you just stay away with what you found yesterday?"

"I didn't find much yesterday. Did read an interesting file on my wife though. Apparently, she had a twin brother. Did you know that? Mr. LeDiv had two kids. That's something the world kept secret. Why'd she keep that from me?"

Archer shrugged. "Maybe it just wasn't that important Max. Maybe it was painful, and she preferred to forget. You can't beat yourself up because of it."

"She's afraid of me. Has been for a few months now. I don't know why. She just started pulling away. Couldn't get her to open up. I've been thinking. Maybe she felt this was coming. Maybe she sensed it. They say a mother always knows. You think that's true?"

"Doesn't matter… What matters is what we're going to do from here… Sorry Max, but I have to ask you a tough question… Was there any chance your wife was having an affair?"

He didn't flinch. "Probably… She hadn't been happy with me for a long time. I tried. Nothing worked. I couldn't please her… So I don't know."

"You're not certain? You just think it's a possibility?"

"It got to the point that I really didn't pay attention. What she did was her business. I quit caring. I don't know how we grew apart. Early on, we had the perfect marriage, but you know what they say about things too good to be true?"

"Yeah. I know. Been there... Max... Another tough question... Do you know where Carson is being held?"

For the first time Max faced him. His look bore resentment. He didn't look defensive. He looked like he was insulted and wanted to retaliate.

"What are you asking me Archer? You really think I could somehow be responsible for the kidnapping of my own son? No wonder you haven't found him."

"Relax. I'm just asking questions. You need to help me sort through this so I can move on... Now why were you coming back here?"

"I was coming back because an FBI agent had been researching the same files and asking the same questions as me. He seemed to be one step ahead and knew details I didn't, so she was pulling all the files he logged out yesterday. I was gonna review them this morning. That's the truth."

"FBI. You sure? The Feds are working your case?"

"I don't know. If they are, they're keeping a low profile. All I know is whatever he was studying got this place toppled."

Archer sullenly faced the sidewalk. "Did she tell you what he was looking into?"

"Not really. He asked about my son. He was looking into

cases of missing children over the past few years. He had linked a couple of them to abductions that I was looking in to. Those are the files I was going to review."

"So, you think because a few kidnappings over the last several years have gone unsolved, it ties to your son's case? You feel there's a serial killer on the loose, preying on young, innocent victims?"

"It's possible, but one so high up that others would do anything to keep his identify concealed. You know, like the theories that Jack the Ripper was really English royalty."

"Max. I hate to ask, but one cop to another, are you off your meds?"

"What? How do you know about my meds?"

"Just a hunch, but your answer tells me that I was right. Now tell me honestly, are you off them?"

"Yes." He shook his head; tears falling down his checks. "I have been for over a week now. Why?"

"Since right about the time your son went missing?"

"I don't like what that insinuates Archer. Watch yourself."

"It's just a thought Max. Are you sure there's not more to this that you're not seeing?"

"What, do you mean? Am I sure I didn't kidnap my son? I'd never do that."

"Another question then. Why'd you name your son after the kid you killed in the warehouse?"

Max stood up. "What I named my child is none of your business. You understand me. It's none of your business."

Archer stood beside him. "Calm down Max. I'm just trying to do my job."

"Archer, I don't expect you or anyone else to believe me, but I'm not crazy. I'm off the meds because I feel more helpless when I'm on them. I need to be alert. To feel alive…

…My son. That's how he made me feel. Like life was worth it. Ya know…

…I can't make it if something happens to him. I can't. Please help me get my boy home safe, and in order to help me, you have to trust me. I'm not involved in this."

Archer was still unsure but decided to play along. "Okay Max. Say for now I do. What's your next move?"

"I gotta continue what I started. I'm gonna investigate my wife and find out what someone doesn't want me to see… What's your move?"

"I guess I'll do the same. I need you to come down to the station soon and work through some things with me."

"In time. I will in time… Last thing… The girl identified the man as Special Agent Garrison Reed. You familiar with that name?"

"No, but I'll look into it. You've got my number. Keep me informed."

With that, he turned to leave. Max called behind him. "Archer, I haven't forgotten what its like to bear the shield.

There's nothing like it. I'd never do anything to disgrace it. It represents something most of the world can't understand. It's a bridge to a better place. I'd never disrespect or misrepresent that. It's the brotherhood man."

Archer closed his eyes and nodded. He knew exactly what Max meant. Once a cop, always a cop, it's in the blood. It causes one to view the world differently. Recognizing the good, but equally discerning the bad. Finding the threat in every room, ever watchful for the boogiemen that only come out at night. Protecting the innocent. The watchmen on the wall while others safely sleep.

Few understand why some risk their lives for such low pay, but it's more than an occupation. It's a place where lives were forged. It's where the worst of times and the best-trained individuals intersect, and the difference between life and death is often the trust you've placed in the man at your back. Max was right; it was a brotherhood.

23

Archer hurried across the chaos to where she was waiting. She breathed an exaggerated sigh of relief when she saw him.

"Where'd you go? You can't leave me like that."

"Sorry. I-"

She looked angrily into his persuasive eyes. "I thought something had happened to you. We have to watch each others back now."

"Regan, I just talked to him."

"Who?"

"Max. He was sitting by the fence behind the camera trucks. It was eerie. He just stared ahead and blankly answered my questions. We had somewhat of a conversation, but he couldn't take his eyes off of the billowing smoke."

"Like he was proud of his handiwork?"

He tightened his lips, contemplating the question. "No. It didn't feel that way. He looked guilty, but not of setting the fire. I think he feels responsible for getting the girl killed."

He motioned for her to walk with him as he started toward the car. He tossed the keys over the hood to her.

"You can drive. I need to think. We're missing something."

"Where we headed?"

"Back to the precinct. I want to review everything again. I called Ronin earlier and told him to meet us. We're running out of time. Max knows it. He's getting desperate. He's teetering on the edge. He'll hurt someone or get himself killed. We can't allow that."

An hour later, Max stood outside the door of Mr. LeDiv's high rise office. Two guards stood at the entrance, refusing to let him in.

"Get him on the buzzer James. It's important that I speak to him. And bring my wife down. I know she's here. I just saw them, with Carson. They've got my son back. You've got to let me see them."

James tried to calm him. "Come on Max. We've known each other a long time. You know whose orders I have to follow. Mr. LeDiv specially told us that if you showed up, we weren't allowed to let you in today. He left this for you."

James reached into his pocket and removed a white sealed envelope that had Max's name eloquently printed in the center. Max opened the envelope and removed a typed letter. His head fell as he read the contents.

"James… What is this? I want to speak to him now. Get him down here. I want to see my son."

"I'm sorry Max, but Carson isn't here. I don't know what you thought you saw, but he's still being held. We don't know where he is."

"I saw her walking with him through the front door. They just walked right past you. Why are you doing this? Let me see my son."

"Max, you're worrying me. Are you okay?"

Max starting shaking. The voices were screaming at him again. He couldn't get rid of them. No, it wasn't his fault.

"Stop it," he yelled. "Leave me alone."

James stepped forward and clutched Max around the right shoulder. "That's enough Max. I tried to do this the easy way, but I'm afraid I'm gonna have to ask you to leave now."

Max fell to his knees. "Why James? Why are they doing this to me? I don't understand. I haven't done anything wrong. Don't let them shut me out."

The loudspeaker next to the doorway crackled. The distinguished voice of Morgan LeDiv echoed from the electronic diaphragm.

"Show a little dignity for God's sake. Act like a man."

Max angrily leapt to his feet. "Come down here, and I'll show you how to act like a man."

The guards both stiffened and slammed him backwards, as he took his first step toward the door. James spun him hard in the opposite direction.

Mr. LeDiv sounded amused. "This is over Max. There's nothing you can do. We'll get Carson back. Don't worry. You'll be seeing him again soon. But until then, don't come back here. Jessica feels like you're a danger to our chances of bringing Carson home alive. She doesn't wish to see you right now."

"But we need each other. She's my wife. And I want to see my son."

"Right now, she's Carson's mother. So don't push it Max. You aren't going to like what you find if you do. Leave it alone."

"Are you threatening me?"

"Just leave it alone Max. It's not a threat. It's a warning. You aren't prepared to handle the truth yet. Just leave it alone."

"Leave it alone? It's my son we're talking about-"

"I know you don't understand, but we're doing this to protect you. We're doing this to give us the best chance of finding Carson. The best thing you can do is just get away from here."

"I'm not leaving until I see my son. I want to see him."

"Don't make this get ugly Max. It doesn't have to. What you

hold in your hand is a temporary restraining order. It will hold up in any court. Don't come within three miles of her until I say otherwise, or I'll have my men detain you until the cops show up to arrest you. You've been served."

"Morgan. You can't do this to me."

"Max. This isn't a game, and I'm not playing. You have twenty seconds to get in your car and get off my property."

The speaker crackled again. LeDiv was gone. Max looked upward into the lens of the security camera above the door. He intently stared, hoping his eyes were boring holes through Jessica's heart. Finally, James moved toward him, placing his hand on Max's shoulder.

"I'm sorry Max. You've always been kind to me. I don't want to have to do this the hard way. Please, don't force me to. I'm asking you nicely one last time. It's time to go."

Max glared at him. For a second it looked like he was going to go for it. That look.

Betrayal.

Anger.

Pain.

Rage.

It often flashes right before a man makes a decision he can't go back on. James recognized it and readied himself. Then, as quickly as it flared, it was gone. The eyes grew gentle and subdued.

"For you James. I'm gonna leave for your sake. But if I don't hear from my wife soon, I'm coming back, and hell itself won't stop me from getting through that door. You tell him that. Restraining order or not."

24

Ronin was waiting in the comfortable chair at the head of the long black table in the conference room. "Don't worry, got nothing better to do than wait on you. I tell you, not much changes. It's me up front, and you bringing up the rear."

Archer laughed. "Usually me solving the crimes while you're sittin' around tryin' to impress the ladies. As usual," he looked toward Regan with a sly grin, "they're not buyin' it."

"I don't know detective. I could do worse," Regan replied. "With those gray hairs come wisdom and experience."

"And I'm sure you'd get a long way living on his pension."

They all laughed. "Guess you got me there. I definitely got nothing to offer with my meager boys' in blue retirement fund."

Archer sat down beside him, exhaling deeply. He closed his

eyes, forcing the air from his lungs again, as if he were forcing the fatigue from his psyche. He opened his eyes.

"Any luck Ronin. We need a break in a bad way. You-"

"You know me. I'm the break you've been waiting for. I've been doing real investigating while you've been chasing fires and talking to shrinks."

"Ronin, I've known you a long time. You only get this comedic when something is bothering you. What's going on?"

His demeanor changed instantly. "You ever regret getting involved with something? You know, it sounds like a good thing until you start looking into it, but by the time you realize you should have left it alone, it's already too late. You're in too deep."

Archer shook his head. He knew the feeling all too well. He'd been feeling it lately. This case. It didn't feel right.

"What is it Ro? What did you find?"

"Arch, it's not what I found. It's what I can't find that's bothering me. There's nothing but dead ends. I-"

"Just start from the beginning. Maybe two other open minds will help you gain perspective."

Ronin spilled the contents of his leather briefcase on the table. He opened a legal sized envelope and removed a note pad. "This is what I've got so far… Or don't have…

…First of all, the suspect that ran his car into the bulldozer, he doesn't exist. Anywhere. I was able to lift prints from the inside of the car. I ran blood from the wreckage. Hair samples.

Dental records, after having the coroner reconstruct the facial bones. Even pulled photos from a couple of traffic cameras. Nothing. There's nil coming back on him. You know me Arch. I've even got friends with access to INTERPOL databases. Either this guy was squeaky clean, or he has some powerful people keeping him under the radar."

"Seems odd that someone would escalate from no criminal activity to kidnapping. Usually one has to build up to that. You sure there's nothing?"

"I'm thorough. Always been good at finding people. You know that… Not this time. I'm afraid I'm looking for a ghost…

…And as to why he killed himself, I have no idea. I've studied every inch of that car and each item recovered from the wreckage. There's nothing that can be used to identify him, and nothing remotely suggesting why he was there. My suggestion would be to ask Max Stanley why he was chasing him. Why'd he believe this character had information."

Archer nodded his agreement. Regan shifted uncomfortably in her chair. No one liked the direction this was heading.

"Secondly, are you totally convinced that Max Stanley has been telling the truth? The more I find on him, his credibility is taking tremendous hits."

"What do you mean?"

"Well, for starters, I interviewed every person I could find that was associated with the places that Max said he encountered the people that warned him that his son would be taken. Workers, customers that employees pegged as regulars, street bums living outside on the corner. You name it, and I questioned them.

Many of them remember seeing Max. They all remember him as highly volatile, erratic, nervous, and agitated. Not one… Arch, not one witness remembers any of the suspects that Max described. It's uncanny."

"What about the video feed from the stores?"

"Arch. I pulled every available feed. I pulled feed from the parking lot. I even pulled feed from traffic cameras and other private businesses for a six-block radius in every direction. I've had my team scouring the images for anyone that resembles their descriptions. There are no matches Arch. None."

"Any chance the tapes were doctored?"

"I mean, anything's possible these days, but the kind of computer savvy and equipment you'd need to completely wipe an entire neighborhood's surveillance equipment and replace it with a cloned feed. You're talking governmental hacker skills."

"Guess we can rule that out."

"At this point, I'm not sure if we can rule anything out. Something dangerous is happening…

…Furthermore, did you know that Mr. LeDiv and his daughter have both filed a restraining order against Max? Something about him being a threat to their safety because he's unstable and needs to be hospitalized. LeDiv told the judge that he's sorry he posted bail. He feels that Max needs to be incarcerated so he doesn't hurt himself or anyone else."

"Are you serious? Why would Jessica Stanley want her husband behind bars? Last time we saw her, she was playing the grieving mother part well enough to win an Oscar. Why-"

"I dunno Arch. Obviously something happened that they aren't saying. I'm trying to find out, but local law enforcement has no details. Or, they're refusing to say."

He looked at Regan, "I even interviewed your uncle. He says he hasn't heard anything either, but he's gonna have his ears open."

He fidgeted through more papers on the table. "Did you know that Max has been taking antidepressants for the last several years?"

Archer tilted his head slightly forward. "I wasn't certain, but I played a hunch. He indicated to me that he'd quit taking them a couple of weeks ago because he felt restricted."

"That could be his biggest mistake. He could very well be delusional. He's taking strong narcotics designed to suppress his... other personalities."

"What?"

Regan slide her chair closer to the files. "May I?"

"Certainly," Ronin replied, "That's like reading Greek."

She looked over the list, her eyes narrowing as she read. "I've never heard of any of these meds. They aren't the classic regimen used to treat depression or multi-personality disorders here in the States. I'll have to see what I can dig up on them."

Ronin cleared his throat. He couldn't seem to get it clear

enough. "I did already. It led me to this."

He pushed a folder in front of her. She opened it. An exquisite, colorful logo was printed on the first page. A cross was faded into the background. Drops of blood shaped like rose petals were falling. A child stood looking upward at its base. Tears fell from his eyes. Various ornamental décor created depth on the emblem.

"What is this? I've never seen it before."

"Either of you ever heard of Vestis Corpus?"

Archer looked at Regan. She answered before he could. "Blanket Corp. I've heard of them. It's a worldwide corporation known for medical research on diseases of unknown etiology and incurability. They're currently working on cures for AIDS, Cancer, Hepatitis, the Ebola Virus, Type I Diabetes, and many other sicknesses plaguing the world. That's pretty much all I know. Their pharmacology practices are highly experimental."

"You said he was taking narcotics used to treat multi-personality disorders. How do you know that?" Archer asked.

"I spoke with the one who prescribed his medication last night. He's been taking it since he saw her a few years ago. She's changed the prescriptions a few times to keep up with current research developments, but she's kept her eyes on him for a long time."

"Who?" he asked, intently looking through the documents.

"Doctor Gale Lloyd. She was his police department shrink. I told her I was working with you on the case. She asked a couple of questions for verification. Then listed the meds for me and told me what they were responsible for. She said she'd forward the list to you this morning with the other documents she was sending. You never got them?"

"Unfortunately, no. Dr. Lloyd was killed in her home last night. Right now it's being ruled a suicide, but we aren't buying it. She intended to get us the information we'd requested."

"This is deep Arch. Too deep… I pulled as much information as I could on Dr. Lloyd. Couldn't find much. I did discover that she was a major contributor to Blanket Corp. She's listed as one of their midlevel research facilitators…

…Blanket Corp's practices are highly confidential. They're protected by various governments and political infrastructures across the globe. They seem to be the one organization besides the United Nations that's untouchable…

…And I do mean untouchable. I can't access financial statements, employment rosters, hierarchy chains, or anything else that gives personal information about this conglomerate. They exist on paper, but as far as leaving a trail, I can't find it."

Archer felt his blood pressure rising. Another dead end. "What other good news you got for me?"

"Well, LeDiv was supposedly getting money to make a drop when Dr. Rees followed him yesterday. I have no record of that either. It's not on any of his accounts. No transfers. No withdrawals. Nothing. Unless he had a large sum of money just lying around his house, it appears the money drop didn't happen."

"Except I saw it," Regan countered.

"You saw nothing. Is it possible you saw only what they wanted you to see? A money exchange that never happened."

"I don't know. I guess so. But I talked to Jessica Stanley in the car. She-"

"She what? Seemed afraid, concerned... Look, I'm just saying it's possible this is bigger than a kidnapping and ransom. It feels bigger...

...By the way Archer. That FBI agent I've been looking for. Nothing. Like everyone else involved in this case. I can't get close. Seems like he's too protected as well."

"Keep digging. Maybe you'll turn something up."

"Honestly, I'm thinking maybe I should just sit this one out kiddo. I'm too old for this much drama. I'm also a little worried."

"What's bothering you Ro? In all the years I've known you, you've never shied away from finding the truth. Why now?"

"Arch. Two hours after I talked to that lady... just two hours. I noticed I had a tail. Black SUV. I took it slow. They followed for a while."

He chuckled, "I took them the long way around. Finally, I turned right onto the Causeway. They turned left. However, another SUV picked me up half a block later. They were doing some serious communicating. If I didn't know what to look for, I'd have had no idea they were back there."

"You positive Ro? No mistakes?"

"None Archer. They were there. And too many people are starting to turn up dead already. I don't think it's in my best interest to finish this one."

"No judgment from me ole fellow," Archer said as he patted Ronin on the back. "You've done enough."

25

Max cowered in fear. He'd gone straight home and fallen asleep on the couch, but not before downing half a bottle of Lucid Absinthe. He'd also found his most recent prescription. He opened the bottle for the first time and rolled two of the firm yellowish pills in his fingers.

This prescription was new. She had said it was the best one yet. Honestly, he wasn't sure if the others had helped at all. He'd continued to take them only because she'd insisted. Jessica had agreed, and he'd stayed on them to keep her happy. That hadn't worked out so well.

Now, he was sitting on the couch, the half opened bottle on the small coffee table. The shimmering, jaundiced panther's eyes on the bottle startled him.

They blinked.

He'd seen it.

Then they rose high above the couch, glaring down from their perch on the ceiling. The angry snarls caused him to try and bury himself in the upholstery.

The menacing eyes watched him like, fixedly staring through seemingly omniscient lenses.

Lucid. What a paradoxical name for such a strong alcoholic beverage. It spoke to clarity of mind. Sobriety. Completely opposite from the way a drink this hard affected the mind. He'd been far removed from clarity after the first few swigs.

Maybe it was the drink causing him to see the devilish cat slink along the ceiling. Its claws dug so deeply into the white texture that it fell like disheveled snowflakes onto the furniture below. He tried to move where the large cat wouldn't be hovering over him, but he couldn't escape its intimidating stare.

Suddenly, it lunged for him. Its body slammed into him full force, knocking him sprawling across the floor. He turned around and lifted his head in time to see the penetrating eyes fade back onto the slender black bottle in a strand of putrid smoke.

He rested his head against the foot of the couch and closed his eyes. He needed rest, but knew it wouldn't come. He prayed he would fall asleep and wake up the next morning to find that life was back to normal. He wished Carson would be back, and his family would be whole. Even as he wished, he knew it wasn't possible. There was no such thing as normal anymore.

He heard the voice speak just before he sensed the movement. The scratchy rasp made it barely intelligible. He discerned the meaning more than understood its entirety.

"Back off Max. We've been more than fair. You have to let go."

He loudly sobbed. "I can't just let go. He's my son. I've never held back. Every time you've asked I've given, but you can't just take my boy."

"We're not asking Max."

"Please, I saw you that night. You took him. I know it was you. They won't believe me."

"Of course they don't. To them I don't exist. I'm just a figment of your imagination. I'm just a part of you that only comes out when others aren't watching."

"Are you just-"

"A figment of your imagination?"

The dark figure moved toward him, staying far enough in the shadows that it wasn't discernible. Max struggled to inch toward it, but the drugs had dampened his strength. The struggle was futile; he couldn't go forward.

It's heinous laugh revoltingly echoed through the perimeter of the room, shattering the slight hope Max had been clinging to.

"Could a figment of your imagination have taken Carson? Of all people, you know I'm real."

"But why? Why'd you take him? Why can't you just leave him alone? Take someone else's kid. I've been loyal. Don't do this to me. Please. I'm begging. Is that what you want? I'm begging you."

"I'm not interested in your false, fear induced humility. What I want, only the boy can give. You don't have it in you."

"I do. I can do whatever you need. I'll get ten more kids for you if you'll just leave mine alone."

"By the harvest moon. Once it casts its crimson radiance across the sleepy hollow of his heart, he'll be taken Max. One life for many."

"How? What do you mean?"

It mocked again. "A story that predates time. A lamb slain. One death to save the world. He could be the one we've waited for. The appointed one."

"He's not. He's my son. Please, give me back my son."

The dark figure moved toward the door. Max willed ever fiber of his body to follow, to reach the figure, to hold him down.

Torture.

Painful

Slow.

He'd do anything to find out where they were holding Carson. However, as fiercely as his mind battled the swarming cloudiness, his body remained subdued to its paralytic influence. The figure faced him, death impenetrably staring through the placid darkness.

"Stop the pursuit Max. What's done is done. One life. Let's not make it two."

The door slammed as the dark figure seemed to float from the room. Max screamed.

Terrified.

Panic-stricken.

Pain.

Regret.

Frustration.

His cries were absorbed by the solitude of his surroundings. His prayers seemed to touch the ears of a dispassionate God. He fell back against the couch.

The bottle boldly stood in the midst of the table. The intrepid, slanted eyes ogled him. They levitated again. Floating upward, before momentarily disappearing into the intense blackness.

Re-emerging, they peered at him, silently and masterfully keeping him subdued.

He lay there for hours vacantly gazing into the hypnotic, brilliant slits on the ceiling. Neither awake nor asleep, he merely existed. Finally, the yellowish globes disappeared, and Max crashed into a deep sleep, dreaming of far away places. Places where he and his son were safe. Places where his family wasn't tormented by the dark figures he'd come to know.

26

Archer sat at his desk, buried behind mountains of paperwork. He occasionally glanced through the glass barricade that separated him from the rest of the office. He'd always been a loner. He hadn't taken a new partner since Ronin had retired years ago. Since he'd left, Archer had preferred and been granted the isolated path.

He propped his feet up and reached for the phone. He wished he had the number on speed dial, but he and the man he was about to call weren't on that level of friendship. They'd met on a case a few years ago that had crossed many jurisdictions.

During the course of the case, two assailants had approached the man from behind. Both were armed, and both had the intent to kill. Archer had been the only thing that had kept him from catching a bullet in the back. The way Archer figured it, the man owed him one.

He opened the desk drawer and removed an index card. It simply read *FBI Paranormal Profiler*. He wasn't sure if this case involved the paranormal or not. In his opinion, Max needed to get back on a daily dose of his meds. However, he wasn't looking for someone to work the case for him. He merely wanted a connection on the inside, someone who could get answers.

The phone rang three times. A tired voice picked up on the other end.

"Yo. This is D-Myles. What's up?"

Archer cleared his throat. "Is this Agent Darryon Myles, with the Federal Bureau of Investigation?"

"Yes. It is. I don't know how you got this number, but you're calling me on a protected personal line. I'm on vacation. Try calling headquarters, they'll connect you to another agent that can help you."

"Wait. I have this number because you gave it to me. You told me to call if I were ever in a bind. You said you'd drop what you were doing and try to help me. I usually don't call in those kind of favors, but I'm desperate-"

"Archer Madsen? Sorry brotha. It's been a minute. How've you been man?"

"Not too well, or I wouldn't be bothering you."

"No prob, I'm just chillin' in the Keys with my wife. What's up?"

"Your wife? That pretty girl you were working with? Always

saw that one coming."

Darryon chuckled, "Guilty. I finally did the right thing. She had to quit the Bureau, but we've made it work. Both happier than ever… but you didn't call to catch up on me. What can I help you with?"

"I need information Agent Myles. In a serious way. My sources all lead to the FBI, but they aren't giving me anything to work with. They're stonewalling me, and I want to know why."

"What kind of information you looking for?"

"You ever heard of Vestis Corpus?"

Darryon let out a long whistle. "Man, you sure don't let a brotha off the hook easy. You goin' after tha big fish. I'm afraid I can't help you much… On the record."

"So you've heard of them?"

Darryon was silent. Archer could hear him discussing something in the background.

"Aight man. Look, what you need to know doesn't need to be discussed over the phone. You still living in that God forsaken city?"

"Haven't moved."

"I'm gonna catch the first flight in. I'll send you flight details. Have someone pick me up at the airport and bring me to you. I'll be coming under the name Jessie Moore."

"I don't want to ruin your vacation. If you're like me, you

don't get many."

Darryon laughed again. "True. But I don't have many people that have saved my life either. I'm repaying a debt. Just have someone pick me up."

"Will do, and thanks Darryon. It'll be good to see you, and even better if you can help me."

"Playa, I'm not sure you'll be thankful once I get there. If you're into what I think you're in to, you're gonna need more help than I can give. Maybe more than the entire FBI can. There's a reason Vestis Corpis remains untouched."

"Well, maybe it's time to change that. I've got a missing kid and a family that wants him home. I've got bodies stacking up from anyone who has been involved. I've even been assaulted, as well as the doctor consulting on this case."

"Sounds like it's startin' to get personal. We both know that's dangerous."

"It was personal the moment I tasted my own blood in my mouth."

"I feel ya. Hang tight. Be careful. Should be to ya in a few hours."

Archer hung up the phone and placed his feet on the floor. He had a feeling when Darryon Myles got there, they were gonna hit the ground running.

27

The twelve sat piously around the executive round table. Ten men and two women silently waited. A digital clock meticulously clicked overhead, a hushed reminder that he was late as usual. Not that they minded. Even if they did, he would never know. No one had the guts to tell him.

They were all powerful people.

Influential.

Important.

Famous.

Wealthy.

Intellectual.

However, he was the one who mattered most. If they were

honest, they were afraid of him. He possessed a power they didn't understand.

The door swung open, and he stepped in. Every face fell. It wasn't so much their countenance, as it was an intense sense of unworthiness. He was of average height, but head and shoulders above in stature. Every woman wanted him, and every man wanted to be him.

He readily took his place. Number thirteen. The head of the round table. As he ceremoniously took his seat, the others chanted indistinguishable words in an unknown dialect.

He removed an item from his bag and placed it in the center of the table. It was a book. Well worn. Its pages crinkled in the corners and discolored from centuries of exposure.

"Unum de multis. Nos es unus of plures," he passionately decreed, gazing from one person to the next. As his commanding eyes fell on the first, the man repeated the mantra in English. "One of many. We are one of many."

Only after each person had personally repeated did he stop to open the book. He abysmally stared into the parched pages like he was afraid to read. Finally, he picked up his head.

A small candle sat in front of each person. The leader removed a candle from his bag and placed it in front of him. It was larger than the others, and proudly displayed the scorched signs of many uses. He ritually removed a special mixture and placed it next to him on the table.

Two cups, each one containing an unholy solution. The gold and brass containers were both filled with a special concoction refined by the high priest himself. It was the only way it could work.

He removed the lid from the two grails, and then stepped away from the table. The others stood in unison, watching intently. He moved toward a rack standing in the corner. As he got there, he slowly unbuttoned his shirt, letting it fall to the floor. His pants followed, as did his remaining clothes.

Completely naked, he removed something from the rack and moved back toward the table. He moved from each person to the next, placing his finger on each person's forehead, while fervently bellowing in an unknown tongue. Every eye was closed, as each person was afraid to behold his nakedness.

Finally, after he'd touched the last one, he unfolded the robe he'd taken from the rack and put it on. He pointed to the young female immediately to his right. Without hesitation, she moved toward the far corner and removed her clothing. Not nearly as intimidating, the others keenly watched.

She removed a robe from the rack and moved close to them, taking her place directly in front of the potentate. He intently examined the front of her body. Then, placing his hand on her right shoulder, he forcefully spun her around and examined her from behind. He ran his fingers through her shoulder length blond hair. As he touched her, she closed her eyes, feeling an intensity she'd rarely felt. He violently pushed her away and motioned for her to take her position. As she took her place, she was allowed to put on the oversized dark brown robe.

In the same movement, he motioned for the second person

to follow the girl's lead. The man went though the same routine. Closely being examined in his nakedness before being allowed to place the robe on.

After every member had been through the routine, the man sat down. The other members remained standing until he raised both hands into the air and gently lowered them. As his hands rested, the others sat down at the table.

"I've been sent to rectify you're dilemma. Someone must be held accountable."

No one spoke.

"This has become an unwanted distraction. Some of your members have strayed. The Concilium wants blood."

The blond in the chair next to him timidly replied, "Sir, we aren't responsible. He's gone rogue. He's trying to position himself. He wants a spot on this Trust. He's trying to prove his allegiance, but he refuses to listen. His disobedience is stifling."

"Excuses. If just one of you had his guts, you would have silenced him already… We've existed through the centuries because we've found a way to kill in silence. We serve our master and do his biding, and no one's the wiser…

…We believed this Trust could govern its own region. We've patiently waited for this Trust to right its own ship. Have we been so foolish?"

Her head lowered, as she eyeballed the floor. "No," she bashfully replied. "You haven't been foolish. We'll get this right?"

"Who suggested that this man be allowed in?"

An elderly gentleman toward the back of the table raised his hand. "It was me. It was many years ago. He was young. On fire. Full of life. And searching for answers. We were able to give him some. He's proved his loyalty. He fulfilled his oath. He's looking for a seat at the table. That's all he wants, to feel that his sacrifice matters."

"This isn't about an individual. Ever. One cannot force the hand of the serpent without getting bitten. Challenge the authority of the Concilium and suffer the consequences. Someone must pay."

The blond responded, "One of us? But why isn't he the one to be punished? It's his fault."

The potentate's marked expression silenced her questioning manner. He thoughtfully constructed his words.

"There's no room for weakness with the Trusts. You were each selected to operate anonymously with your Trust because we felt you could each handle the responsibility…

…However, Trusts are ever evolving. They're highly volatile. The Concilium is constantly re-evaluating each individual's standing in the Realm…

…He's made mistakes. That's true. He's placed his own interests above the whole. But that doesn't reflect badly on him"

He thrashed the words into their midst. "It looks bad for you. With proper mentoring, we'd not be having this discussion. Someone must pay for the sins of this group."

He poured the two solutions into the bowl of his candle. He touched the wick with his fingertip, and it erupted. He carefully placed the burning candle into the center of table.

"Permissum incendia ostendo sum verum."

The blond next to him looked at the others. "Let the fire reveal truth."

He thrust his hands through the flame and unfolded them in a throwing motion toward the other candles around the table. All but three instantly burst into a bluish flicker. The blond, the elderly gentleman, and the other woman incredulously beheld their empty wicks.

"It's down to three," the potentate decreed. He removed nine crooked daggers from his bag and clanged them into the center of the table. "You have one minute. Then it must be done. It's up to you to decide which of the three must die."

28

Regan moved toward Archer. "I've got good news Arch. We found one of them. The information I gave you yesterday paid off. They're waiting for you to make entry."

"What?" The words almost exploded from his mouth, "They found one of the kidnappers?"

"Yes. His name is Scott Halford. Twenty-four. A mechanic. Working right now at that expensive automotive repair place on Estherwood. My uncle sent a couple of undercover units to keep an eye on the place until we get there."

He walked to his desk and picked up a duffel bag from the floor. He opened it and removed a navy vest. He tossed the heavy pack to Regan.

"Put that on. You're not going near the action unless you're wearing it."

He reached into the bag again and removed another one, fastening it around his chest. Zipping the bag and dropping it to the floor, he reached for his radio with the other hand. He flipped the switch on.

"Channel five," Regan stated. "It our surveillance frequency."

He flipped it to five. There was no chatter. He pressed the button on the side and heard the familiar squelch.

"Do we have eyes on the suspect?"

Someone gave a squelched reply. "Sure do. He's under a red Corvette right now. Doesn't look like he's going anywhere soon. What's your eta?"

"Be there in ten. Keep your eyes open. He's our only lead."

Eight minutes later, Archer parked his car two blocks away. He and Regan quickly moved toward the site. As he approached, an undercover officer moved toward him from an unmarked car.

"He's still in there. Same car. He's hardly moved over the last twenty minutes."

Archer took the binoculars and pointed them toward the auto shop. He quickly found the suspect. His legs were barely visible from under the red sports car. Archer thoughtfully studied him.

"Has he moved at all?"

"Nope. Been working under there the entire time."

Archer swore. "Where are the other workers? Why is there no movement down there?"

"I don't know. Come to think of it, I haven't seen anyone in a while."

Archer handed the binoculars back to the undercover. "I'm going in. Be ready. Get your men in position."

Archer moved forward, quickly crossing the street. As he neared the entrance, he drew his gun. He moved into the building. The radio cackled. It was Regan's voice.

"Archer, there's no movement outside. I'm still not seeing any movement in there either."

"10-4," Archer replied as he moved further in. He made his way to the car and aimed his gun at the man under it.

"Scott Halford, I'm Detective Archer Madsen. Police Department. I need you to slide out from under the car please."

There was no movement.

Nothing shifted.

"Sir. I'm not gonna ask you again to come out from under that car with your hands up."

Nothing.

Archer moved quickly forward. He grabbed the man by his pants leg and pulled him from underneath the car. Two events transpired in that moment. The first is that he recognized the man as the one in the photo. This was definitely Scott

Halford, or what was left of him. He'd been shot, at least six times. Professionally killed. Three holes in the space of a quarter near the heart. Three in the forehead, as evenly spaced.

The second event was the unmistakable sound of a pin being pulled when he moved the body. A clear string was attached to the victim's chest. It was designed to remove the pin from its other end when the body was moved. Archer had walked right into the trap. He'd removed the body without thinking. He'd also recognized it in half a second.

He immediately sprinted toward the entrance, wildly yelling and swinging his arms. He'd just cleared the open garage when the building burst into flames. The force of the eruption picked him up and threw him. He landed hard on the concrete twenty feet from where he'd been standing.

He rolled over. His ears were ringing. His vision was blurred. His head was pounding. He remembered exactly what had happened. He'd moved the body, and that had triggered a massive explosion.

He moved around to see it. There was nothing left. The building was in ruins. The surrounding two businesses were also going up in flames. He heard voices beside him. It took a few seconds to recognize them.

"Archer, are you okay? Archer?"

He tried to sit up but couldn't muster the strength. "Help me up," he said, as he swore again.

"No. Stay down. You were hit hard. You need to be checked out."

He could already hear the sirens wailing in the distance. "Was anyone else hurt?"

"No. No one else followed you in. We were all watching from outside… Arch, you're lucky to be alive."

"Just help me up," he said as he reached for her arm.

"Arch please," she begged, as he used her for leverage while wobbling to his feet.

The Lieutenant ran toward them both. "Are you two okay?"

Archer looked at him, "Somebody doesn't want us to discover the truth. That kid, he never had a chance. Six shots. Three to the forehead. Three to the chest. All from point blank range. Somebody wanted to make sure he didn't talk. One more time we get a lead only to have it slammed in our face… Someone on the inside has a big mouth, and I'm going to find out who."

"Arch, calm down. There's no mole. I'd vouch for any of my men. There's no way information came from inside this department."

"Sorry, but someone has been toying with us. They're always one step ahead. We keep getting the door slammed in our face…

…This kid was alive until we discovered him. Regan picked him from a photo book. How could they have known that without a department snitch? You need to plug the leak. Because if I have to, God help whoever it is."

"Archer, calm down. You're no good like this."

"Calm down. I almost got my head taken off. If there hadn't been a slight delay in the mechanism, or if I didn't recognize that sound, I'd be a dead man...

...And you realize that Regan could have been with me. If she'd have followed me in, we'd both be unidentifiable right now."

The Lieutenant grimly nodded. As he looked away, he recognized the blue and white van pulling into the lot. He kicked at a rock, sending it skipping across the ground.

"Great. The press. I'm gonna run interference. You calm down. I can't have you getting distracted. Stay focused on your task."

As he walked away, Regan leaned in, "Arch, are you sure the dead man was the one from the photo?"

"If the photo you showed me earlier was Scott Halford, there's no doubt. By the look of things, he'd only been dead a couple of hours.

He paused and looked at her. She could see the hamster wheels spinning in his mind.

"What are you thinking Arch?"

"Regan, who was there when you recognized the suspect in that photo?"

"No one. Why?"

"How long ago was that?"

"About two-and-a-half, maybe three hours. Why?"

"Think Regan, during that time, who did you tell? Who knew you'd made a positive i.d.?"

She looked toward her uncle and reluctantly turned back to face him. "No. Archer. Stop what you're thinking. It's not possible."

"Did you tell anyone else?"

She looked at the ground, her mind now racing too.

"Regan. Think. Did you tell anyone else?"

"No. Arch. I told him. That was it. I told no one else until I told you later."

Archer looked angry. He shook his head in disgust and walked toward the EMTs that had just arrived.

"Anyone have anything that'll keep me awake but stop the pounding?"

Regan stared after him. Her uncle couldn't be responsible. He wasn't that kind of man. She would never believe it. Archer was thinking irrationally. The case was getting to him. She just couldn't wait for it to be over.

29

Two hours later Regan drove his unmarked unit in silence. He sat crossly in the passenger seat. He was in pain. That was obvious, but he'd never admit it to her.

"Arch, why don't you let me take you to the ER? You were almost pulverized by a military grade explosive. You need to be in bed, letting some cute, little nurse patch you up."

"No. This isn't over, so neither am I."

"That's crazy. At least recline your seat and take a nap. I'll wake you up when we get there."

He didn't argue; he just leaned back against the headrest. She smiled, hoping he'd take her advice. He didn't. There wasn't time.

After several minutes he spoke, "Max confirmed what Jess told you; this has happened to the LeDiv family before."

"You mean, he wasn't aware of it 'til now?"

"No. He was beating himself up, wondering why she didn't trust him enough to tell him. I told him that it was probably too painful; something one spends their entire life running from. But I don't know. It seems like something that would've come up in a normal marriage. Right?"

"I think so. I don't know any healthy couples that aren't blessed with the art of communication. If they don't trust each other enough to share their most intimate details, they don't last long these days. It's the missing link in most marriages. The simple art of sharing your basic feelings, experiencing each other's day, and discussing life."

"Doesn't sound like they had any of that. Perhaps that's why they seem to be in trouble. I sort of get the impression he was given the cold shoulder."

"I don't know Arch. I'd like to know more. I get the feeling he was giving her emotional popsicles as well. I don't know if she should shoulder most of the blame. I'm having a difficult time assessing their condition."

"Max also indicated that he read his wife's record from the D.A.'s office. It sounded like her file was pretty detailed. I wonder if anyone around here would know about it."

"You ask my uncle?"

"I'm not asking him anything. I don't know who to trust. Honestly, I don't trust anyone but you, and that's because you're right beside me. I don't-"

"Arch, it's a lonely road you're walkin'-"

"It's the only one I know. You don't get this far by trustin' everyone that pretends to have your best interest-"

"And that's what you think I'm doing? Pretendin?"

"Stop. I don't mean it that way. All I'm saying is that we both know this isn't gonna turn out pretty."

"So you're just waiting for the other shoe to fall. That's it? You don't know what's gonna happen, but you know it's bad?"

"Pretty much. And I have the feelin' that when this all comes out, there's going to be a lot of people get hurt. This is much deeper than we think."

"What do you mean?"

"It's not a kidnapping-"

"What? You don't believe we're after a missing kid?"

"Oh. Yes. I still suppose we're after a missing child. However, I believe he's the tip of the iceberg. We're uncovering something that's been expertly buried, and someone doesn't want it uncovered."

"And you think that someone is extremely powerful?"

"I think that someone goes higher that we could imagine. How else do you explain everything that's taken place? Why is the FBI involved in a two-day-old missing person's case? Why did an arrogant doctor offer you a job, spend half the night preparing files, only to kill herself before she went to bed the same night? How does our only suspect end up dead less than two hours after you identify him?"

"I don't know Arch. Even the man Max chased ran himself into a bulldozer. There have been several unbelievable points to this case. I don't know what to say-"

"Then say nothing. Our only solution is to keep digging. Eventually the snake will be forced to surface, and then it'll be exposed."

"What then? What if its venom is deadlier than we think?"

"Then I'll be waiting, and they'll find I'm not what they think either."

"What's that mean Archer? You can't do something you'll regret."

"I don't live with regrets Regan. Weighs a man down. If I make the decision, I just live with the consequences."

"Please. Promise me you won't do anything illegal."

"I'm sworn to defend the law, not break it."

He cleared his throat, an obvious attempt to change the subject. "What do you think about this being in the LeDiv family before? Isn't that a bit odd?"

"I think you'd have a better chance of being struck by lightning, unless someone were intentionally targeting your family. Or, it could be a self-fulfilling prophecy."

He smiled, "I won't even pretend to understand what that means."

"Maybe Jessica lived in fear to the point that she created this. Not that she intentionally planned it, but it's came to fruition because she's lived a certain way."

He scowled back. "Or maybe it's just old fashioned karma. She's lived like a devil and has to reap the whirlwind."

"Why so cynical Arch? That's not you."

He ignored the question. "I guess we still have the license plate of the motorcycle. They're still trying to track it. Then there's your mysterious cowboy. Two possibilities."

Neither of them spoke. They both knew whatever they were chasing didn't leave loose ends. If those men were traceable, they were dead. No evidence. No witnesses. No case.

Archer closed his eyes. He hadn't faltered last time when there hadn't been a case, and he wouldn't this time either. He'd find that missing child, and whoever was responsible would pay.

30

The man lay on his back in a hammock. The two trees holding the swaying bed were centuries old. Worn and tested, they had weathered every storm, standing as ferocious reminders on the power of consistency.

Patience. It's more mental fortitude than any other attribute. That's why he continued to work for these people even we placed among amateurs. He was a hired gun, a mercenary. He went to the highest bidder. It just so happened the highest bidder had always been his current proprietors.

This time had been different. They'd never had him work with the people he was assigned to kill. They knew he preferred to work alone.

He had known from the beginning that this one wasn't going to work in his favor. He was a professional. The two men he was hired to work with were in over their heads.

That's why he'd protested at first. Strongly in fact, until the voice on the other end of the line had agreed to double his salary. Money talks when logic and wisdom argue otherwise.

He knew exceptionally little about his employers. They never contacted him from a traceable line. In fact, he rarely spoke to one of them directly. His messages were usually encoded on his private computer network. He'd decipher the files and prepare his tactics based on their instructions.

He was a cleaner. He waited until the expendable hires completed their part of the plan, and then he'd make sure they disappeared without a trace. He took pride in his handiwork. He left nothing uncovered. Every fiber of evidence was buried so deeply that it would never be discovered.

He had to admit that his employers didn't discriminate. He'd killed all kinds. No one was out of his employer's reach.

Men.

Women.

Children occasionally. Nothing makes a stronger statement than the senseless murder of a child. There's just something about innocence betrayed that breaks the heart of those involved in a case of such magnitude.

He'd done a few hits that he wasn't proud of, but nothing that he lost sleep over. Cash with blood on it spends just as easily as an honest living. He preferred the quick route, and he found killing just as easy as breathing.

He kicked his cowboy boots off and closed his eyes. He knew they'd come for him one day. He lived every second prepared for that moment. He was an ultimate loose end. They'd allow him to live in their financial bliss until he grew too old or slow to keep up, then they'd burn him like he'd burned so many others. He'd reap what he had sown, of that he had no doubt.

His burn phone vibrated in his pocket. He got a new one at the beginning of every job, and discarded it at the end. It was their means of communication. A way to stay connected without establishing a tangible connection. If he were caught, they couldn't be traced.

He picked it up. "Yeah."

"The job done?"

"Been done. They'll find the motorcycle, but it's only gonna lead to more questions. They won't find the one who was really driving it. He's taken care of…

…I used the other one for bait. Might even take care of those investigators if we're lucky."

The voice on the other end sounded agitated. "Your lure almost worked, but he survived. The building is gone, the body is gone, but he made it out in time."

"What would you have me do? I played that one beautifully."

"You screwed up, but we've decided to give you another chance to convince them to stop pursuing this."

"How?"

"It's time to end the life of a certain psychologist. If you played your cards right, you should know exactly how to find her. Make sure tonight is her last."

The call ended. He looked down in disbelief. Murdering the family of an influential city cop wasn't a smart idea. They were usually much more low profile. It was obvious that they were getting desperate.

Oh well. Money earned. A new target meant a new price. He picked up his electronic tablet and emailed a message to an anonymous account. It only had one word. An exceptionally high figure. He smiled. They'd never disagreed with his suggested fee before. They'd always paid him.

After a few seconds, the tablet gave an audible beep. He opened the reply. It read one word.

Done.

He shrugged and pulled his boots back on. Who needed sleep? He knew a woman who was about to die in a tragic accident. He knew a man who was about to be incredibly rich. And that's all that mattered.

31

Max nervously paced the tile floor of the nursing home. How had he not been aware of this for all the years he'd been married? It had been right there, available for discovery if he'd have been interested.

He'd found her easily. He hadn't even had to hire an investigator. A legit computer search had turned up her name. She was supposed to be dead, killed in a car accident when Jess was a child. It was one of the many tragedies he thought his wife had been forced to endure. Life had supposedly been so unfortunate. She'd told him that he was the only good thing that had ever happened to her. That was until Carson was born.

Carson had changed everything. His smile lit up the room. She had cried the first few months when she would look at him. He was the perfect bundle of joy. The radiant first that would make any mother more than willing to adventure into the depths of rearing "children" instead of a "child."

He was a momma's boy and had been from the beginning. "Mom" had been his first word. He went to her to fix all his problems. He wanted her to tuck him in at night and read his bedtime stories. Dad was loved, but there was something special about the bond that Carson and Jessica shared. Max had been amazed and completely happy by his wife and son's relationship.

He wasn't jealous. He never had been. He was glad Carson had a mother that loved and cared for him so completely. He did find it odd that she over thought things at times, but figured it was because Carson was their first child. She wanted to give him the best care. He would much prefer that to being married to a woman that placed her own needs above her children's. That seemed to be the trend more and more these days.

Now, he wondered why she seemed to be such a perfect mother but such a dishonest wife? How could she lie to him about such immense events?

She'd had a brother that he'd never known about. It was true that she had never directly lied about having one, but she'd never been honest and told him either. To him, partial disclosure was just as crucial as being dishonest. Now, he'd discovered that Jessica's mother was alive. Apparently, the story of the fiery crash had been untrue.

He'd desperately dialed her number, and she'd reluctantly agreed to meet him. He had scorching questions that he couldn't wrap his mind around. Why at the age of Mr. Morgan LeDiv had she been placed in a long-term care facility? Why was she no longer part of her daughter's life? What information could she shed on the kidnapping of her son? Was their anything she knew that could help find Carson? Were these cases related, or was it merely coincidental that his wife had lost a brother and now a son?

He needed answers, and she was probably the only person outside of Jessica and Morgan that could give them, and they weren't talking.

Max hesitantly walked down the hallway toward the nurse's station. He'd almost worn a path in the floor from an hour of incessant marching. Finally, he worked up the courage to face the overweight, overworked, underpaid, and subsequently excessively irritable nurse behind the counter. She was a rotund black girl with an attitude. Her gum popped between sentences, barely heard over the chomping from her unprofessional destruction of the gum in her mouth.

"My name is Max Stanley. I'm here to see Mrs. LeDiv. She's expecting me."

"LeDiv? Dere ain't no LeDiv stay here."

Max looked confused. "But, I spoke with her on the phone earlier. I tracked her to this facility. I called this number. They transferred me to her room. We talked for twenty minutes."

"I don't know who ya thank ya spoke wit', but we ain't got no LeDiv. You sho ya got tha right name? Maybe ya spoke wit' someone else."

He struggled, fighting for composure. It was happening again. He could feel it. He squeezed his shoulders toward his neck and almost convulsed. The voices were back. This time they were laughing at him.

Mocking.

Discouraging.

Humiliating.

"Stop it," he screamed. "Stop making fun of me."

The girl rose from the desk. The cushioned seat heavily sighed a squeaky relief as she removed herself from its surface.

"I don' know what's yo prob, but if ya don' leave nah, I'm callin' security."

She rolled her eyes. "Talkin' bout makin' funna you. I got betta thangs ta do wit' my time."

"I'm sorry. Don't call security. It's not you."

She had one hand on the phone. The dial tone pulsed, as it was halfway to her ear. Reluctantly, she placed it back down.

"Wish I culd hep, but there ain't no LeDiv's livin' here."

He craned his neck, forcefully battling the voices pillaging his mind.

"And you're certain? Would you mind to check your records? Just to be sure you didn't miss anything?"

She placed the papers in her hand down slightly harder than she normally would have. With a heavy sigh she typed, gazing into the screen. Her gum annoyingly continued to pop as she nervously chewed. He subtly leaned to the left, trying to read off the screen, but it had one of those protectors that completely obscured his view.

"Sorry. There ain't no LeDiv's. Now, when ya say ya spoke wit her?"

"I spoke with her a couple of hours ago. She agreed to meet me. Said they'd let me right in. She described the front gate and everything. Gave me her room number. I just don't remember it."

"What numba ya called?"

He removed a piece of paper from his pocket and shoved it across the desktop. She scrutinized it.

"That be tha right numba. It woulda dialed direck ta dis phone. I been right here fo hours. Ain't got no call from you. Ya sho ya dial tha right numba?"

He took the crumpled paper and compared it with the number in the call list of his cell phone.

"Look ma'am. It's the same number. It shows I spoke with someone here for twenty-five minutes."

She took the phone and looked at it. She turned around and looked down the long hall and motioned for a male orderly. He quickly stopped what he was doing and briskly walked toward them. As he approached, she raised her voice toward Max.

"I don' know wat game you be playin', but you betta leave now."

She spun the phone in his direction across the countertop.

The top call he had seen only moments before was missing.

"No. What did you do? You erased my call."

The male orderly arrived beside him. "What's going on here? You need help with something Shawndra?"

"Dis man was jus' leavin'."

The voices again.

Raging.

Angry.

Contempt.

Scorn.

Max screamed, "What did you do? Why'd you erase my call?"

"I ain't done nuttin'. You thank I did dat den bring back a printed phone bill… Ya need he'p. Get yaself sum he'p."

Max glared at her through raging eyes. The voices wouldn't stop.

Kill her Max.

She played you.

You can never find your son. She knows something, and she's hiding it from you.

You should beat it out of her Max.

Don't let her do this to you.

Show her Max. Kill her.

Max violently shook his head from side to side and covered his ears with his hands. As if stopping external sound from leaking through the auditory pathway would silence the malicious voices residing inside.

He was going crazy. There were too many signs lately that he couldn't deny. Too many pieces were falling through the cracks. Maybe he hadn't placed the call. Maybe he hadn't spoken with her.

The male orderly placed his hand on Max's shoulder. "C'mon man. You alright?"

Max jumped, knocking the man's arm away from him. The woman picked up the phone again.

"I'm callin' tha police."

The orderly motioned for her to stop. "Put the phone down Shawndra. He's okay. Right sir?"

The voices grew fainter. He uncovered his ears and sobbed. "I'm sorry ma'am. I'm leaving," he said, as he disbelievingly examined his phone again.

The orderly moved toward him. "I'll escort you out sir."

"That won't be necessary. I walked in. I'm sure I can find my way back out. It's one hallway, then turn right."

"I insist. It would be my pleasure," the orderly non-assumingly replied.

Max grunted and turned to leave. The orderly followed him

all the way down the corridor. Max turned at the end and looked back toward Shawndra. She was fervently discussing something on the phone. It looked heated. He could only imagine what she was discussing about him, and whom it was with.

The orderly motioned to the right, snapping his attention from her direction.

"Sorry," he mouthed, as he moved toward the exit door. Once out of sight, the orderly touched him on the shoulder.

"Max Stanley. Are you Max Stanley?"

Max wheeled to face him. "Yes. How'd you know my name?"

The man smiled. "Mrs. LeDiv wishes to speak with you. She was afraid this might happen. She asked me to make sure you got to see her if you showed up."

"She's here?"

"Yes. She's been here for several years. I'm not sure why they're lying to you. But I've gotta make sure you get to see her. We just have to slip back across the hall without being noticed."

"Why are you doing this? Why would you help me?"

"I'm not helping you sir. I'm helping Mrs. LeDiv. She's a sweetheart. If she needs to speak with you, then I'm gonna make sure it happens."

Max's rigid expression turned into a smile. "How much is she paying you?"

The man laughed. "Enough… She calls me her angel. She pays me to keep my eyes and ears open. I make sure she's taken care of."

"Just get me to her. There's a lot we need to discuss."

32

His hair was a mess. Black smudges streaked both sides of his face. Sweat mingled with blood caked his wrinkle lines. She was impressed how stoically he was handling this experience. Like a gallant warrior, he marched headlong onto the field of battle, even when peering into the merciless eyes of death.

His cell phone rang, breaking her girlish idolization. He answered. "Tell me ya got something?"

"It's too soon to tell from the scene here, but we've confirmed that the device was triggered when you moved the body. It did have a backup mechanism as well. It could have been triggered from a cell phone."

Archer slammed his head back. "You mean someone was watching us? Just waiting for the right moment to place a call and kill us all?"

"That's how it appears. Judging by the grade of the weapon.

We're guessing they had to be within a quarter-mile radius. I'd say the trigger on the body was more a secondary device. The killer was hoping a group would enter together. Boom!"

"It's a good thing I'm a loner… Anything else?"

"Yeah. The Lieutenant put Conrad back on the case. He's running down different angles… Don't worry; you're still the primary. He's support. The Lieutenant is going to fill you in. I just didn't want you to be surprised."

"Thanks… What's he working on?"

"He's following up on a couple of leads. Tracking down that cowboy that Regan told us about. Also, he's trying to track down that motorcycle. It's registered to Tyler Wiggins."

"Are you kidding me? Tyler Wiggins, the son of Congressman Wiggins?"

"One and the same. Conrad is searching for him, trying to establish a connection. All he knows so far is that it wasn't reported stolen. So on paper, it's still in Tyler's possession. Actually, on paper the Congressman owns it. I'm afraid this could get messy."

Archer chuckled, "It's already messy. Just keep me in the loop, and let Conrad know he's to forward anything pertaining to this case straight to me. I won't have him running his own investigation."

He clicked the phone closed and spoke to Regan without facing her.

"The motorcycle you saw comes back to a United States

Congressman. You know how to pick 'em don't you?"

"Arch. I highly doubt a Congressman would be involved with a low profile kidnapping during a major election."

"I keep telling you, it's more than a kidnapping."

Her eyes crinkled in the corners as she turned to him. "I don't care what you say Arch. I'm taking you home. You need a shower and some fresh clothes. Then we'll get back on this."

He didn't argue, just placed his head back in the seat. He closed his eyes and within seconds was asleep.

33

Max sat in a rocking chair facing a slim woman in a hospital bed. She was restrained with four white straps, keeping her loosely incarcerated in the blanketed prison. Her eyes told a story. They were sad, creased with worry.

Sickening fear.

Confusion.

She seemed to be an empty shell, only remnants of a life that used to exist. If he didn't know she was living, he'd have sworn he was conjuring a ghost.

An inspection of the room revealed bottles of pills lining the dresser. Each was a different prescription, but all from the same pharmaceutical company. She was taking at least seven different kinds of medications. No wonder she appeared so lost.

She also looked much older than he expected. Knowing Morgan LeDiv, he'd pictured a woman so painfully beautiful that she was still seductive after the years had past. However, drug exposure and seclusion had robbed her of whatever beauty she had once possessed. She reminded him of a drug addict he'd met in college, a methhead that had lost control and been killed by accidentally overdosing on a mixture of illegal narcotics and prescription pain pills.

The male orderly was still standing with him. Finally, he broke the silence. "Mrs. LeDiv?"

The woman sullenly stared, her eyes glazed.

"Mrs. LeDiv, are you okay?"

No reply. Just the cold and empty expression.

"Mrs. LeDiv, Max Stanley is here for you. You told me you wanted to speak with him."

She slowly and vacuously faced him. Her hand came up and slowly pointed. She tried to voice words that wouldn't articulate.

"Mrs. LeDiv. I have to go now. I'll put down that I've already checked on you and administered your afternoon meds. That should buy you a couple of hours. I'm gonna lock you in. I'll come back to get him when it's safe."

He turned toward Max. "Sorry, but in order to make sure all goes well I'm gonna have to lock you in. The deadbolt is on a safety alert network. If it's not locked, it'll buzz the front desk."

Max nodded his head. "I understand… That's interesting. How long has this facility had that technology?"

"It doesn't. It's just Mrs. LeDiv, and for as long as I can remember it's been that way. I never ask questions."

"You mean she's confined to this room?"

"Unless she has a couple of orderlies escort her outside, she's locked in here." He sort of laughed. "She calls them her prison guards. She calls Mrs. Shawnya the warden. I never thought how awful that sounds 'til now."

Max looked repulsed. "What kind of person would keep their family in a place like this? I'm afraid I don't know my wife at all," he mumbled.

The orderly stepped to the door. "I'm leaving Mrs. LeDiv. I can't come back for a couple hours. You should be left alone by the others though."

He looked back at Max. "I'm gonna stop back by the nurse's station and tell her you were escorted off the premises. Please don't do anything to place my job in jeopardy. I've got a family to feed."

Max nodded. "Thank you. For everything."

The door closed behind him, and Max heard the metallic clink of the deadbolt. Two hours of silence wasn't gonna be fun. More time was being wasted. Less chance he'd ever find Carson alive.

He undecidedly studied the woman in front of him. "Mrs. LeDiv, I'm Max Stanley."

She flashed her head toward him. "I know who you are. I've tried to keep up. You look better in life than those pictures. Off course they were grainy. Not the best quality. You seem like a good man."

"I try to be…"

He was thoughtful, but ended his intellectual process by just asking, "Why the charade Mrs. LeDiv?"

"Please. Call me Sandra. And whatever do you mean son?"

"C'mon Mrs. LeDiv… Sandra… Why do you pretend you're out of it? As soon as he left, you're at least coherent enough to talk to me."

She breathed heavily. "I don't trust anyone. Been here too long. I pay him enough to keep him honest. He helps me out, gives me a little extra attention, but he's not gonna risk his life for me. Not that he knows anyway. Just doing this would get him killed if they found out."

"Morgan?"

She laughed. It caught him off guard.

"Morgan. He's in over his head. Morgan is just a pawn."

"Ma'am. Since you've been in here, Morgan has become an extremely influential man. He's powerful now."

"He was always powerful son, but I'm telling you that he's just a big fish in a small pond. He'll be devoured by the sharks. I doubt he even has rank yet."

"Rank?"

"Yes, rank. He wanted to be one of them. They're what this is all about."

"Who? Who are you talking about?"

She looked distant again, like she were remembering something, or trying to. Finally, she broke the strangeness of her stare.

"I don't know. I could never remember."

"Please. Mrs. LeDiv-"

"Told you. It's Sandra. Don't call me by that name."

"Sorry. Sandra. I'll try not to do it again-"

"Try. We don't try. Tryin' is for the weak and unintelligent."

"Yes ma'am... Do you know who you're talking about Mrs. Sandra?"

She grimaced. "No. I told you. I don't remember. I'm afraid I never did. I just knew they existed. I heard them talking one night. I heard them talking to Morgan. Morgan was pleading with them. They told him it was the only way. He could have the power he'd always wanted, but he had to prove himself."

"What did that mean? What did he have to do?"

"I don't know. I can't remember."

"Mrs. Sandra... Was that right before your child was taken?"

"Oh, no. It was long before that. Matter-a-fact, it was long before my children were even born. That was back when Morgan said he didn't want kids. They only weigh people down and cost too much money. That's what he said."

Max expressionlessly looked through her. "Do you mind to tell me about it? About the kidnapping I mean."

"Tell you what? He was taken. We never found him. What else is there to tell?"

"I don't know."

"I don't either. The kidnapping isn't important. It was never solved."

"I still need to know. I'm sort of hoping I can change that. I think the two cases might be connected. I need your help deciding. I'll do everything I can to make sure those responsible are brought to justice-"

"Justice. You think I care about justice. That won't bring him back. That won't change years of pain and frustration. That won't get me out of this penitentiary I've been hidden in."

"Sorry, I-"

She scoffed, "Justice. It's just a pretty word to cover a repulsive idea. We don't want justice. We want retribution. Revenge. We want to watch the guilty get what's coming to them. We want someone to suffer because we've suffered. Don't kid yourself Max Stanley, we're just as guilty as they are."

"I disagree ma'am. We're trying to make the world a better place. If these people are ripping kids from their homes, they need to be stopped. If they aren't stopped, it's only gonna happen again and again. At what point does someone rise up and end the madness. You call it revenge. I call it justice. Call it whatever you want. At least it stops the disease from spreading-"

"Stops it? You can't be serious. Take a look around son. Read the papers. Watch the news. The disease never stops. It's called humanity. As long as people exist, their irrationality will continue to cause problems."

"Sorry. I don't share your cynicism. We can make the world better-"

"You're just an idealist. There's no light at the end of the tunnel, only more tunnels, leading to deeper and darker places."

"Maybe, but at least I've got a dream. Something to live for."

"Yeah, well I'd rather have something worth dying for. And that was taken from me a long time ago. There's not much left."

"Please. Tell me about it then. If not for revenge, then for Carson."

"Carson?"

"You know… my son… the grandson you've never seen. He could still be alive, and I'm not stopping until I know for sure. As long as there's a chance he could still be breathing, I'm not giving up."

"Ah, the beauty of innocence. How romantic?"

"There's no innocence here. My life is full of regrets, but Carson isn't one of them."

She thought for a moment, before swigging down a glass of ice tea. She harshly placed the cup down on the glass-topped table.

"Okay... Max Stanley... What do you want to know?"

"For starters, why are you here? You seem coherent enough to take care of yourself. So, why are you in a highly guarded, prisonish long-term facility? Why the restraints?"

"Because, I couldn't find my son. I lost it. Morgan fell out of love. Said I was too preoccupied with the past. He thought I belonged here, where I could wallow in my self-pity. Can you believe my husband had the audacity to look me in the eyes and tell me that?"

Max shuttered. "I'm sorry."

"Don't be. I forgave him long ago. No use letting bitterness sink its vile fangs in you forever. It only corrupts. Turns everything good into something unholy."

"Do they ever visit you? I mean Morgan? Jessica?"

She painfully shook her head. "Morgan did at first, but that only lasted a few months. Heard he'd moved on to some bimbo much younger than me. He never came back. Changed his numbers so I couldn't contact him anymore. I haven't seen him in years. He continued to pay for my care, so I can't hate him too much."

"What about Jessica?"

"No. Morgan told me that I was dead to her. He didn't want her having to deal with knowing what her mother had become. So he refused to bring her. She doesn't know I'm alive."

"I'm sorry-"

"Quit apologizing child. You had nothing to do with any of that. From what I understand, you've been a good man for my daughter, and a better father for her child. You've got no reason to apologize."

"I'm still sorry this has happened to you. I want to help you get out of here. And Jessica should know that you're alive."

She snapped her head around. "Oh, no. You must promise you'll never tell. That's why I quietly stay here. They told me if I ever contacted her, they'd kill her. They're powerful enough to reach her. Anywhere."

"Who? Who are they?"

She seemed angry. "Don't ask me that. I don't know. I already told you that I don't know. Leave it alone."

"Okay," he soothingly reassured her. "I won't mention it."

At least that answered some of his pressing questions. Jessica had not mentioned her mother being alive because she honestly thought Sandra was dead. Maybe he'd been judging her unfairly. He did have a habit of making decisions based on emotion.

"Why do you think two boys were taken from the same family? That can't just be happenstance can it?"

"Don't believe in chance. Everything happens for a reason. Every part of life is somehow connected. Sometimes we must find the connection, but it's always there."

"Can you talk about it? The kidnapping I mean? Tell me everything you remember. If there's a connection, I want to find it. Please?"

"After all these years, there's none left to find. It's long since been buried, I can promise you. They're extremely thorough-"

"But you remember something. You must remember-"

"Memories are inconsistent. You know that. People remember what they need to help them survive. Other memories are conveniently misplaced in an unsearchable abyss."

"Then tell me what you think you remember."

"You don't get it do you? I don't remember. Those days were like a dream. The images are hazy at best. I can't break through. I haven't been able to-"

"Or haven't wanted to because you're afraid of what you'll see. You're so afraid of protecting what used to be that you're ignoring what is right now. You're willing to let your daughter's only son share whatever fate your son did, and we're urgently uncertain about that...

...Or do you know? Is that why you've chosen this? You don't want to remember. It hurts too much."

"It's worse on a mother not knowing. I wished a million times over that I knew. I've prayed for years that God would just show me in a dream. I've wasted my life on empty attempts to conjure recollections that won't come…

…so don't talk to me about not wanting to remember. Not wanting to know. I'd give anything to know if he suffered, or if they just killed him. Do you know the terrified thoughts that ravage a parent's mind? They haunt you. They possess you and never let go."

"Then help me. I don't want to stay here. I can't stay here. I've got to find him." He broke down and sobbed. She just sat there.

Emotionless.

Compassionless.

Max urgently looked toward her. "Mrs. Sandra. Please. Anything. Tell me anything."

"What I can tell you doesn't make sense Max Stanley. What I have to share is what landed me here in the first place. I've got nothing you want to hear."

"I'll take anything."

She paused, before nervously continuing, "The spirit took him. The devil stole my child."

She said it matter-a-factly. There was no reluctance. No hesitation. She was convinced. Max studied her for a moment. She too seemed to be studying him, readying herself for the backlash.

When he spoke it was broken, as if he were trying to compose his thoughts and his voice at once. "Please, explain.

What do you mean the devil took him?"

"I saw him Max. Dressed in black. Eyes like a serpent. Nothing discernible. The heinous laugh. The penetrating gaze that peered into my soul."

Max moved forward and sat on the end of her bed. "A dark figure. Are you sure?"

She lowered her head. This was it. Another rejection. "Yes. I'm sure, although no one ever believed me. I-"

"I believe you Sandra."

With those words the ice melted. She sat up as far as she could and shifted her pillows behind her. "You do?"

"Yes," he said, as he touched her hand with his, "I do."

"Okay Max, let me tell you everything…

…The night he went missing, I fell asleep in the room with him. We were just lying there. Morgan had been called out in the middle of the night. That wasn't uncommon. He was just starting his business, and we knew it was going to be a lucrative one. We knew he was gonna have to work long hours and deal with difficult clients in order to grow it the way we'd envisioned…

…He wasn't there. It was just me and the kids. Jessica was asleep in the bed with me. Morgan Jr. was sleeping on a small pallet I'd made him. He liked to 'camp out.' That's what he called the times I'd pull out his sleeping bag and let him sleep on the floor…

…I heard movement. A gentle scraping across the

hardwood floor. I lurched from the bed and fell hard. Something was wrong. I couldn't move. I'd been able to rise, but I crumpled the moment my foot hit the ground."

She uncomfortably shifted. Max recognized the fear written across her cheekbones. He clutched her hand more tightly. "It's okay Mrs. Sandra. Take your time."

"I've had years. Don't need time Max. Just still so frightful… I fell. Then I rolled onto my back. When I did, he was standing over me. A dark form. I couldn't see his face. Only those eyes. I heard his steely laughter. He was mocking me…

…I heard his gritty little voice. He spoke to me several times, and I was helpless to move.

What's wrong? Can't move?

Are you afraid of me? You should be.

I'm gonna take one of your kids Sandra LeDiv.

You choose which one. Will it be the girl?

He touched the skin on her cheek. I tried to scream, but I couldn't. Hot tears burned my skin, but I couldn't move. The tears were the only part of me that had motion. And really, what good are tears?

Or should I take the boy?

I could do great things with him. Oh what a price you're gonna pay.

I couldn't choose. What kind of sick person does that? Who would ask a mother to choose between her children? What mother in her right mind could decide?"

She burst into tears, trying to control them so others outside the room wouldn't hear. Max gently nudged her hand again, reminding her that he was there.

"I'm sorry Max."

"What happened Sandra? I need to know."

"The devil looked at me. He moved back beside me, and leaned closely. He kissed me on the forehead. I felt his hot breath and the repulsive sting of his lips, but I couldn't see anything but his eyes. Those sickly eyes...

...Then he stood up and kicked me. He kicked me in the rib cage. I later learned that he had cracked a couple of them. Of course, the police, Morgan, and the detectives assigned to investigate believed I had tried to stop the assailants and been injured. I must have hit my head. They wouldn't believe a spirit had entered my-"

"Sorry, but Sandra, I need to know what happened."

She cried again. "He kicked me. Then, as I struggled to catch my breath and move away from him, he picked my little boy up and placed him on the bed next to her...

You pick one. It's up to you.

You pick one, or I'm taking them both.

Pick one now. Or you'll never see either of them again.

I told him I couldn't. I told him it wasn't fair.

He picked them both up and moved toward the door. I couldn't get up. I was terrified. Before I knew it I was screaming. I still don't know why. I told him. Leave the girl. Please, just leave my daughter."

She fell into her pillow and cried uncontrollably. He put his arms around her. After a couple of minutes she resurfaced, her eyes streaked with the tears of yesterday's broken dreams. She pitifully looked into his eyes.

"Now you know my secret. Now you know why my husband hates me. I chose which child the demon would take. I chose which child would be sacrificed. I chose, his only son."

Max sat speechless. He wanted to do something. Anything. He wanted to wrap her in his arms and let her know that it was going to be okay. However, the words weren't coming. Of all the stories he could've imagined, this wasn't one of them.

She continued to look into his warm eyes.

"I can't be forgiven. It's too late for me. God himself wouldn't pardon me for what I've done."

"Sandra. You were in an impossible situation. You handled it the best you could. You stopped him from taking both of your children. You have to consider that. You may have lost one, but you also saved one. I have a family today because you protected one of them."

"If only Morgan would've believed that. My life was taken because he couldn't forgive me. He blames me for what happened."

"Morgan is a hard man. He's unreasonable. You know that."

"Oh. No. That's not the Morgan I know at all. Time has changed him I'm afraid. It's hardened him. I was afraid of that...

...The Morgan I knew was adventurous, charming, and full of life. I'm afraid this sort of adversity didn't suit him. It didn't suit any of us. It turned me into a fragment of what I had been, and it turned Morgan into an unforgiving, cutthroat businessman."

"Were there ever any ransom demands? Is that why they didn't believe you about the supernatural nature of the crime?"

"I never heard them directly. Morgan handled that aspect of the case. The investigators believed it though. They had the sting operation all planned out. They were gonna take the bad guys down at the drop and bring him back in one piece. They went to the drop alright, but no one ever showed. They went to retrieve the money were they'd left it, but it was missing. The brief case was there, but when they opened it, it was empty."

"They never discovered what happened to the money?"

"No. The investigators claimed that one of their guys had eyes on it the entire time. Stated that no one ever touched it."

"They didn't find that suspicious?"

"Of course. They looked into it. Although, probably not that hard. After a while, they figured we'd grieved enough. Said we couldn't heal as a family if they didn't allow us to have closure. So they dropped the case. Like that would bring closure to an anguished mother."

"And you, did you drop the case?"

"I had to. There was nothing I could do. But I was convinced there was more to it. I knew something else was going on. Something they didn't want me to find…

…Morgan grew distant. More so than just because of my choice. He hated me because of that. But there was something else. He was hiding something. I could tell."

"What did you think it was?"

"I don't know. At first I thought it had something to do with the money. Later, I thought maybe it was the kidnapping itself."

"What? Like he had something to do with it?"

She reluctantly nodded her head. "I think he might have. Of course, I searched every possibility and chased down every lead. I found nothing."

"What about you? Anything strange happen to you afterward?"

She moved her head backward, away from him. "How'd you know?"

"I dunno. Just a hunch. What happened?"

"I had strange dreams during the night. Hallucinations during the day. Sometimes, I heard voices. They wouldn't leave me alone. They kept pressing me to do bad things. I couldn't get rid of them…

…I tried to pursue the supernatural angle more, but no one

would listen. Morgan convinced them I was crazy. But, Max, I'm not delusional."

Max stood up. "Hallucinations?"

"Yes. Spiritual things. Demons out to get me. I think they were trying to intimidate me into silence. I guess it eventually worked. I kept quiet, and they think I'm more insane than ever."

She pointed toward her nightstand littered with pill containers.

"They prescribed all that. Multiple personality meds. Bipolar meds. ADD meds. You name it, I think I'm on it."

Max flinched. "This story is all too familiar. It could be mine. The hallucinations, the nightmares, the voices; even seeing the dark figure take my child. I've experienced it all."

"You know what bothers me most?"

Max shook his head.

"What bothers me most is that this has ruined my life. I've lost it all.

Respect

Decency

Trust

Independence.

My child.

And Morgan. Like I mentioned, he changed. He did. But he grew into a more complete person. Shortly after we lost our son, his business exploded. He became powerful, influential, and extremely wealthy. And I hated him for it."

"Three more questions, if I may?"

"Sure. Why not?"

"After the ransom drop, were you ever contacted again? I mean, did you have a second chance to procure your son, or was that it?"

"No. I'm afraid that was it. Never heard anything from them again. Morgan said they just dropped it. The authorities think we spooked them, so they killed him and moved on to new victims somewhere else. They just apologized and said that's how these sort of people work."

"Okay. Were there any more attempts at contact from the other side? The dark figure I mean?"

"No. Saw him that night. And never again."

"Okay, was there ever a deadline given that you remember? Perhaps a certain amount of time."

"The days or hours I don't recall. I forgot those details a long time ago son. However, one thing I'll never forget. They set the deadline as midnight, under the harvest moon…

…I can't forget. I still cry every time I'm standing underneath one's reddish glow…

…It's hell you know. Losing a child. Don't give up on him Max. Keep fighting them."

The lock suddenly fidgeted and the door swung open. Max hopped from the bed and moved in that direction. The male orderly walked in.

"Hurry. Mrs. LeDiv, you rest now."

He looked worriedly at Max. "Sir, you've got to go. They spotted your car outside and ran the plates. She's getting a security team to look for you now."

Max followed the orderly from the room and down the dark corridor. The man led him to a door in the furthest corner of the east wing.

"The wood line is thirty feet outside. Make a run for it. Head east. The highway is about a mile. It's a straight shot. If you hurry, you should have no trouble making it. They'll be searching the building at least twenty minutes. That should be plenty of time."

Max took two steps and whirled around to face the man. "You left her door unlocked. The alarm."

The orderly instinctively reached for his keys and swore. "Run. I'll try to keep them away as long as I can."

"Thanks," Max replied, and fearfully bolted toward the trees.

34

Detective Conrad Randall made his way to the sizeable platform that had been set up outside the new hospital construction site. It was ground breaking news. The local hospital was expanding, and the government had provided the land and given a grant for healthcare development.

Conrad casually strolled past the security detail guarding the stage. They were there to make sure no one planted electronic or explosive devices near the area the Senator would be speaking. He hoped they wouldn't be interested in a local cop. He flipped his badge as he moved past, not wasting time for a reply.

The first one approached with a burst, "Excuse me sir. You can't go up there."

"I need to have a conversation with the Senator."

"Everyone wants to see the Senator right now. Take a number and get in line."

"Does everyone want to see him because of his involvement in a Federal kidnapping investigation?"

The man sharply eyed him. "That's impossible. What are you trynna pull?"

"Not a thing. Now get the Senator here, or take me to him. If I haven't talked with him in the next five minutes, I'm gonna come for you. You'll be taking a ride for impeding my investigation. Make a decision, you're wasting my time."

"Look man. Put yourself in my shoes. I'm guarding a United States Senator two weeks before his re-election campaign comes to a head. I can't just let people approach him with outlandish allegations two hours before his primetime speech. He's wrapping up final preparations."

Conrad took three steps away from the stage. "Okay. Just give my regards to the Senator. Tell him a lot of voters are going to be interested to find out why he was too busy to help a local detective investigate the case of a missing boy. Tell him to prepare for that speech as well."

He turned back and walked toward his car. The guard followed him, his mind racing. What was the better move? He'd been given express directions that the Senator was not to be disturbed. However, the staff hadn't counted on a hotheaded detective investigating a case with Federal implications. If the man were telling the truth, this could directly impact the campaign.

"Wait... Stop!"

Conrad abruptly paused and turned to face him. "Make up your mind. Letting me talk to him would be easier, but I've always enjoyed the hard way. You're call."

"What's his involvement in your questioning?"

"That's between me and the Senator. You just get him in front of me. Clock's ticking."

The man moaned and slowly moved toward the stage, approaching a group clustered in the far corner. A pretty, petite brunette met him slightly away from the others. He whispered, nodding his head in Conrad's direction. She looked toward him, looking away when she recognized her gaze hadn't been as subtle as she'd have liked.

After a brief altercation, the woman moved toward the rest of the group. She emerged with a distinguished looking gentleman at her side. He was in his late fifties to early sixties. Clean cut and honest looking. He listened to her obvious concerns, then briskly turned and moved in the direction of the detective.

He extended his hand as he approached.

"Congressman Wiggins. Detective Randall I presume? What can I do for you this afternoon?"

The brunette was standing right beside him, a little too close Conrad thought. The signs were there, and she was an extremely striking young woman. Eye candy. Every good senator needs some, he thought with a smug grin.

"Do you two think people don't notice? If you don't want the other side going public with this affair, I'd suggest working on the body language between the two of you. It screams inappropriate behavior."

She abruptly stepped back, eliciting another minor smirk. The Senator neither smiled nor scowled. He displayed no emotional change whatsoever.

He was good. Conrad had to give him that. Years of political posturing and answering ridiculous questions had prepared him for almost anything. Therefore, Conrad's only choice was to catch him off guard by being overwhelmingly blunt.

"Senator? If that's your response to this line of questioning, I'd also suggest prepping your children for life without a father at home. From what I understand, Mrs. Wiggins is an independent and intelligent woman who won't tolerate being made a fool of."

The Senator motioned for the woman to leave them completely. He stepped toward Conrad. "Whatever your questions are detective, my private life is none of your concern. I'm kindly granting you ten minutes. If you want to waste it, I'd suggest you subscribe to one of the major tabloids. You can hear all the juicy rumors about me that you'd like. My family knows what kind of man I am, and furthermore, so do the thousands of people fighting to re-elect me."

"So you're telling me the comfort level that I just noticed between you and your hot, young aid is purely platonic?"

"I'm very comfortable with her if you must know, but why don't you address that line of questioning to my sister. She'll be here a little later."

"You're sister-"

"Yes. Head of my campaign. That hot, young aid that you're concerned about is my professionally brilliant niece. Is our relationship purely platonic? No it isn't. Try familial."

Conrad smiled. "Nice defense. I didn't see that one coming."

"Detective, is there something I can help you with? If not, I need to get back to my speech prep-"

"Yes. Senator Wiggins, why was a motorcycle registered in your name connected to a Federal kidnapping case this afternoon?"

"What? That's ridiculous. I don't even own a motorcycle."

"You're correct. You actually own three."

He extended the paperwork toward the Senator. "You recognize the signatures sir?"

"Of course I do, they're my sons," he replied, stiffening even as the last words fell from his lips. He handed the papers back to the detective.

"I'm not saying another word without my attorney, and don't you speak with my son either. I forbid it. He must have an attorney present as well."

"I'm afraid you're a little late for that Senator. He was picked up an hour ago. He's already waved his rights. He's writing a statement as we speak."

The Senator removed his cell phone and held down a speed dial button. He panickedly held it down again when it became apparent that his son hadn't answered.

"Reception is horrible at the station. Probably isn't getting your calls."

The Senator had fright in his eyes. He timidly faced Conrad. "Those motorcycles aren't my sons. I lied. They belong to me. All of them belong to me. You hear me? I'm involved. Just leave my son out of this."

"You sure about that? You really ready to throw your career away for some trailer trash crack-head."

"Watch yourself detective. That's my son you're talking about."

"A kid who has been arrested four times for drug related charges. No wonder you're against the three strikes law in this state. We catch 'em, and you're all about turning 'em back on the streets. No wonder the department can't expect stricter enforcement from you, your own son would be a life-timer."

"Again, my family dynamics are none of your business."

"In this case, I'm afraid they are. You're son has been in trouble before. He's been so addicted in the past that he's proven prone to violence when chasing a fix."

"That was reduced to a misdemeanor theft charge."

"Because you happen to be a political representative. If not for your position, he'd have been thrown in jail 'til he rotted."

"I'm not sure what you've got against me. If it's a policy difference, I assure you I'll not apologize for my political agenda. I'd advise you to stop this bullish behavior and vote against me like my other opponents. Pay big bucks and take out an accusatory commercial. But don't come after us legally unless you have legitimate proof."

"I've got more than enough. A signed confession isn't gonna be easy to get out of."

"If you have questions for me, ask them. If not, I need to get back to posturing that matters."

"As a matter-a-fact, I do have a few questions. I need your whereabouts for the past two weeks. I need access to your phone records. I need permission to cycle through your email accounts."

"I assume you have a warrant?"

"I assumed you wouldn't want me going through the proper channels to get one. Lots of paper work. Contacts. Hands the papers shuffle through. It would be a tragedy if the wrong person saw the information and decided to sell it to Governor Carter's camp."

"I see. So you don't have a warrant, but you think the threat of political espionage will force me to answer your questions. That about sum it up?"

Conrad flashed a deviant smiled. "And here I thought we'd turned this into a friendly chat. I have nothing but your best interest at heart. I assure you."

"You're a snake in the grass."

" And you've got a campaign to win. You don't need any embarrassments or setbacks.

"You son of a-"

"My. Wouldn't the Christian right love to hear the end of that statement. That would probably lose you a few votes from your sanctimonious following."

"Excuse me detective," Senator Wiggins stated as he pushed past him back toward the staging. "I was told you needed to question me about the disappearance of a missing child. I would do anything I can to help with that. However, I'll not be harassed because you don't agree with my policies or share the views of my supporters. You have a good day sir."

"I wouldn't if I were you."

"Why's that?"

"What if I told you that five hundred thousand dollars in unmarked bills has been found in one of your campaign headquarters?"

"I'd say you were lying."

Conrad pushed a photo toward him. "You recognize this place?"

"Of course I do…"

He had that panicked expression again. "But I promise you, that's not my money. I've never seen that before."

"So... Let's get this straight-"

"I can see how this looks Detective Randall. Do you think I'd really have anything to do with a kidnapping when I'm two weeks away from being re-elected? Why would I be that stupid?"

"Maybe you were telling the truth earlier. Maybe the motorcycles do belong to your son. Now you're covering for him because you don't want to see him go to prison. Nothing like the kindred protection of a father."

"No! Tyler wouldn't do that. He's changed."

Conrad removed another photo and nonchalantly placed it in the Senator's hand. The Senator physically flinched.

"You recognize the hot brunette? And what's that in her hand? That doesn't look like a normal cigarette to me. And, what's that she's wearing. She's got that bad girl image thing down to an art. Guess she knows how to party."

"That was a long time ago. Look at the time stamp."

Conrad removed another photo. "Good observation, but this one is from last week. And look who is with her. My, isn't that Tyler Wiggins, and what's that he's holding?"

The Senator turned pale. He gasped for air. The political posturing hadn't prepared him for the revelation of family infidelities. He physically staggered backward.

"I didn't know anything about this. You have to believe me."

Conrad pushed forward, "Okay, now that I've got your

attention. I'm not interested in your policies. I could care less about what your employees or family do in their private time. They want to smoke a little pot, that's their business."

"Then what's this about?"

"It's about exactly what I said from the beginning. Questions about a missing kid."

"I don't understand? Why take the long way around? Why not just ask your questions?"

"Because we need to have an understanding. I don't care about destroying you. All I care about is getting information to find this kid. However, I don't care about not destroying you either. You stall me. Stand in my way. Or force me to cut through political red tape, and shortness of breath is gonna be the least of your problems. The bad dream you just glimpsed is gonna become a nightmare. Follow me?"

The Senator nodded. After a few seconds he nervously grinned. "You ever consider a career in politics. You'd be better than most."

Conrad smirked, "I'll keep that in mind. They say all you need is arrogance, attitude, and agenda."

The Senator tried to laugh, then stopped, "You mean what you say Detective? You aren't interested in destroying my campaign?"

Conrad nodded, "Just help me. I'm the only one who has these pictures. These are the only copies. They're yours under two conditions."

"They are?"

"First, you clean up your ship. Get your son and niece some help."

"Done. What's the second?"

"Don't lie to me. I find out you're not telling the truth, and all bets are off. I'm coming after you with everything I've got."

"Okay, what do you need to know?"

The detective pulled two more forms from a folder he'd been carrying.

"These are some of your financial records for your campaign. All legally obtained. Public record you know."

The Senator nodded again. "I'm aware of that."

"So you're also aware that your re-election fund has been running low the past few weeks. Are you certain that no one in your campaign could have carried out an elaborate scheme to replenish your dwindling budget? Desperate times sort of thing."

"Absolutely not. We've had weekly meetings, almost daily, concerning our financial crisis. There have been no signs of economic upturn. We've continued to struggle. We're worse now than when we started."

"And you're certain that no one has indicated a change is on the horizon?"

"Not at all. Everyone's nervous. We don't want it getting leaked, but the outlook is bleak. We're just hoping to survive the next couple of weeks."

"How'd the money get in your campaign headquarters?"

"I don't know. I swear. I have no idea."

Senator Wiggins gazed thoughtfully into the distant clouds. "If you don't mind me asking, how'd you go about finding it there?"

"We had a BOLO out on a motorcycle seen leaving a money exchange. The motorcycle came back registered to you. We had units investigate every location associated with your campaign. One of the officers found the motorcycle parked in an alley behind your building…

…As you can imagine, it didn't take long to get a warrant. A quick search yielded a duffel bag full of cash. Approximately half a mil."

"You fingerprint the money? The bag? The motorcycle?"

"They're being processed now. I don't have to tell you how damning it's gonna be if they lift prints that come back to anyone in your campaign. I can't promise you secrecy then."

"I know. I know. Wouldn't ask you to."

"You sure you don't want to change anything about your story? This is a one-time offer."

"There's nothing to change. I'm telling you the truth.

He painfully looked toward the clouds again.

"How old is he? The missing boy I mean?

"Seven… Eight maybe… Too young to be involved in all this."

"His family, who are they?"

"You know I can't reveal the details of an ongoing investigation."

"Why hasn't there been an Amber alert? Seems the family would want the word out."

"The kidnappers have been in contact. Already had some sort of money exchange. The amount that was exchanged is the amount that was recovered at your headquarters. So you can see the dilemma."

Conrad shifted his stance. "Are you gonna provide your and your son's whereabouts for the past couple of weeks, as well as the phone records and email addresses I requested?"

"Of course. Anything you need."

"I'll need a sample of your prints and a DNA swab. I'll also need the same from every employee and member of your staff. How you keep them quiet about the investigation is up to you?"

"Should I just come forward and make a statement?"

"I wouldn't. The kidnappers would feel threatened if they feel this is public information. We need that slight edge. It's all we've got."

"I understand. So by talking to me about this, you're assuming I'm not tied to them?"

"I still need to rule you out sir, and we're watching your campaign and your son. If anyone gets spooked and tries to run, we'll get them."

Senator Wiggins nodded and motioned for the brunette to come back.

"Reschedule tonight's speech. Apologize to the hospital administration. Tell them an unfortunate emergency has come up. We'll be there tomorrow morning-"

"But sir, they've been major contribu-"

"Just do it. I trust you to smooth it over the best you can... Then get everyone together at Main Headquarters. A mandatory emergency meeting."

She shot the detective an ugly glance, and then looked back toward her uncle. "Sure," she said as she reluctantly walked away.

Conrad extended his hand. "I'll have a team there in a couple hours. Make sure they all show please."

"They will... My son detective... Has he admitted to anything illegal? Is there anything I should be aware of? I'm not asking as a politician. I'm asking as a concerned father."

"How well do you know your son? You think he's capable of crimes of this magnitude?"

"Honestly... no... I don't, but I guess from your perspective no father ever does."

"You can relax for now Senator. I was bluffing. He's not down at the station. We haven't been able to locate him."

The Senator shook his head, half relieved and half surprised.

"How'd you know he wouldn't answer my call?"

"I didn't. Rolled the dice. Sometimes it pays to take a risk."

"You ever decide to give politics a chance, there'll be a place for you on my staff."

"I don't need an interview?"

"You just had one... See you in an hour detective."

Senator Wiggins motioned for his guards, who escorted him to a limo waiting by the curb. Conrad walked toward his beat-up Toyota Camry. It was nothing special, but had been faithful. He sat down in the cushioned seat and picked up his phone. He was supposed to make the call.

Oh well, he wasn't one for following the rules. He'd call when he had more. For now, he was going to follow this one through on his own. He didn't need anyone calling the shots for him. He was good enough on his own.

He started the car and merged into traffic. He didn't notice the man in the cowboy hat merging behind him.

35

Tyler Wiggins wasn't supposed to be home, yet he lay on his plush bed, under his infamous silk sheets. He'd told his boss he wasn't feeling well today. A stomach virus was contagious. He'd be glad to come in, but just didn't want to risk making others sick during such a pivotal time. Management had agreed. His best choice was to stay home and let the virus run its course. Better to let one employee rest than be forced to rest ten later.

The truth was that he wasn't sick. He was hung-over from too much drinking the night before. He barely remembered getting home. At least he'd been careful. He remembered making right decisions. Well, except for the excessive drinking part. However, he'd been drinking at a friend's house, away from the public eye. He was trying to be considerate of his father's campaign. He'd even remembered to ask the only sober girl in the room to take him home. He'd barely known her, but he knew her much better now. She was part of the reason he was staying home. He learned that most young girls wanted their turn with the Senator's son. Being Tyler Wiggins was a drag most of the time, but it definitely had its perks.

He'd been sleeping soundly when a noise from the living room had awakened him. He'd rolled over, expecting to feel her next to him, but she was gone. It wasn't her movement that he was hearing either. There was something peculiar about the sound. There's a barely discernible acoustic difference about the noise made when someone is trying to not be heard. The noise had awakened him, but the overly hushed quality is what caused the alarms to pulse through his tired brain. He forced himself to stand up and slowly moved toward the bedroom door.

His apartment wasn't large. Out of the bedroom, there was six feet of hallway that opened into the living room. The kitchen was in the same area, only cordoned off by a mini-wall divider. A bathroom door was two feet down the hallway on the opposite side. That was it, about eight hundred square feet of real estate.

He heard voices as he got close to the door. His heart leapt in his chest. This couldn't be happening. He'd locked the doors. No one should be inside without a key. They must have broken in. Yet, there were two distinct male voices urgently discussing something in his living room.

He fumbled with the cell phone. Why wasn't it working? He couldn't get the numbers to dial properly. Once he did, the phone refused to operate. There was no dial tone. He didn't have a landline. Like most young Americans, he lived by the power of his smart phone.

He panicked. Someone was interfering with his signal. His phone acted like this every time he was on the university campus. The rumor was that the school utilized a cell phone jammer. Whoever was in his house obviously had the same type of contraption.

That meant a couple of things. First of all, this wasn't just a simple robbery. It was too organized. They were after something. Only two people in the world knew he kept a private stash of weed, and he doubted anyone would be dumb enough to break in for the small amount he kept. It couldn't be that.

Secondly, it meant that whoever was out there had an agenda that included more than a quick exit. They didn't want him making phone calls. So, they weren't planning on leaving quickly.

Thirdly, if the girl from last night had stayed like she'd promised, she was in danger. She'd lied to her boss too, but she wasn't in the bedroom with him now. She must have either locked herself in the bathroom, or they had her already.

He struggled to listen through the distance but could barely understand the words. He moved closer, slowing inching his way down the hall. He held his breath; afraid they might hear if he exhaled too loudly.

Finally, he heard one speak. "Let's just finish this and get out of here. It looks bad enough."

He heard the distinct beeps of someone punching the keys

on a cell phone. He checked his again. The signal was good. They had turned the jammer off to make a call. He slowly retreated toward the bedroom so they couldn't hear him. He'd taken two steps backward when he heard the voice.

"Yes. This is an emergency. I was jogging past the Livingston Apartments. I heard someone screaming for help from inside the building. Then a loud crack. It sounded like room 103 or 104."

Tyler panicked. He lived in apartment 104. Someone was setting him up. He heard the front door close and immediately burst from the room. He tried to dial the emergency number, but his phone wasn't working again. They jammer was back on.

He rounded the corner. There she was.

Beautiful.

Seductively clad.

Remarkably peaceful.

Dead.

Blood pooled around her from an open wound in her chest. A knife lay on the kitchen floor a few feet away. The sick cowards had stabbed her and watched her bleed out on his leather couch. Her right arm hung loosely beside her. Her long hair drifted gently over the armrest. He moved toward the knife. The blade had no sign of blood.

Did they think he was stupid? He wasn't going to pick it up. He'd watched enough movies to know that was a perfect set up. They'd placed the call and wanted him to further incriminate himself. He was too smart for that.

He heard movement outside the window. Peering in were two strangers that he somehow knew had just been inside. They locked eyes.

He bolted for the closet door. He removed the twenty-two handgun from the shelf and quickly loaded the six cylinders. He wasn't going to let them get away. Tears rushed down his face. His blood pressure turned his cheeks a violent red. He moved quickly from the closet to the front door, gun in hand.

He glanced through the window as he passed.

Nothing.

They were gone.

He heard heavy footsteps moving toward the back of the house. They were making a run for it through the backyard. He rapidly moved toward the end of the hallway, checking his cell phone for signal, and again turning it away dejectedly.

Adrenaline propelled him toward the door. He was almost there when it flew open two feet in front of him. It opened so suddenly that he didn't have time to stop before colliding with someone charging in. The gun fell from his hand, and he lunged for it.

His body jolted uncontrollably. Hot urine trickled down his leg. His face painfully contorted, as the jagged tips of the electrode pack forced him to the ground. Even after the electrical current stopped pulsing, he could stop trembling. Couldn't catch his breath. Couldn't stop the heavy thumping in his chest.

Finally, his senses dulled enough so he could make out the words being screamed at him. His attackers were identifying themselves as police officers. They were strongly urging him to stay on the ground. His hands were forced behind his back. The cuffs were pushed so hard that his circulation slowed.

He finally managed to speak.

"She's dead. I've been trying to call you."

The cop immediately in front of him picked up his cell phone and started to place it in a plastic evidence bag.

"Please, I was trying to call you."

The man picked up the twenty-two handgun, sealing it in a separate bag.

They heard someone yell from the living room, "Jesus. Jackson, get in here. Andrews. Oh, God."

Two uniformed officers rushed past. The younger one threw up as he entered the living area. The older one laughed, chiding the rookie for his weak stomach. He then turned and walked back up the hallway toward them.

He looked at the man holding Tyler. "Call HQ. Tell them send homicide out. This one's ugly."

The first policeman nodded and kicked Tyler in the face as he stepped past him. "Oops, I tripped."

Tyler spat blood on his carpet. "I didn't do this. You've got to believe me."

Twenty minutes later, Detective Conrad Randall approached Tyler, who was still uncomfortably sitting in the hallway.

"Tyler Wiggins. I'm Detective Randall. You're in deep-"

"I didn't do it. I swear. I didn't-"

"Don't interrupt me again. I don't care if you did or not. Right now. All the evidence is pointing at you. So save us the trouble. Why'd you kill her?"

Tyler wailed uncontrollably, "I didn't do anything. I didn't kill her. You have to-"

"I don't have to do anything. This is my crime scene. It's not some rich kid frat party. The silver spoon isn't gonna save you this time."

He let his words linger. Finally, he pressed harder. "Why'd you murder this girl Tyler? You realize that she was too good for you? She was too much to handle, but you didn't want anyone else handling her either? Or was she one of the only ones to ever tell you no?"

He screamed again, tears streaking down his cheeks. "I didn't-"

"What? You didn't give her a chance? You killed her before she could move on with her life. What? Was she too beautiful for you to possess, so you murdered her for it?"

"Stop it!"

"You couldn't stand the thought that she was turning you

away and going to be with one of your friends. That it? You wanted her all for yourself?"

"It's not like that. I didn't even know her."

"C'mon Tyler. You can do better than that. The sheets are telling me you knew her pretty well. So well you couldn't let this one get away. What? Did she laugh at you or something? Spoiled rich kid got his feelings hurt so somebody had to pay."

Tyler wanted to explain it all, but he couldn't. The words weren't there. Conrad moved toward him and lifted him off his feet from the handcuffs behind his back. Tyler groaned in pain.

"You'll live you sick puke," Conrad stated, as he moved Tyler into the living room.

"Look at her Tyler. Look into her eyes. Tell her you're sorry."

Tyler looked sick. His eyes watered uncontrollably.

"That's right. You can't tell her. She can't hear you, because you took her life. Did you know she has a younger sister that idolizes her? Did you know she has a mother and father that will be getting a phone call any moment telling them that their daughter won't be coming home. Ever. Because some sicko pervert had his way with her and then discarded her like yesterday's newspaper."

"Stop it. I didn't do it. I-"

Conrad lifted his fist and pretended to punch him. Tyler jumped backward, and tripped, landing in the kitchen on his back. Conrad motioned for one of the policemen to bring a chair and have Tyler sit.

He then walked toward the body. The coroner was doing his final examinations before taking the body to the lab.

"Such a waste," the coroner stated. "So young and pretty."

"As opposed to an older and more rotund girl?"

The coroner blushed. "Not at all. I just meant-"

"Just give me the facts doc," Conrad interrupted.

The coroner composed himself. "Okay. She hasn't been dead that long. Fifteen to thirty minutes. Tops."

"C.O.D.?"

"Small handgun. Appears to be twenty-two caliber."

The coroner paused and eyed Tyler, who was now sitting in a chair a few feet away. "There was one recovered at the scene."

"What?" Tyler yelled. "That's impossible. She was stabbed. I saw the blade lying on the floor. Right over there."

Conrad walked where he was pointing and looked around the tile surface. There was nothing there.

"Tyler, did you pick the knife up by any chance?"

"No. I'm not stupid. I left it there for you to find. I knew you'd be getting here soon. I heard someone call the police."

"Not stupid. Tyler... C'mon... you can kiss your daddy's

campaign chances goodbye, because you had to party."

He looked toward the officer again. "If you find a knife, get it to trace. Bring the gun to ballistics. Get someone to run a GSR test on the kid."

He looked back toward Tyler. "You better pray that God performs a miracle, cuz if your hands test positive for gun residue, no attorney in this world will be able to save you."

Tyler burst into tears again. "They will."

"Is that an admission of guilt?"

"No. I didn't do anything wrong."

"Then why will they test positive Tyler?"

"Because I shot my gun a lot yesterday. I went to Shooters. Fired over two hundred rounds. There's probably GSR all over me now."

"If you think that defense is gonna fly, you're sadly mistaken," Conrad almost laughed. "As smart as you are, I was expecting a little more creativity than that."

"I'm not makin' this up man. You gotta-"

"I don't gotta do nothin' bro. Sit there and keep your mouth shut."

"C'mon man. I know my rights. Just give me my phone call. I'm gonna call my dad. He'll-"

"He'll what Tyler? Wave some magic wand and make the evidence go away. I don't think so. I'm coming at you so hard you'll never see the light of day again. I'm gonna personally make sure of that."

He put his face an inch away from Tyler's. "I'm gonna ask the D.A.'s office not to seek the death penalty. You know why? Because I'm gonna make sure they know who you are and what you did. By the time they're done with you, you'll be begging for isolation. Plenty of inmates in the third cell block would love to get their hands on the pretty son of a politician."

Tyler un-assuredly stammered, "What evidence? There's no evidence. I ain't done nothin' wrong. You can't have anything on me."

"Wrong son… How'd you get that blood on your shirt?"

Tyler looked down. He hadn't noticed it before, but his shirt was smeared in blood that was rapidly drying.

"I don't…" his voice trailed off, as reality snapped him to attention. He was in trouble. There wasn't gonna be an easy way out of this.

One of the officers pulled him out of his thoughts. "Look what we found here. He tossed something onto the table in front of Conrad. Conrad picked it up. He repulsively looked away.

"Pictures of young girls in compromising positions. Most of these don't even look like they know they were being watched. Tyler, what were you in to?"

"What? I don't know what you're talking about."

Conrad flipped through the images, his lips turning up with each one.

"And here's a few of our vic. Looks like you'd been following her around for a while. How long did it take you to plan this?"

"I never saw her before tonight. You gotta believe me. I-"

"I don't believe you Tyler. Why would I?"

The policeman came back in the room. "We found more," he said, as he placed a small container in front of them. Conrad pulled an item out of the box.

"A camera. What do you bet these pics match that camera? You want to change your story Tyler. I'm giving you one chance."

"I want my attorney."

"That's how you react to the hand trying to feed you. One chance, and you just blew it. You coulda worked with me. I'd have tried to help you kid. But sorry. Deals off the table now."

"You don't want to help me. You want to bury me. That's not my stuff. You're planting evidence."

"I guess we're planting this too," the cop said, as he removed a sandwich baggie of marijuana from the contents. "That's intent to distribute."

Conrad turned away from Tyler and looked toward the two cops in front of him.

"Get him to the station. As quietly as possible. The press

will be all over this at any moment. Surprised they aren't here already… Get him processed as soon as you get him there. Full panel. DNA off of her and him. GSR. Trace. Keep this quiet. No leaks."

"Don't take anything for granted. Dig so deep that no jury on earth could let him walk, political father figure or not. He ain't getting off for lack of evidence. Make sure you follow every procedure. I'll be there shortly."

Tyler screamed as they rushed him out the door. Conrad shook his head. It always amazed him. The Senator didn't seem to be a bad guy. Sometimes the apple really does fall far from the tree. How do kids go that wrong?

He picked up his phone and punched the number. The pretty girl from the Senator's campaign picked up. Conrad recognized her voice and warmly spoke.

"This is Detective Randall again. Tell the Senator to skip the meeting we had set up. He needs to get downtown to the station. His son is in trouble."

"Trouble? For what?"

"He's being arrested on suspicion of murder. Tell the Senator this is a courtesy call, but not to expect any more favors."

"Okay. How does it look for him, detective?"

"In all honesty. Doesn't look good. Just get the Senator downtown. It could be the last time he sees his son for a while."

He pressed the end button and rapidly punched the buttons for another call. He hated to do it, but he was tired of being in trouble. Better to just suck it up and get it over with.

36

Archer was alerted from his desk by a commotion in the hallway. The futile resistance echoed off the walls.

Seated at the opposite side of his desk, Regan cringed at the squabble outside. They both stepped into the hallway to witness the cause of such commotion. Archer shook his head in disgust.

"It's Tyler Wiggins. We've had run-ins with him before. He's never acted like this. Lemme see what's going on."

He waved one of the officers over. "What's the problem?"

"The boy's being arrested on suspicion of murder."

"Arrested? By who? This kid has ties to my case. It's not gonna get screwed up by someone with a passion for publicity."

"Detective Randall, sir. He had him detained."

"Thank you," Archer said, as he slammed the door closed.

He looked at Regan. "This has got to stop. That man almost got himself killed yesterday. Now he's running my case as the primary investigator. He's a loose cannon."

Regan crinkled her nose and curiously lifted her eyebrows. "Takes one to know one they say."

He snorted. "Don't start. You've been working with me all of two days and you're already applying labels. I thought you were better than that."

"I don't share your history with each other. I'm just wondering why every time his name is mentioned you bristle."

"Long story."

"Complicated? Or just boys being boys?"

He cracked a half smile. "Little of both honestly."

She looked through the blinds into the crowded office outside. "You know. I've heard he's a bit rugged, but he gets results."

"Can't argue with that. Guess I'm just not partial to rugged."

"You're on the same team Arch. It takes all kinds. You'd do well to remember that. You should give him a chance, and you can start right now. He's heading this way," she said, as she noticed his approach through the glass divider.

Two seconds later there was a hard knock at the door.

"Come in," Archer gruffly bellowed.

The door opened and Conrad stepped through. "Arch. Dr. Rees. Sorry for the commotion."

Arch stood up from his desk. "Conrad, what are you doing? You can't just bust Senator Wiggins' son like he's a common criminal. I hate politics just as much as you, but you answer to people that aren't going to be happy with this."

"That's sweet of ya Arch. I didn't know you cared."

Archer just shook his head. "I thought you were told to keep me in the loop Conrad. You're lucky you weren't suspended for that fiasco yesterday. I shouldn't have to waste valuable time putting out your careless fires."

"Have you checked your phone Arch? I tried this time. You didn't answer, and I had no choice but to bring him in. He's covered in blood. He was found running out of the back door with the murder weapon in his hand. I didn't have much of a choice."

Archer didn't even check. He looked at Regan, who was pleading with her eyes for him to calm down. He sighed.

"My apologies. We're both trying to get the kid back home. We might as well play nice. Now explain why he's here."

Conrad spent the next several minutes recapping the evening's events. Archer jotted detailed notes, carefully chronicling the boy's arrest. He was just finishing up when Senator Wiggins entered the building with his legal entourage.

"What's he doing here?"

"Sorry Arch. I took the liberty of letting him know his son had been arrested. I was hoping it would make him more cooperative and possibly save the department some trouble later."

Arch moved toward the door. "Regan, please accompany Detective Randall into the interrogation room. Conrad, you continue your obvious charm with Tyler Wiggins. I'm going to discuss this with the Senator."

"Arch. You do know I consider him a suspect. He's not been cleared yet. It's feasible that he could have concocted this plan to aid his campaign. Especially if he can swoop in at the end and help find the child. He'd be a savior. His approval rating would go through the roof. This is expected to be the tightest election we've had in four decades."

"I'll keep that in mind, but right now I want you focused on the son. His record has escalated to murder. Premeditated kidnapping for monetary gain isn't far from that."

Conrad nodded and motioned for Regan to follow. She gave Arch a slight wink as she passed. Archer followed them and turned toward the group quickly approaching.

"Senator Wiggins. I'm Detective Archer Madsen. I'm in charge of the investigation against your son."

"Detective. These are my attorneys. I want them in the room with my son now."

"Of course. Right this way," he said, as he led them toward the interrogation room. "However, I'll need you to stay with me Senator. I've got some questions of my own for you."

Archer opened the door and motioned the three high priced lawyers into the room. He then led the Senator to another room in the back.

"I don't know how long we can hold off the vultures. We'll do the best we can. I've already briefed our people not to leak this. They understand that their jobs are at stake, so they're taking this seriously."

"Thank you sir."

"I've got to be honest. It doesn't look good for Tyler. Did Detective Randall give you any details?"

"None. I was told that Tyler had been arrested for murdering a girl in his home. It doesn't make sense. He'd never hurt anyone. He's always been more a lover than a fighter."

"Sure. The problem is that it's only been four hours since the police burst into his home. The evidence is mounting quickly. It's atypical for a case to unfold this neatly in such a short time. He wasn't careful at all. It appears to be an honest crime of passion."

"What's the evidence?"

"I can't say right now…

…Senator. Have a seat please." He pulled up a chair for himself around the large table.

"I'm gonna need you to answer some questions for me. Please speak very candidly. I need your answers as straight as possible."

"Okay."

"Where were you last night?"

Down the hall, Tyler wasn't cooperating.

"For the hundredth time, I didn't kill that girl. Look. I'm a disgusting person. I'll admit that. I was with her last night. She liked it enough to stay with me today….

…You want to know her name, but I'm such a jerk that I never thought to ask it. If she told me I don't remember. I didn't want a relationship. She was beautiful, and I've got needs…

…But you know what. We both liked it that way. No strings attached. It was fun while it lasted, but then we'd move on to the next good time. That's what we both agreed on."

"Only she didn't get to move on. You did. How's that look?"

"I don't care how it looks. I'm telling you, I didn't kill that girl."

Regan gently interrupted, "Tyler, do you want to know her name? You want to know who she was? Her family is right outside. They need an explanation. Maybe you could-"

He looked stunned. "No. No. I can't do that. She was just a good time. I can't tell her parents what we were doing. They didn't know. I won't tell them."

"It's not like she's alive Tyler. She'd never know."

"You people are demented. There's something wrong with

you. It's not just about her. They don't deserve to go through that. They've lost her. Isn't that enough?"

Conrad interrupted, "C'mon man. Don't think I'm buying the reformed prisoner routine. I heard you found religion during your last incarceration. The jury wont buy it either, you're gonna go down for this."

Regan pushed him aside. "Tyler. Listen to me. We can fix this. I know it seems like we can't, but we can make it better. I'll help you."

"Be honest. How bad does it look?"

"It doesn't look good right now."

"That's the understatement of the year," Conrad interrupted. "It looks like you'll be hanged in the back room as soon as the jury meets you. You're dead in the water."

Tyler's eyes were confused and pleading for help. He looked from one of the next. Finally, Conrad slammed a file down in front of him. This is what I've got. I've got you're DNA under her fingernails-"

The attorney in charge stepped forward. "My client hasn't denied intense intercourse. There's no crime against that."

Conrad smugly glanced at him. "I'm not providing evidence in isolation. I've got enough to put him away."

The attorney wasn't convinced, nor swayed by Conrad's strong rebuttal. "Then get on with it."

Conrad turned back to Tyler. "You want to explain the GSR residue all over your body? The fingerprints on the gun? The same gun you were holding in your hands when we burst through the door. The same gun that's been ballistically matched to the bullet that stole the young girl's life five minutes before we got there."

The attorney interrupted, "My client doesn't deny firing the weapon. He admitted that he target practiced at a gun club most of yesterday afternoon."

"With a twenty-two? Seriously! What kind of man takes a twenty-two to a firing range? I'd be embarrassed if that were my defense."

"Embarrassed or not, the amount of GSR on my client suggests that he's telling the truth. I will provide video evidence that he was there, just as he states. He owns the gun, so his fingerprints would be all over it. You have no proof that he fired that weapon at the victim tonight."

"The explain why it was in his hands when we got there?"

"My client found the girl murdered in a pool of blood. He thought she'd been stabbed. He grabbed the only weapon he possesses. He then saw two men leaving his apartment. He was pursuing them."

"He was trying to run out the back door when we came in! Where were you running Tyler?"

"Don't answer that-"

"I'd answer the questions if I were you son. These hotshot pricks don't care about you. They're only interested in daddy's money."

The attorney smugly shifted in his chair. "These hotshot pricks don't have to care about him Detective. We aren't paid to care. We're paid to make sure young Mr. Wiggins here doesn't spend time in prison. You've got nothing. So I think this interview is over. It's time to release him."

"Oh. I don't think so," Conrad condescendingly replied. "I've got twenty-four hours to get him to tell the truth, and I'm just getting started. I'm afraid it's gonna be a long night for you boys. Might want to get a cup of coffee."

The attorney was half standing. He slouched back in the chair. "Enjoy calling the shots now Detective Randall, because come trial, I'm gonna eat you alive."

Conrad pushed another folder toward Tyler, "The pictures Tyler. They match your camera. Who are the other girls in the photos?"

He fidgeted with the water bottle in front of him. "I don't know. Never seen them. And that's not my camera."

"But you've seen this one haven't you," he said, as he slid a few pictures of the victim toward him. "How long did you hunt her? What made you pick her? Her parents are gonna want to know. How many others are there?"

Tyler started to cry. "I don't know. These aren't... not."

The gentle trickle turned to a downpour. He cupped his face in his hands, hiding the best he could.

Conrad leaned close to him. "Just tell me what happened Tyler. We just want the truth. Tell us the truth."

Tyler lurched forward and almost yelled. "I'm telling you the truth. I don't know anything about those pictures."

The attorney interrupted again, "I'm assuming you had them ran for prints, since you printed everything else in the house. Why aren't they listed?"

Conrad hesitated. The attorney smiled. "You didn't find his prints on them did you? Isn't it strange how you only find evidence on the stuff that actually belongs to my client? It's painfully obvious that someone is trying to blackmail him and ruin his father's political campaign. Your gung-ho attitude to get yourself in the news isn't helping. Why don't you really do your job and find out who's responsible for trying to pull this off."

"Nice defense, but do you really expect a jury to believe that your client, with an extensive history of drug abuse, found with enough marijuana in his house to be charged with distribution…

…Do you really believe they're gonna buy your conspiracy theory defense? That's desperate. I hope this does go to court. It'll be the easiest case the district attorney ever processed."

"The weed was planted. Not my clients. He's been clean for a few weeks now. Drug testing is being analyzed now from urine and hair samples. You have nothing."

"Wow, you are desper-"

"Stop it," Tyler yelled. "The weed was mine."

"I'm advising you not to say anything else."

"No. I have to. I didn't kill that girl. There were two men in my apartment. I've never seen them before, but I know they set me up. I'll accept responsibility for what's mine. The drugs are for my own use. Purely recreational. I don't sell."

. . .

Archer sternly watched the Senator. "I understand what you're saying. I can agree with most of it. However, I still don't understand where the money came from? Half a million. That's a lot of dough."

"I don't know, but I can assure you it didn't come from anyone in my campaign. I honestly believe I'm being set up. Why would I leave that kind of money just lying around in the open for anyone to find? The first thing we do with all major contributions is to bank it."

"Legal contributions, but I don't think you'd be foolish enough to bank the exact amount you'd asked for in a ransom demand."

"And I hope you don't think I'd be foolish enough to allow that exact amount to sit in the open at my campaign headquarters."

"Senator, I'm going to ask you one more time as nicely as I can, where's the boy?"

The Senator hung his head, before strongly lifting it and glaring in Archer's direction. "I'm afraid I've been more than patient. I've tried to answer your questions. I've allowed my son to be harassed in the next room. I've done everything a reasonable person in my position would. I've bent over backwards for the past two hours to tell you what I know, but the truth is, we're no closer to the truth than when we started-"

"That's your fault Senator. Not mine-"

"You want to continue wasting what little time that boy's got left badgering me, go ahead. But, when the truth comes out, and it will, you'll have to tell the boy's parents that you were more interested in getting your name on Channel Ten than getting their child safely home...

...You got any reason to hold me?" He asked as he stood up.

Archer shook his head. "Don't leave town."

"What about my son?"

"He's not going anywhere. We've got more than enough to hold him."

. . .

Conrad had been sitting quietly. Sometimes it's best to let them wallow in their own nervousness. They often rethink what they've said. If they've lied, their attempts become more elaborate, until their stories delineate. Then you go back to the beginning, remind them of the lies, and you have them.

He shifted forward, "Anything else to add, before I throw away the key."

He looked away and started to say something, but Regan interrupted with a tug on his arm. She leaned toward Tyler, her face only inches from his.

"Tyler, what is it? What are you hiding?"

He shook his head, obviously disturbed.

"Tyler, look at me."

He faced her, his eyes wide with surprise.

"What are you hiding? I can see it. Something you don't want us to know."

"Exactly," Conrad trumpeted. "He killed the girl. He kidnapped the kid and brought the money to the headquarters. Then he went with her to party. What happened then? You got too intoxicated and bragged about what you did? Then you had to kill her because she was gonna tell?"

"I didn't kill that girl. I didn't kidnap no kid. I wouldn't do that. I-"

"No," Regan sternly replied. "That's not it… Tyler, I'm not interested in hurting you. I'm not a detective. I just want the truth. If you're telling the truth, and you didn't kill that girl, help me prove it."

"I can't"

"You can. It's obvious you're hiding something."

He sobbed. "Have someone check the alarm clock on my nightstand."

Conrad slid forward, "We already went over that place with a fine tooth comb. There's nothing there."

"Just check it again."

His head fell on the table. "I'm in so much trouble."

Regan pushed away from the table and walked toward the door.

He lifted his head again. "The proof is in the clock."

Forty minutes later, Senator Wiggins sat at a desk with Regan, Archer, and Conrad.

Archer stood up. "I'm afraid this isn't going to be easy Senator. We know that you and your son aren't responsible for kidnapping the kid or murdering the girl."

"Then what's the hard part? Just let us sign some papers and get out of here."

"We can't. You're free to go, but we'll still be holding onto your son."

"I don't understand."

Archer removed an iPad 2 from its case and turned it sideways. He pressed play on the screen and a video started. After a few seconds, the Senator turned his head away.

"That's enough. I don't want to see anymore."

"I'm afraid he was using a dummy alarm clock. It was a hidden camera. Pretty high tech. As you can see, excellent quality. It saves hours of video. It's also motion activated."

"Hence the reason it's activated there," Conrad scorned. "Lot's of movement. As you can see, this was your son with the victim."

Archer hit another button and the images moved quickly forward. After a few seconds he hit play again. The room was dark. It was clear that Tyler and the victim were still both lying in bed. After a few seconds, two men were seen entering the room. Both in masks. They removed the girl from the bed so effortlessly that she couldn't make a sound. Tyler hadn't even stirred. Just as quickly, they'd escorted her out of the room, shutting the door behind them.

"That's great news," the Senator said, sounding relieved. "Is that enough to cast suspicion from him?"

"That. Plus we had a witness come forward. A neighborhood watchman. He says he saw two men get in a parked car. They still had their masks on. Also, traffic cams show the car the man described in the area around that time. Seems he was telling the truth."

"That's great."

"That part is. This part, not so much."

He pushed another button, and another video started playing. Another girl. Young and pretty. Innocent. The Senator turned from the noises and actions on the screen. Archer pressed the button again, and another image replaced it. Then another. And another.

The Senator stumbled to the trashcan in the corner. He fell to his knees, his stomach contents erupting into the empty can. He looked up from his knees.

"How many?"

"He illegally videotaped his escapades with over thirty girls that we know of. He's confessed sir. He's innocent of murder, but he's been running an illegal website for profit. Using himself as a porn star."

"You're sure they weren't complicate? None of them knew they were being videotaped?"

"No. That makes it more exciting to the voyeurs. But, that's not the worst part sir."

The Senator stood up. "What is?"

"Over ten of them are under fifteen. Your son has been visually prostituting minors."

. . .

Later, Archer stood alone with Regan and Conrad. "I feel bad for the Senator. He's probably going to withdraw from the race, citing personal family issues."

Conrad half-laughed. "You know the world we live in. Every one will assume that he was having an affair and got busted."

Regan shook her head. "I was almost hoping they'd be guilty so we'd be a step closer to bringing Carson home."

"We are anyway. We've got two of them on video. Good quality. Two men in mask, carrying her out over their shoulders. Sounds like what Max witnessed with Carson. I'm having our techies record the body movements and analyze it against anyone we suspect could be involved."

Conrad turned uncharacteristically serious. "We also learned that whoever is behind this is clever. This type of planning usually takes weeks. They did it in a day."

"And it was elaborate," Archer agreed. "We wasted half a day chasing our tails. At least their plan to waste our time by framing the Senator's son could be what ultimately gets them. They had no idea he was making sex tapes."

"Not to be the bearer of more bad news Arch, but the Harvest Moon is tomorrow night. If this stays true to form, we've got one day to find him."

Archer's cell phone lit up. He immediately read the text and turned to them. "Darryon just landed. I'm going to pick him up. Conrad, just do what you do. Regan, get some rest. Good work tonight. I'll need you sharp tomorrow."

They split up. A block away, the man in the cowboy hat smiled. They were leaving her alone. This was gonna be fun. Lots of fun.

37

Regan stopped at the red light. She was surprised how little traffic was on the road. She guessed it was much more highly traveled on weekends. She pressed the black, plastic dial on the radio. It came to life. A female reporter was excitedly clamoring over the airwaves.

Breaking news. Police are investigating the murder of a couple found in a wooded area just south of Lexington Park. The woman has yet to be identified. She was young, mid to late thirties. Petite, estimated at one hundred and fifteen to one hundred and twenty-five pounds. Blond, shoulder length hair. Details of the cause of death are being withheld at this time. However, anonymous sources within the department are saying it's the most gruesome scene they've ever worked. They described it as grisly, saying it was littered with primitive weapons.

The male has been identified as Maurice Hammond, an orderly from Willow Creek Long Term Care Facility. He was last seen leaving his job with a man who moments earlier had caused a commotion in the home.

Witnesses say they were afraid. The man seemed highly irrational, agitated, and violent. The victim and the man were last seen heading north on Highway 33. No make or model of the vehicle has become available.

Police have indicated that the suspect is Max Stanley, the son-in-law of investment guru and high-priced defense attorney Morgan LeDiv. Mr. LeDiv is reported unavailable for comment. If anyone has news about the whereabouts of Mr. Stanley, please do not approach him. He is considered armed, highly volatile, and extremely dangerous. Please call your local police department and pass along any information that you would consider vital. For cash reward, remember you can contact the police department via the Tip Hotline. Further information will be on your local news at ten.

The light turned green, and Regan started forward. She picked up the phone. She highly doubted that Archer listened to the radio. She was hitting the third number when a sudden blur in her peripheral vision caught her attention. She recognized the massive mini-van running through the intersection a fraction of a second before it slammed into her passenger door.

Her small car was pushed one hundred feet, before it curled off the grill of the van, flipped three times, and then landed upside down on the left side of the road. She struggled to fight the cobwebs circling her. She felt like she was going to pass out.

She fought against the seatbelt that kept her restrained, holding her suspended in the air. It wouldn't give. Her neck ached, and her head was bleeding profusely. The thick gas from both air bags was making her gag. She tried, but couldn't reach the button to lower the windows, allowing the vapors to escape into the evening air. She fought back tears.

She was sure her arm was broken. It was turned at an awkward angle and hurt worse than any pain she'd ever felt.

"Help me," she yelled. "Someone help me."

Someone was approaching. She could see the jeans moving toward her. Amazing how different everything looks when flipped over.

"Please hurry. I can't get out."

"Are you okay ma'am? What can I do?"

He stood beside the car, lowering himself to look in. She felt a surge of adrenaline pulse through her body. She recognized them. The cowboy boots.

It couldn't be him. She reached into the center console and removed the weapon she had the permit to carry. She pulled it down and held it closely by her side.

The man peered into the car, as his face fell to window level. She tried to recognize him through her blurred vision and smoke in the car.

He was wearing the hat. What arrogance. He wasn't even trying to hide. He was unnaturally bold. Probably a psychopath.

"How can I help you ma'am?"

"Please sir. Just call 9-1-1-. Get an ambulance. I think my arm is shattered. I can't breathe, so I've probably got some cracked ribs. Please, get an ambulance."

"Already on the way," he reassured her. "It was the first thing I did."

She frantically looked around; praying someone else would be close. She couldn't see anyone near and didn't hear the sounds of approaching vehicles.

"What happened?" the man asked. "I didn't see. Just heard a terrible crash."

"Did you check on the other driver? Are they okay?"

"My wife is a registered nurse, she's checking on them now. You look like you took the worst of it, so I came here."

He stood up. She couldn't see what he was doing, but she heard him shuffling around.

"What are you doing? What's going on? Please, just get me out of here."

"Just checking on the best way to do that."

She suddenly smelled it. Gas. He was pouring gas on the undercarriage of her car.

"This isn't good," he said. "Your gas tank is leaking. If it sparks, there's gonna be an explosion."

"Sir. I might not make it. I'm working with the police department, and I've got key evidence that needs to be turned over to my supervisor. Can I trust you to make sure it gets to him? Please, it's important."

"Sure," he said, as he leaned down, his face peering through the window again.

He recognized the gun blur upward a moment too late. He staggered back just as the muzzle flashed. The first bullet clipped the top of his right shoulder. The second barely missed, careening off the door to the left. The third hit him solidly in the chest. He was knocked into the street. After a few seconds, he moved, struggling to pick himself back up.

He pulled the gun from his waistband and swung it toward the overturned car. She fired again, barely missing, the bullet ricocheting off the concrete and shattering a storefront window behind them. She squeezed hard again, just as his gun lined up with her door.

His muzzle flashed, just as the gun leapt in her hands. Her gun slipped from her grasp as she felt a burning sensation on her neck. She violently thrashed downward, trying to reach the gun that was now just out of reach.

Two inches. That was the difference between life and death. She couldn't get it. She'd pressed as far as she could, and it wasn't enough. She dreadfully turned to face him.

He was floundering, still unable to get up. Finally, he lay still. She could hear him vehemently cursing. In the distance, she was just beginning to hear the welcome sound of sirens' wail. Someone had called for help.

She cried.

Faced with death, she recognized the value of life.

He choked, clearing his head. Then he wheezed, spitting

blood onto the concrete.

"You think you've won, but it's all for nothing. The kid is done."

"Where is he? Do the right thing. You're dying. Please, here's your chance for leniency. May God have mercy on you."

He laughed, spitting blood between breaths. "I've done too much to be cleansed by one act of honesty."

"If you won't do it for yourself, do it for his family. They-"

"His family... The cause can't convict the... " He choked again, and then his voice trailed off before he could finish.

"The cause? What does that mean?"

He lifted his gun one final time. Carefully aiming toward the car. His arm was shaking so severely that he couldn't steady it. She helplessly watched, as the gun was pointed in her direction. The barrel seemed a mile wide, as she waited for the bullet to fly.

He fired, and his gun immediately clanged to the ground. She breathed a sigh of relief. She hadn't felt anything. The bullet had missed.

He muttered, "You might be too good to burn in hell, but you're not too good to burn here."

"Tell me where the kid is?"

"Don't worry, you'll be joining him soon."

He gasped one last time, before his head grew too heavy and landed hard against the pavement.

She felt the heat almost as instantly as she heard the vaporous hissing above her head. She had been wrong. Dead wrong. He hadn't aimed for her. He'd aimed for the gas, and he hadn't missed.

38

The morning sun was rapidly devouring the dew left behind by the night's gentle nourishing. Last night hadn't been easy. It had been hellish. Two men stood in the lobby of an expensive hotel ten miles from where the accident had occurred.

The first one spoke, "We need to just eliminate the entire Trust. They're an embarrassment."

"It's being considered as we speak brother. The Concilium doesn't tolerate such gross negligence."

"I can't believe he's gone."

"He must have gotten careless. We're already in the process of finding a new reaper."

"He was the best we've had in years. Killed by a woman. Not even a real cop. What a travesty. More proof that this entire situation reeks of amateurism. It's a wonder they haven't exposed us all."

"Any word if she died?"

"No. She still lives. The rescuers got there moments before the fire got to her. He was already dead in the street."

"Any chance he can be connected to us?"

"None. It'll be days before they identify him, if they even do. If so, he'll reflect nothing on our people."

"We're certain?"

"Absolutely."

"Any chance he could've talked before he died?"

"Not if he wanted his family to live. He knew the rules. You get caught. You die before you talk, because if you talk, your family pays the price you should've."

The last man who talked had been forced to watch his family get brutally murdered. He'd then had his own tongue ripped from his mouth before he'd been executed himself.

The man grunted. "That hasn't stopped 'em all from talking."

"It has everyone that knew enough to matter, because they're the ones who know we're dangerous enough to follow through with our threats."

The man sat down. He was powerful. Arguably, the most powerful man on the planet. His dominion went beyond what most men would have been comfortable with. He wasn't always in the limelight, but his influence was widespread.

The other man thoughtfully looked in his direction. "Do you think it's wise to move forward with the conference?"

"I think it would be more suspicious to cancel the festivities now, after so many months of planning. We have to move forward. Besides, the harvest moon appears in its fullness tonight. There will be cause for much celebration later."

"Have the children been prepared?"

"Yes," the authoritative man replied. "All of them."

39

Darryon drove the car he'd commandeered from the department compound yard. Archer sat silently in the passenger seat. They'd spent the night checking on Regan at the hospital and reprocessing the scene of the supposed accident.

She'd killed him. He'd plotted to trap her and make it look like an accident. There was no denying his elite skills as a professional killer. The scene was beautifully constructed. If she had burned alive, it would have easily been passed off as a fatal accident caused by a drunk who'd blown through a red light. The plan had been detailed enough to involve a man who'd been drugged and left in the van's driver's seat. His prior DUI record made him the perfect patsy.

The killer had been careless. He'd been fooled by Regan's girlish charm. However, he'd cruelly found out that he wasn't messing with an ordinary woman. She was a survivor, and survivors find ways to stay alive.

"Where you taking me," Archer tiredly asked.

"What do you know about Vestis Corpis?"

"Very little. They're a worldwide pharmaceutical retailer, reported to be working on a cure for most of the major diseases around the world."

"Yes. They've received several humanitarian awards from various countries. They're known for *spending all to wage ware against the microscopic killers that eliminate more of humanity than all the major wars combined*."

"That's an impressive agenda, but what exactly do they have to do with this case? They must be pretty powerful to make you travel all the way here from a vacation."

"They aren't just powerful. They're intimidating and even untouchable. We've heard lots of rumors over the years. We've tried to investigate many of them. Never got close to finding anything useful. Every time someone gets close, they either disappear or end up dead. Natural causes or freak accidents."

"Is there another way to die?"

Darryon snickered. "I guess not, but perfectly healthy forty-year-old men dropping like flies from strokes and heart attacks seems highly unlikely."

"How many?"

"Our agency, as well as several others around the world, have tried to decipher the mystery of Blanket Corp. We've all suffered loses."

"Not coincidental?"

"Twenty-three."

"Twenty-three? What's that?

"The number of deaths reported over the last two years from agencies who were either directly or indirectly investigating Blanket Corp."

Archer whistled. "That many? Why doesn't someone do something, put an end to it?"

"Not much can be done. The leadership is invisible. Anyone we've actually touched would rather die than expose the intricate details of the cooperation. We've not been able to penetrate the peripheral. We're still so far outside that we can't see in. We've latched onto the tail, but the serpent strikes before we can expose it."

"Has there ever been evidence of wrong doing?"

"Purely speculative. However, their actions are highly unusual. Almost cultish."

"What about membership? How many people are we talking about?"

"No one knows for sure. The organization reaches around the world, so their numbers extend into the multiple thousands. They have highly visible recruiters, usually high profile political types, athletes, doctors, lawyers, or other mega-millionaires."

"And from such a large pool of members, no one has been able to turn up the heat enough to make one roll over?"

"Not one. It's highly unusual. But no one talks negatively about the company. Every employee appears to be highly motivated, ambitious, and in tune with the heartbeat of the corporation. The experience is surreal, almost religious."

"Odd choice of words... Religious?"

"Yes, they bear many similarities to modern Christianity."

"How so?"

"Their constitution lists a strict guideline of sound moral principles that each employee must adhere to, on paper anyway. They elicit large followings everywhere they travel. They try to heal the sick and speak of bringing life to places long since considered the domain of death. They attempt to birth miracles and fight to make them commonplace. They call for devoted volunteers that are willing to sacrifice everything to trumpet the cause of superiority and freedom-"

"So all they're missing is a Messiah?"

"No. They've got one, although no one knows who he is. He leads Blanket Corp with the passion of a fuhrer. We've heard of him, but have no evidence that he exist. He's a shadow."

"That shouldn't be hard for the FBI. How much power can a shadow wield?"

Darryon exhaled sharply. "The most. There are whispers that he's one of the most powerful and connected men on the planet."

"How? Surely we'd be able to connect the dots if that were

the case. He'd have to leave some kind of trail."

"He doesn't. We know his reaches extend from the White House to the Kremlin. Some have even associated him with the Vatican."

"In what capacity?"

"Don't know. There are many theories, but nothing concrete. We've been trying for years."

"So, the leader of Blanket Corp could be anyone?"

"Precisely. We know he's risen in power over the last several years. The effects of his control have been realized through the ever-evolving laws and growing propaganda that influence the medical field worldwide."

"Sorry Darryon, I'm not a conspiracy theorist. What are you saying?"

"I'm saying that whoever is the Wizard behind the curtain at Blanket Corp, he's influential enough to manipulate the global market. Some think he's the president of the United States. Others feel he's one of the leaders at The United Nations. Archer, some even suggest he's the Pope. Whoever he is, he doesn't show himself, and we can't find him."

Archer shook his head. "I'm lost. You mean to tell me that what we're trying to solve in this city is at the forefront of a universal revolution?"

"Definitely a key piece of the puzzle. I don't know exactly how, but my intel has confirmed that something huge is happening, and it's going down now."

"Now?"

"Tomorrow night, under the Harvest moon."

"Darryon, tell me precisely what you know."

"I'm trying. Truth is we don't know much. No one but my team has even connected this much. We haven't taken it to our supervisors yet, because we don't trust anyone but each other. I shouldn't even be telling you. This information could get us both killed."

Archer shifted without saying a word.

Darryon pulled into a public park and exited the car. Archer followed. Darryon moved toward a concrete picnic table forty yards into a remote wooded area. He motioned for Archer to follow. They both sat down on the concrete bench opposite each other.

There was a gently flowing, manmade lake over Archer's left shoulder. The low splash of a fountain could be heard in the distance. A few birds nonchalantly chirped their gaiety across the crisp and cool morning air. Occasional joggers moved past them at various speeds, getting exercise on the hiking trails circling the recreational area. Children's laughter could be heard from the playground across the lake. A few empty swings moved back in forth in the subtle wind; lonely reminders of better times, or visual promises of the joys ahead. It all depends on how one views life.

Darryon looked across the table, his eyes full of uncertainty.

"Archer. You don't know what you've gotten yourself in to. I don't even know. There's a segment of Blanket Corp that we discovered a couple of years ago. According to Blanket Corp spokesmen, this group is one of the links that they've considered disbanding. They fear this link has gone rogue."

"Links?"

"According to the spokesmen, they compare the corporation to a chain. Each link in the chain is called a Trust. Each Trust is operated independently, but falls under subjection to the whole. Each has its own mission, handed down from the top. Each is made up of twelve extremely powerful figures from the region…

…The Trusts are supposed to be highly anonymous. Secrecy is always at the heart of these types of organizations. The less the public knows, the more mysterious and powerful the conglomerate appears. It's basic sociology."

"What does this have to do with finding Carson Stanley?"

"I believe that someone wants to gain access to the Trust that's operating in your area. The only way to do that is through extreme sacrifice. It's written in the Verbum Concilium."

"The what?"

"It's like the Ten Commandments of Blanket Corp. The 'Word of the Council'."

"So sacrifice is the only way to the top?"

"Yes. Intereo Vivo. Die to live. I'm afraid it's the only way, and whoever is responsible for Carson's kidnapping appears hell-bent on creating a major disturbance on Blanket Corp's radar..."

...Blanket Corp's public relations director has indicated that whoever kidnapped Carson has done so without the endorsement of their governing body. They state that they're just as adamantly seeking Carson's safe passage home as we are."

"If you know so much, you must have a suspect."

"We did. A huge one. Provided by Blanket Corp. I'm afraid you know him well."

"Morgan?"

"The one and only Mr. LeDiv. We thought he was the one we'd been tracking. However, that's been most difficult to prove. Too many circumstances preclude him from the focus of our investigation. Blanket Corp has also turned over evidence verifying our findings. Morgan LeDiv is not the person leading this rogue group that we believe is responsible for the kidnappings-"

"Wait! Kidnappings?"

Darryon recoiled. "Yes. Kidnappings. I'm afraid that Carson Stanley isn't the only child that's missing. This is much bigger than your case Archer."

Archer stood up and leaned across the table, his knuckles nervously digging into the concrete tabletop. "How many?"

"Ten. There's always ten."

"Always?"

"Yes, every eight years Blanket Corp has a mega-conference that ends with a community gathering. It always falls on the evening of the Harvest Moon, and it's so big that key leaders from the organization attend…

…What we uncovered is that every eight years there's another phenomenon that simultaneously occurs."

"Which is?"

"Ten kids. Within a five hundred mile radius of the conference, ten kids are always reported missing, and all within the two weeks leading up to the Harvest Moon."

"How far back have you traced this?"

"Over thirty years."

"I'm lost. You think a rogue group that you just found out about two years ago is responsible for all of this?"

"No, I don't. I think Blanket Corp is caught in the crosshairs, and they're lying to cover themselves. I think Morgan LeDiv was handpicked to lead the Trust in this region. However, because so much attention has been generated, he's been blacklisted. Now, they're pretending this group has turned against them. But, I'm not buying it."

"What do you think-?"

"I think Morgan is out as the leader. He's just a pawn in the game. He's been skipped over, and they've been forced to choose a stronger, lessor known leader for this Trust…

…However, I don't believe this Trust is acting outside of Blanket Corp's authority. I think their actions are fully sanctioned…

…LeDiv is being set up as the fall guy by someone more deceptive and deadly than he is. But he's too arrogant to sense or see it."

"So Blanket Corp is complicit in multiple kidnappings that date back over thirty years?"

"At least thirty years. Some evidence predates the turn of the Twentieth Century."

"Why the kids? Why are they taking them?"

"We don't know, and we've no evidence to confront them. Unless we can uncover something by tonight, we won't have another chance for eight years. Once the window closes, all evidence disappears. We must get them tonight."

40

Max thoughtfully sat on the couch, peering into the crystalline fluid of Everclear. He'd been unsuccessfully trying to drown his sorrows in a shroud of intoxication. He hadn't had much luck.

Frustrated, he'd reluctantly freed his phone from the tightness of his front pocket. He'd dialed the number and asked for the man to come. He'd been stood up even then. The man had sent someone else instead. Another investigator. Extremely thorough he'd been promised.

Now, painfully studying Conrad Randall, Max was uncertain that Archer had been telling the truth. He didn't want to risk his or his son's life on the fact that Archer knew what he was talking about.

"You sure you're as good as he says?"

"I'm better. Now, what can I do for you? You know I'm supposed to be bringing you in for murder. You're a suspect in two homicide investigations."

Max scoffed. "Morgan. He's an evil man."

"That's what people keep telling me, but he's not the one wanted for murder Max. I'm afraid I'm gonna have to bring you in. Archer wants to see you."

"You think I'm stupid? I ain't goin' with you. As soon as I show up, it's over for me. I'm not stopping until I find my son."

He put his head down beside the bottle on the table. "I guess they really got me this time."

"Max, you're gonna have to come with me. There's no other way."

Max shook his head, contemplating his options. He was woozy. He was tired. He was incoherent. Frankly, he didn't stand a chance against a younger and stronger Conrad Randall. He knew he'd be arrested. There was nothing he could do.

He could try to run, but he wouldn't get to the end of the hall before he'd be tackled from behind. He could fight, but that would only make it worse. He was caught between the proverbial rock and hard spot. When that happens, one mustn't quit. It's always beneficial to know the art of negotiation.

He labored to put his words together. "Please. I'll go with you, but first, do one thing for me. Please take me back to the facility I visited yesterday. There's a woman I want protected.

A witness I left behind. I want you to meet her. Introduce her to Detective Madsen. She could answer a lot of questions.

"How far out of the way is this place?"

"So you'll consider it? Maybe I should've asked for more."

"Don't push your luck Max. Just come with me, and we'll discuss it on the way."

"Not happening. The place is ten miles out of town. Twenty miles. That's all I'm asking for. Twenty miles that could blow your case wide open. I think she knows more than she's even told me."

"Who is she?"

"She's Mrs. Sandra LeDiv, the forgotten and presumed to be dead ex-wife of Morgan LeDiv. The mother of my wife, and Carson's grandmother."

Conrad's eyebrows narrowed. He crossed his arms and lifted his forehead in concentration. After a couple of seconds, it was apparent he'd made up his mind.

"Okay Max. We'll check it out. I'm going to trust you on this. In one condition. As an act of good faith on your part, because you know I have to bring you in, you're going to wear the bracelets."

Max turned around and placed his hands behind his back. "Do what you have to detective. I've put those on enough people in my time. I guess what goes around comes around."

Conrad smiled and clicked both locks into place. "Guess so. Now explain where we're going."

Twenty minutes later, Conrad led Max down the long corridor to the nurse's station in the center of the isle.

"Why he back? We don' want him, heh. He caused enough trouble da las' time...

...It true he kill Maurice?"

"I didn't kill anybody. He was alive when I left him in here, and you know it."

She looked at Conrad, "Suh, we don' want him causin' no disturbance. He terrified tha patients and residents las' time."

Conrad lifted up the handcuffs from behind, creating pressure on Max's shoulder.

"He won't be causing trouble now. I can assure you. I just have a few questions, and then we'll be leaving."

"Fa Sho." She reluctantly agreed, showing her agitation. "Just make sho ya keep dat dawg on his leash."

Conrad grunted. "You've never read how to win friends and influence people have you?"

"Just axe yo questions."

"First of all can you tell me what happened last time... uh... my dawg was here?"

Max started to say something but a quick lift on the cuffs forced him to keep his mouth shut. The girl opened a pack of gum and popped a piece in her mouth, immediately chomping it between her oversized teeth.

"The las' time dat man came in here he went postal. He put me on blast in front of da residents because he wuz lookin' for a lady dat don't be heh."

"Mrs. LeDiv?"

"Yeah. Tha's what he said. He come up here ackin' all cracked out. Nuttin' up like he wuz trippin' on sum bad cookie."

"I'm not sure what you just said," Conrad said without smiling.

She popped her gum with extra emphasis. "Den send uh brotha ta axe dez questions."

Conrad ignored the comment.

"Ma'am, Did he get physical with you?"

"Yeah. He did. He tried to grab my colla'. I holla'd for da orderly at da end of da hall. He got heh quick. Took ya boy outside. Dat's tha las' we saw eider a dem."

"Til now? You haven't seen either of them until I brought this man back today?"

"No. Well, except on da news. Dey said dat Maurice body was foun'. He been killed."

She looked away, her voice choking. "I feel guilty, but I'm jus' glad it wasn't me."

"You felt threatened?"

"I jus' knew he was gonna hurt me."

Max leapt toward the table, but was slammed down hard by Conrad onto its hard surface.

"Apologize to the lady Max. This is no way to act."

Max struggled to free himself, but Conrad's grip was far too sturdy. The young woman smiled at him, almost tauntingly.

Max outwardly calmed, but his eyes raged. "Let's solve this once and for all. Take me to her room and let's ask her."

"Suh. I don' know what you talkin' bout. For tha hundredth time, there ain't no LeDiv heh."

"Detective, go to room 1711. That's her room number. I talked to her. She'll tell you the truth."

She hurriedly searched through a binder. "1711. That's Mrs. Pierce room. You can't go in there."

Max broke free from Conrad and scampered down the hall, awkwardly swaying as he moved with his hands clasped tightly behind him. Conrad pursued, only three steps back. He reached to grab his arm just as Max turned down an empty hallway.

The light's flickered brilliantly as he moved down the corridor. For a second he thought he'd made it, until something slammed into his back. Conrad came down on him with his full weight, knocking him to the floor. He had nothing to break the fall, and his head smashed into the solid tile.

He fought to regain his wits as more footsteps echoed toward him. Before he could completely gather himself,

Conrad jerked him to his feet. With a closed fist, Conrad punched him in the stomach, doubling him over and knocking the little wind he had left out. He swallowed hard to keep himself from throwing up.

"Get him outta here," the girl from the desk yelled.

Two armed guards were standing by her, spaced on either side of the hall as far apart as it would allow. Both had their hands resting on their gun belts, inches away from being able to pull it if necessary.

Conrad quickly assessed the situation, and it didn't look favorable. Both had the look of men acquainted with danger. Neither blinked with trouble staring them in the face. They spaced themselves appropriately and staggered their depth. If shooting erupted, he couldn't get them both. It was too much ground to cover. These weren't normal minimum wage security guards. They had professional training.

He calmly removed the radio from a clip on his belt and hit the button. "D-77. I need assistance at Willow Creek Long Term Care Facility."

The radio squawked back, "10-4. All available units. Willow Creek Long Term Care Facility."

"I'm axen you two to leave, dis is a privately owned franchise. You ain't got no authority here."

The two men shifted slightly further apart.

Conrad didn't step backward; he slightly moved his hand toward his gun as well, resting it on the top. He coolly eyed them. He knew he should back down, but something bothered him. He had that nagging feeling men sometimes get when they know something isn't right. He'd never seen armed guards assigned to a nursing home before.

"Let's not get carried away. There's no need for this to get ugly."

The girl stepped toward him. "Leave now and there won't be no trouble. You're on private property."

Conrad contemplated a careful retreat, but there was a reason they were pressing him so hard to leave. "I'm afraid I can't do that."

The guard closest to them inched forward. "Can't? Or won't?"

"Either way. Doesn't matter."

"You have no authority here."

"I'm a police officer. I have authority where I feel there's something happening in a public venue against the laws of this state."

"Not without a warrant."

"Don't need one. You invited me in, and I'm standing in a public place."

"You've already been told, this building and its enterprises are privately owned."

"Maybe privately owned, but not privately funded. Unless you're ready to revoke your tax exemption status, I'm telling you to stand down. This state's government is your main financial contributor. It's your call. Of course, changing your tax status will take weeks, and I'm not standing in the hallway that long."

The guard's hand edged closer to his weapon. He had that crazed look in his eyes. The look a rabid dog has when it instinctively knows it shouldn't attack, but just can't help itself.

Conrad leaned closely to Max, slipping the key into one side of the handcuffs. He never broke eye contact while slowing turning it, loosening the hold on Max's wrist.

He whispered, "I'm trusting you. If trouble. Left ankle. Gun. Take the man on the right."

Max felt the cuff slide from his wrist, but he kept his hands behind his back like he was still trapped in Conrad's grasp. The guard kept fidgeting with his gun handle, tipping back and forth on the balls of his feet.

Conrad calmly smiled, "Just so you know, if y'all decide to start shooting," he looked directly at Shawnya, "I'm going to kill you first."

The second guard lurched forward. "You can't do that. She's not even armed."

Conrad ignored him, continuing to look directly at her. "I don't like you much, if I'm dying, you're dying."

Her smug gum popping turned to a sour scowl. She looked like she was going to turn and run.

"Don't do it. A sudden movement might be interpreted a lot of different ways, and my nerves are on end. You jump, and my twitching trigger finger might take that as a sign of aggression."

She contemplated his threat and deducted that he would do exactly as he said. She reluctantly replied, "Alright. Whatcha want den?"

Conrad looked up. Max had fallen down two doors away from 1711. He took a few steps backward, never taking his eyes from them. He stopped in front of the room.

"I want to look behind door number one."

The girl stepped toward him. She motioned for him to come near her. When he was two feet away, she leaned forward and put her lips near his ear.

"You sho ya want ta do dat? Ya only feedin' tha duh-lusion."

Conrad shot her a half smile. "I think I'll take my chances."

"Fine, but first, at least look at dis."

She pushed her smart phone in front of him. There were photos of Max at the nurse's station in a heated discussion. Papers were strewn across the floor. The final images were of Max and Maurice walking down the hall together.

"He ackin like some uh dem patients we have on da third flo. Jumpin' back and forth in his mind. He ain't right in da head."

She took her phone back and moved past him, turning the doorknob. The door pushed open, and they stepped into the room. Max peered in disbelief. He looked at Shawnya.

"Where's the lock that keeps her in? The one that sends an alarm whenever it's not set? You had it changed out?"

She moved away from them. "Control dat. I don' want him hurtin' me."

Conrad pulled back on Max's arm, pretending to be handling him by the handcuffs again. Max craned his neck and looked toward Mrs. LeDiv on her hospital cot.

A nice, queen-sized bed had replaced the prior restraints. A beautifully quilted throw lay across its end. The woman lying asleep in the bed wasn't the one he'd seen earlier. She looked slightly similar, but there was no doubt they weren't the same.

"That's not her," Max shouted. "That's not the woman that was here last time."

"Shhh! Ya gonna wake her. She sleepin' peacefully. Let her rest."

It was too late. The elderly woman stirred under the sheets. She gasped, obviously panicked by the sight of so many people unexpectedly standing in her room.

"What's happening? Mrs. Shawnya, Is everything alright?"

Shawnya moved toward her, and helped her sit up, gently rubbing her hand over the elderly woman's shoulder.

"It's okay Mrs. Pierce. These gentlemen just asked to speak to you. That's all."

She eyed them suspiciously.

"What do they want with me? I don't have no money, and

I'm not interested in Jehovah's witnesses. I got too much to read already."

"Mrs. Pierce, you should be ashamed of yaself," Shawnya laughed.

"Ma'am, I'm Detective Conrad Randall."

He moved Max forward so she could clearly see him. "This is Mr. Max Stanley."

She shuddered, weakly pushing backward into the bed as far as she could. Her eyes widened.

"I know him. I remember when he came. He was throwing stuff. He was angry. He scared us all."

Conrad pulled Max away from her. "It's okay ma'am. You can relax. He's in my custody. He won't bother you anymore. I do have some questions."

She nervously relaxed. "What about?"

"About the other day. Do you know why he was acting so irrationally?"

She thought for a second, her hand coming to her chin. She lowered her head after a few moments and looked away.

"I'm afraid I don't recall. He was just yelling and throwing papers from the nurse's desk. He went outside with Mr. Maurice. That man. He's so pleasant. Haven't seen him around since then. Wonder where he's been."

"You actually saw them leave together?"

"Well, I don't leave my room much. You understand. It takes a lot just to make it down to the cafeteria. I was on my way back from eating and saw them together. They were walking kind of fast. They seemed nervous, but Mr. Maurice wouldn't do nothing wrong. He's such a nice man."

Conrad suspiciously eyed Max, and then looked back toward the elderly woman.

"Mrs. Pierce, how long have you been here at Willow Creek?"

"Long enough. Uh. Let's see... going on ten years now."

"Ten years. That's a long time. How do you like it here?"

"Yes. It's ten years. Ten years since my husband died. He was the Reverend Fervor Pierce. He was the pastor at the First Baptist Church on Main Street. He was the pastor for over thirty years. When he died, my kids decided this was the best place for me. Guess they didn't want to be bothered. But, it was a good choice. I like it just fine. They treat us so nice. Ms. Shawnya makes us feel so special."

Shawnya rubbed her shoulder again. "Mrs. Pierce. Des men don' have tha time for history lessons."

"Oh. I'm sorry. I don't mean to be a bother. I just get carried away sometimes."

"It's okay ma'am. You have a wonderful day now. We're gonna be on our way. Thanks for your time."

He pulled Max by the arm and cautiously made his way toward the door. He looked toward the guards and pulled his radio up.

"It's code four. Cancel all units to Willow Creek."

He nodded toward Shawnya. "Sorry to have bothered you today."

He pushed Max through the doorway. As Max passed through the jam, Conrad turned around.

"Mrs. Pierce a couple more things."

Shawnya's mellow expression turned anxious.

"I was just wondering, how long have you been in this room?

"Since I got here. 1711, my little Heaven. That's what I used to say. I've been here ever since."

Shawnya stepped between them. "Thank you Mrs. Pierce. You can go back to sleep now."

Conrad half raised his hand. "Wait! Mrs. Pierce, I have one more question. In all your time here at Willow Creek, was there ever anyone here by the name Sandra LeDiv?"

Mrs. Pierce slightly coughed, and then closed her eyes.

Shawnya staggered forward, "It's okay Mrs. Pierce. Sir, I'm afraid this interview is over. You have to leave now."

He looked toward the lady on the bed. "Mrs. Pierce? You ever know anyone by that name?"

Shawnya hurriedly moved toward them, physically herding him completely through the door. The guards moved with her, one of them pushing Conrad in the shoulder.

Conrad stopped in the hallway. She stepped out with the guards and closed the door behind her.

"We've been more than fair. You upset her. If you want anything else, get a warrant."

"Fine," Conrad glaringly retorted, "but the next one of you that puts a hand on me is going to jail for assaulting a police officer. I don't need a warrant for that."

He glared at the three of them. They each stood in front of the door, guarding it like their lives depended on it not being opened again.

"C'mon Max. I've seen enough. Let's get back to the station," he said as he quickly clicked the cuff back into place.

Max momentarily resisted, but realized it was too late. He'd already been restrained.

"After all this, you're still arresting-"

"After all what Max? All you did was almost get me killed. You were wrong about the woman. Wrong about the room. Wrong about the lock. My hands are tied."

"They're lying, surely you can see that."

"I'm not seeing anything clearly now, not clearly at all."

41

Archer milled through a stack of folders pertaining to missing children. Darryon had been right. Ten. That was the number of children reported missing within the past fourteen days within a five hundred mile radius.

There was no obvious connection between victims or families. They came from various backgrounds. Two were black; two were Hispanic; one was Asian American, and one was Eastern European. The remaining children were all white and born within the borders of the United States.

Other than that, there appeared to be no similarities. They shared nothing in common. In his experience, every case involving multiple victims consist of a pattern for how the killer chooses his victims. It's never random. The choices may appear arbitrary to the casual observer, but most victims are selected for a reason.

Most often, that reason is innate to them. Perhaps it's the peripheral fruit of an emotion birthed from a heart mired in bitterness. There's usually a root cause for every sadistic action. The key to every investigation is to find the familiar thread, the tie that binds the estranged pieces together.

The onus of responsibility falls on the investigator to see what others don't, to feel what others can't, to persist when others fail, and to press when others are weakened by lack of evidence. Ultimately, he or she must follow the trail until it leads to answers that others haven't discovered.

This case was the most compelling and frightening he'd ever worked. He'd almost been killed. Twice. Regan almost had her life ended the night before. The FBI thought the head of the corporation he was going after extended the thresholds of D.C. or Rome.

What he'd viewed as a single kidnapping had turned out to be the entrance to an international secret better protected than the Davinci Code. Why were children kidnapped every eight years? Why had evidence of this been found stretching almost one hundred years?

He'd read the limited research that Darryon's team had compiled. Two hard years of investigation, and they'd discovered that every few years kids were being kidnapped around the location of a commercialized cultish gathering. Beginning as early as the 1920's, it was only in the 1970's that these gatherings became prominently directed and hosted by Blanket Corp.

Why were the leaders of Blanket Corp impossible to trace? Every major company in the world publicly parades their leader, flaunting him as the face of the franchise, using him to champion the cause of the conglomerate.

However, Blanket Corp used little known voices as their mouthpiece. This was highly effective at hiding their true leaders behind the deluge of the worshipping press. They stayed veiled, as if masked behind a Romulan cloaking device. They never surfaced; content to forever remain in obscurity.

Pride wouldn't be their downfall. The means by which investigator's most often catch the most difficult unsubs are because the narcissistic criminal violates life's most basic principles.

Pride usually accompanies their fall. Several serial killers have finally been caught merely because their cockiness led to carelessness. It's not that they wanted to be caught. It's that with each new successful crime, their sense of superiority soared. They thought they'd grown above the law, as if fate was now protecting them.

The two-year investigation had led Darryon's unit to Morgan LeDiv. However, they no longer suspected that he was the face behind the veil. Someone else was pulling the strings. Piece by piece, Archer had read components of the case that ruled out Morgan as the architect of Carson's kidnapping. Perhaps he wasn't completely innocent, but according to the file, he wasn't ultimately responsible either. Possibly complicit, he wasn't the planner. It wasn't his pattern. He didn't fit their profile.

Archer wasn't convinced that their profile was accurate. He still believed that Morgan was ultimately responsible. The bottom line was that there was a one in a million chance that they'd ever see Carson Stanley again. None of the other kidnap victims had ever been found.

What were the odds? Over one hundred and twenty missing children through the years, and not one had ever been recovered. He'd always been hopefully optimistic. In the tradition of Lloyd Christmas, one in a million, at least there was still a chance.

42

Conrad shoved Max into the lone available chair in booking. He looked at the attendant behind the desk.

"Archer's waiting. Keep an eye on him," he said, as he nodded his head toward Max.

Archer stood up, as Conrad walked into the room. Darryon remained seated but waved a hello from the chair. He barely looked up from the mountain of papers stacked in front of him. Archer didn't waste time.

"You find anything useful?"

"Not sure. I'm starting to believe this talk about Max not being on the up and up. Nothing he told me panned out at Willow Creek...

...But, there was something odd about that place. Have you ever seen armed guards at what basically amounts to a nursing home for the wealthy? I never have…

…It was also painfully obvious that they were hiding something. I asked one of the residents if anyone named Sandra LeDiv had ever lived there, and they pretty much rushed me off the premises without giving her a chance to answer…

…Yet, the girl running the show had clear photographic evidence that Max had caused a scene there earlier. He threw papers everywhere and did in fact walk to the exit with the man found in the park. You know, the double homicide."

"Bring him in."

Conrad left for a few moments, and then returned with Max.

"Un-cuff him. He's an ex-cop."

He looked at Max for a few moments. Finally, their eyes locked.

"Max. Don't take my courtesy for granted. I'll retract it in a heartbeat."

"I won't, but we both know this is Carson's last day alive. We have to find him. I'm beyond desperate."

"His best chances are for us to remain calm. You know that. Attachment only clouds judgment. Clear your head Max. Whatever is creating that shroud of uncertainty, you have to fight it off. I need to know what's going on with you Max. I need to know if you're involved with this."

"I am involved, but only so far as because it's my son that's missing. If it weren't him, I wouldn't even be on your radar."

"Okay Max, this is going to be tough, but I need you to remain calm and answer some questions."

"Sure."

"Are you certain that you've had no involvement in the kidnapping of your son?"

Max started to interrupt, but he couldn't speak. The voices in his head were magnifying in intensity to the point he couldn't think.

They know Max.

They know you took him.

They know you have him hidden somewhere.

Tell them where he is Max.

Tell them that you killed your son.

"No!" Max stood up. "I don't know about my son. I didn't kill him. I didn't hurt him."

"What? Max, no one said anything about you hurting or killing your son."

"The voices. They don't stop. I have to stop the voices," Max said, throwing his fingers over his ears.

Conrad moved closer to Max. Archer waved him off. He then stepped toward the now aggressive man moaning in front of him.

"Listen. Max, would you be willing to talk to Dr. Regan Rees? I think she may be able to help you. She may be able to… silence the voices."

Don't do it.

It's a trick Max.

She wants to get in your head.

She wants to hurt Carson.

She's one of them Max.

Don't talk to her. Keep away from her.

Max began to tremble. Small tremors coursed through his agitated body. The skin under his left eye pulsed. He abruptly turned, his head tilted down, and his eyes tilted upward, directly in line with Archer.

"She's one of them. You can't trust her."

"Regan? What makes you say that?"

"She wants to kill Carson. I won't let her. I'll kill her first."

His eyes flared, the volcanic eruption barely contained beneath the fragile surface of his emotions.

Archer moved toward him. He gently placed his hand on Max's shoulder. He spoke, holding his voice low and calm.

"I wouldn't trust anyone else but her with this. She's okay Max. Are the voices telling you not to listen to her? Are they telling you that she wants to kill your son?"

His head rapidly jolted from side to side. His body was almost convulsing.

"Yes. The voices."

Get out of here Max.

They want to control you.

Go for his gun. Kill him.

You can do it. We'll help you.

We won't let you die. Kill them all Max. Kill them all.

Max eyed Archer. His eyes dropped to the gun by Archer's side. Archer recognized it and didn't hesitate. He thrust his right leg quickly back and covered his sidearm with his right hand. He swung his left arm with a perfect backhand strike that caught Max on the chin.

Max staggered backward, the blow knocking him unsteady. He caught his composure and hurriedly attempted to clear his head. He angrily spun around.

Darryon had leapt from the desk and was closing in. Conrad had positioned himself directly behind him.

The gun.

On his ankle.

Go for it.

Take them down.

End the madness.

Max rolled to his right, positioning himself closer to Conrad. In one fluid motion, he lunged for Conrad's leg, pinning it against the wall. He lifted hard with both arms, at the same time swiping at Conrad's opposite leg with his foot. He barely brushed Conrad's thigh, but the momentum of both actions toppled Conrad to the floor.

He lifted the pants leg upward and grabbed around the ankle. The realization of what he was doing struck Archer and Darryon at the same time. Both drew their handguns and lifted them toward Max. Max wheeled to face them.

"Hold your fire," Conrad yelled. "He's unarmed."

Conrad raised himself from the floor and grabbed Max around the neck. The expert chokehold took his breath away, and he lay down, almost passing out from oxygen deprivation.

Archer holstered his weapon. Darryon did the same and moved to beside Max.

"That's enough detective... Detective Randall, that's enough. He's subdued."

Conrad gave him an extra squeeze, and then shoved him hard in the opposite direction.

Max gasped for air.

"Did you really think I'd tell you about my secondary weapon, and then keep it there for you to grab later. C'mon Max. Burn me once, shame on me, burn me-"

"I'll kill you. I'll kill you all."

Archer sat down beside Max on the floor.

"Max, have you been taking your meds like we talked about? You'd said you'd been skipping them. Did you start taking them again?"

Don't tell him Max.

He wants to hurt you.

"Max. Snap out of it," Archer said, shaking him by the shoulder.

Max looked dazed. He slurred his words.

"What? Did I what?"

"Your meds-"

"Yes. I've been taking them since you told me. I-"

"And the voices are stronger?"

Max nodded. "I can't control them. They're too strong."

Four officers had entered the room because of the commotion. Archer pointed toward them.

"Go with them Max. They're going to isolate you in detox. I'm going to have someone check your pills. Something isn't right."

Don't let them take you Max.

You can't be taken alive.

Carson will have to pay if they take you.

"Max. The voices. They lie to you. They try to control you. I haven't led you wrong yet. Trust me."

Max stood to his feet. "You better be right Archer Madsen. My kid's life is in your hands. Whatever happens to him, I'm holding you responsible."

43

12:00 p.m.

Thirty minutes passed since Max had been detained. The booking officer had already called to report that Max was calming. Archer stood in a neatly organized high-rise office. The man he'd scheduled to meet walked confidently into the room. He didn't seem overly cheerful about the meeting, but at least he was cordial.

He stepped to his crystal-topped desk and sat down, motioning for Archer to do the same on the opposite side. He looked out of his window toward the other tall buildings. The view was breathtaking, opening into a magnificent panorama of the city.

"I'm assuming because you're here talking to me that you haven't found the kid yet? Tragic."

"No sir, but that's actually why I'm here."

"If you've come to accuse me again, I think you should leave. I won't have a repeat. My son is going to prison because of this. I'm withdrawing from the campaign. What more do you want?"

"That's why I'm here. I've come to ask you not to."

"Why? You didn't care when you and your team were ripping my campaign chances apart, threatening to expose me as a child kidnapper. Why would you ask me to keep running?"

Archer considered his response before answering.

"Honestly, because we need people like you in high places-"

"People like me? I won't be a puppet-"

"No puppet Senator Wiggins. That's not what I mean at all-"

"Then explain. Because frankly my patience is paper thin."

"Sir, I've been thinking. There's a reason that whoever is behind this went after you. There are so many missing pieces to this puzzle that it hasn't even begun to come together. One thing I know for certain, they fear you-"

"That's outrageous. I have people that aren't fans, but I can't think of any that would resort to kidnapping and espionage to halt my re-election bid."

"Senator, I know this is a long shot, but are you familiar with Blanket Corp?"

"Of course. Who isn't? They're world renowned in the medical industry. What do they have to do with this?"

"I'm not certain, but I know they're in play-"

"You're talking about a mega-billion dollar corporation. One that has done more good in medical research over the last six years than all the other pharmaceutical companies combined over the last twenty. They are working on cures for the world's most devastating illnesses and diseases, as well as universal antidotes as an answer to chemical warfare. I wouldn't suggest using their name lightly."

"I understand. What I don't understand is why their leadership remains anonymous. We only get glimpses of small time leaders. The Trusts, they call them. If they are on the up and up, why don't we know who they are? The United States government is arguably the most commanding influence in the world, yet we can't even touch them. That doesn't feel right."

"I fail to understand what my staying in the election has to do with Blanket Corp."

"Senator, I think we're uncovering a conspiracy that reaches deeper than any this country has ever known. The shooter on the grassy knoll and the magic bullet are child's play compared to this. If what I feel is right, we're going to need good men, powerful men, that can help steer us in the right direction-"

"I don't follow."

"I think they're gearing for war. I think they've been preparing for decades. They're trying to keep men like you out of power. They don't want you getting re-elected, because somehow, you pose a threat to them."

The Senator rolled his eyes. "I must admit, you're one of the greatest conspiracy theorists I've ever met, and I've heard some doozies. To accuse the largest independently owned conglomerate of viable medical research and technology of an evil so vile that we can't comprehend is-"

"Have you been on the forefront of any policies lately? The last couple of years I mean?"

"What do my policies have to do-"

"Please, just answer the question. Have you spearheaded any major policies that have to do with pharmaceuticals?"

"I've been a vocal antagonist of the president's healthcare reform. I've also been a proponent of using taxpayer dollars to ensure that Medicare remains a viable option for the elderly long into the future. Those have been the most controversial topics."

"Senator, I'm telling you, someone in Blanket Corp has an agenda that needs men like you out of the equation. I don't know who is behind this. Honestly, I don't know if we'll ever know. It's not looking good right now, but I'll tell you what I do know. I do know that if the men behind the mask want people like you out of power, I'm fighting to make sure you stay in."

"That's admirable. I respect your enthusiasm, but my reputation is tarnished. If I keep my name in this election, the governor will smear it across the headlines. My son's atrocities will be on the forefront of every major news' channel in

America-"

"Or, you could run the story first. You did the right thing. You found out he was responsible, and you haven't lifted a finger to get him out of trouble. You haven't attempted to use your political power to take justice away from the victims and families hurt by this. You're an honest man, a man of values and integrity. This only further proves that you're the type of person this country needs to help get it righted. You-"

"A local detective selling me the virtues of politics. Never thought I'd see the day."

"Senator, the facts are astounding. I'm having my secretary draw up the documents for you. Everyone that investigates Blanket Corp disappears or mysteriously dies. Please, just promise me that before you make a decision, you'll take a look at what we've found."

The Senator reluctantly extended his hand. "I'll look at it. It's a long shot, but it's the best I can offer."

"Actually sir, there's one more thing you can do for me, if you'd be willing?"

"Mmph. I knew there had to be more to it."

"Go with me. Just see for yourself. Feel it out."

"Feel what out?"

"Blanket Corp. It will be in the papers I'll have sent later, but they have conventions every eight years. Ten kids are always kidnapped within striking distance of where the conference is held-"

"And you think the Medical Festival downtown is the catalyst of your kidnapped child? You really are out on a limb aren't you?"

"Except for the fact that ten kids from our region have been reported missing in the past two weeks. I'm telling you Senator, there's something to this."

"Honestly, why do you need me?"

Archer grinned, "Well, because this event is a major fundraiser for their various causes. Not just anyone is granted access to the inner party. I need your Senatorial status to get us there."

"I'm not gonna-"

"Sir, if they're responsible for what's happened, let's not let them see you sweat. Let's put the ball right back in their court. If they're not involved, we've lost nothing. If they are, we've possibly gained everything. Please, it might be a Hail Mary, but at least I'm taking a shot at the end zone."

The Senator stood, "Thanks for stopping in detective-"

"So... you won't help me?"

"Of course, I'll meet you on sight at six o'clock."

44

1:30 p.m.

Conrad stood in the lab by one of the techs. She was an attractive girl. Her black hair stopped six inches below her slender shoulders. It slightly curled up at the ends and bounced when she walked. She was a little taller than most girls he knew, probably five feet, eleven inches if he had to guess. There was just something about her, although he had to admit, he'd always been partial to girls in scrubs.

He watched her until she turned around and made eye contact. "You aren't gonna get results any faster detective. I can't change the speed of the machine."

He turned away, slightly embarrassed. He was pretty sure she'd noticed that he'd been unable to tear his eyes away from her.

"Not rushing you Courtney, but how much longer would you guess?"

"About fifteen minutes, and yes you are," she replied with a laugh.

He laughed back, and walked into the hall to give her space. He stopped at the vending machine and slid his first quarter into the slot. The lightly salted cashews at E6 were calling his name. He slid the second quarter in. As it clanked its way down the bumpy trail to the receptor, the door opened twenty feet behind him at the head of the hall.

Two men stepped through, passing without a second glance. The second nodded in his direction as he walked by, his sunglasses filled with an eerie reflection from the iridescent bulbs on the ceiling.

Conrad dropped the third quarter into the slot. It mechanically bounced its way down. It was almost to the bottom when he recognized them.

The two guards from the nursing home.

The dangerous duo that hadn't belonged there.

They didn't belong here either.

The second one looked back, immediately placing him as well.

Conrad noticed his acknowledgment and saw his arm flash inside his jacket. Conrad instinctively reached for his gun. The soft sound of the Glock passing through its leather holster was enough to alert the first man. The second cleared his weapon, just as the first spun to remove his.

The hall was narrow. That could be his only salvation. They didn't have room to fan out. His first shot missed, clipping the wall about a foot in front of the second assailant. Sheetrock shards splattered in every direction. The bullet ricocheted through the wall, leaving several large cracks along its porous surface.

The second shot hit home, knocking the man backward, spraying his blood onto the wall. Conrad felt an intense heat in his right thigh. He struggled to keep his balance, as a bullet tore through his leg, coming cleanly out the other side.

He steadied himself and fired again, taking careful aim at the first man. He missed, as a second slug pounded his left shoulder a fraction of a second before he pulled the trigger.

This time he fell. As he did, he felt the hot pain of lead piercing his skin again. This time his right hip was assaulted. He lifted his weapon, unable to aim because of the speed with which the perpetrator down the hall was firing at him. He simply pointed in the right direction and squeezed, spraying the remainder of his clip at staggered points.

The first man went down, landing near the other. The second wasn't moving, but the first contorted his body, rolling over and steadying his gun again.

The door opened behind the man, and the attractive lab tech was visible, horror written across her previously naive face. The man heard the door and wheeled to face the danger. His gun was coming up. Conrad hollered for her to get down. The suspect fired his weapon, just as she dove for cover.

Conrad couldn't tell if she'd been hit or not. He had little time to worry either. The man was rapidly turning his weapon around. Conrad quickly slid the release, his empty clip slipping from the handle. He inserted his backup clip and racked the gun just as the man fired again. He was hit… hard.

Through the mind-searing pain, he forced his gun up, keeping it low toward the floor and firing at the mass of men opposite him. He recognized the hollow thud of bullets into flesh and knew he'd connected. He forced himself onto his side to look. Both men were down.

The door opened and people were running toward him from both sides. His weapon slid from his hands and his head fell. The blood pooled around him. He could feel its warmth on his skin. The world was suddenly swimming. Eventually the vibrant colors around him grew to dim shades of gray. Finally, he closed his eyes and lost sensation.

Voices.

Fear.

Crying.

Nothing.

45

3:07 p.m.

Archer stood beside the white-blanketed bed and held her hand.

"I'm glad you're okay. We didn't know if you were going to pull through. The doctor said the surgery was iffy at best. You had us worried."

She weakly smiled.

"You know I'm a fighter. I couldn't just slip away."

He squeezed tightly.

"I wouldn't expect anything less. I'm… I'm glad you're-"

She cut the tension developing between them. "I heard about Conrad. What happened?"

"Two men walked into the lab, apparently to seize evidence."

"What was he working on?"

"Max's meds. We wanted to see what Max was actually taking. We believe he was given something that caused him to hear voices and act irrationally as a result."

"That would explain the bizarre behavior."

"There are still too many events left unexplained."

"Like?"

"His insistence that an evil spirit took his son. His continual assertion that he was warned about the kidnapping by random strangers. None of that makes sense."

"He could have been drugged then too."

"But by whom?"

"That's the million dollar question."

"Well, why does he tell us stories that are entirely fabricated? There's no way he could be telling the truth."

"Maybe they aren't fabricated to him. Maybe he's confabulating. That's a medical possibility. I haven't heard much research in the area of drug influence, but its definitely possible."

"So he's telling a lie that he believes is true. He's lying to us, but he doesn't realize he's lying."

"Yes. He believes the delusion to be real. What's real to him, he wants to make real to you. It's a known side effect of psychological disorders like schizophrenia and Alzheimer's."

"In your experience, is that a rational explanation, or do you think it's a stretch to justify his lucid behavior?"

"Honestly, I've no idea. It's hard to say. My heart tells me to trust that he isn't intentionally lying. He wants to be with his son. My instinct agrees. However, my logic tells me not to get emotionally involved."

"How is it possible that he believes he saw an evil spirit carry his son away?"

"The most reasonable explanation would be that he was influenced by a mind altering drug. He could have been taking one unaware."

He handed her a piece of paper. "I believe he was. This is what Conrad was killed for. It's the analysis of Max's medications. I leafed through them, but I didn't understand what I was reading."

She smiled, taking the paper and studying the results. "I've never heard of these drugs either. The emblem beside their names means that they're all experimental. The FDA or EMA has approved none of them...

...Three of the four have traces of psilocin, a volatile hallucinogen. Even small quantities can create an altered sense of reality. When you combine the quantity in each pill, there's definitely enough to cause Max to believe some incredibly warped perspectives."

Archer looked blankly at the papers. "So, theoretically Max

could whole heartedly believe his version of the truth although it never actually happened? He could have witnessed something else entirely, but his mind has convinced him that he saw an evil spirit?"

"Yes, or he could have seen nothing at all. He could have slept the entire night and never awakened. Then when he discovered that Max was missing, his brain, affected by the drugs, created a false reality that would at least offer him an explanation."

"Even if that explanation is so unfeasible?"

"The way the brain works is a mystery yet to be solved. The way it works when influenced by strong narcotics is another beast altogether. Most of the time there are no logical answers. The only reason they make sense is because the person believes they actually witnessed it. They feel the rest of the world can't believe them only because they didn't see it for themselves."

"So LeDiv and Jessica are telling the truth. You were right about the money drop…

…What's the typical response of a person who comes out of this type of hallucinogenic fantasy? How does one respond when reality is introduced in direct contradiction to the truth as they know it?"

"Depends on their state of mind at the time. If they're still influenced by the narcotic, they could very well continue to believe the lie no matter what evidence suggest otherwise. In extreme cases, which this could be, the person may believe that others are fabricating events to make them follow a lie.

They become irrational, violent, and desperate. Few things are as dangerous as a mentally unstable person who feels the world is completely against him…

…You know, there's still something I don't understand about this… If Dr. Lloyd was working with whoever is ultimately responsible, then why was she murdered?"

Archer smiled. It was his turn to be the professional authority on the subject.

"She was a hired gun. That's what she amounted to. Crime organizations do it all the time. They have hired muscle that commits their most visible crimes. Then, they send a cleaner to eradicate all loose ends. The moment we talked to her, we signed her death sentence."

She continued looking straight ahead. "Do you think she was killed by the same person who came after me?"

"Most likely. They usually only trust one person as the cleaner. They keep him, until he's expendable, and then they have him cleaned by their new hire. It's the way of the world. No loyalty except at the top."

"I guess that's how they survive so long. No one can touch them because the leaders never get their hands dirty. Organized criminals are definitely intelligent. If they'd only put it to good use, they could help change the world."

"Yes, they could, and that kind of behavior isn't only modeled in high level crime families. It's modeled in lower street levels as well. Most patrol units see it routinely."

"How?"

"Even basic, low-level drug dealers mimic this behavior. They hire underage kids to smuggle their drugs. Sometimes, they even recruit them as dealers-"

"That's sick. And weak."

"Unless the laws change, its ingenious. When the kids are caught, they're released soon after. The system doesn't punish young perpetrators like they're adults. Since there's no bite to the proverbial bark, dealers know that as long as the kid's don't rat them out, there's no danger. They live off the profit of underage labor."

"As I said, that's sick-"

"Well, the system is broken. It allows the real masterminds to hide behind layers of red tape, while turning kids and money hungry adults into victims-"

"So, the man I killed, he was probably one of their cleaners?"

"I'd say that, with almost one hundred percent certainty. He came after you hard, and we've not come close to identifying him. There's no record of him in any criminal database that we have access to. Some powerful people protected him. He existed and died completely off our radar."

"Will they try again?"

"Not if you stay out of this. We only have til midnight tonight. You're a non-factor. By the time you're able to get involved again, this will be a distant memory."

"I don't want to stay out. Isn't there something I can do

from here?"

"Possibly, but I'm not sure you need to get into anything. You should probably just stay away from this."

"Not a chance. I feel just like you did when they blew that building up. It's not over, so I'm not either. So tell me how I can help, or I'll try to get inventive."

He considered her statement. "Maybe inventive is what we need. Couldn't hurt-"

"Or maybe you could just let me help from here. I know there's something I could be doing."

"I'll have the files from Darryon Myles' team sent to you for review. I'll also try to contact Jessica LeDiv one last time and try to talk some sense into her. If I can, I'll get her in here to see you. As a last resort, I'll send Max in, if I can get him detoxed soon enough."

"What are you gonna do?"

"We're going straight to the source. We're gonna flush the toilet and see what floats to the top."

46

3:30 p.m.

Jessica Stanley stood with her father. He looked exhausted and worn. The frustration was evident along the lines of his face. There was something else there as well.

Panic.

They'd done everything they'd been asked to, but the kidnappers hadn't released Carson. He'd made the money drop. He'd met three of their transporters face to face. He'd stayed away from police interviews. He'd done everything exactly as they'd scripted.

Today was the day. Carson was supposed to have been released to his custody that morning, but he hadn't been. To further complicate matters, he'd been trying for the past six hours to contact them at the number they'd left. He'd been told to wait and call that number the day of Carson's release. They'd tell him where to go. So far, all he'd gotten was the broken promises of empty dial tones.

He couldn't go through this again. He'd spent his adult life learning the art of interrogation and hostage negotiation, just in case history repeated itself. It had, but now it seemed like all the preparation had been for naught. He'd done everything by the book, but nothing had gone as planned. Sometimes the best-laid plan does little against the preposterous nature of true criminals.

"I'm sorry honey," he whimpered. "I'm trying."

"Please daddy. Don't give up. I can't lose my son."

He lowered his head. "And I can't go through this again. I've already lost so much. I just knew we were doing the right thing."

She slapped him hard in the chest.

"I trusted you. I let you do it your way. We should have listened to the police. We should have let them handle this."

"Please. Jessica. Don't blame me-"

"Don't blame you. You convinced me not to listen to them. You told me you knew what you were doing. Daddy knows best. Well not this time. I should have-"

"That's not fair. I thought I could pay them-"

"Money doesn't buy everything. I hate you. I-"

He lowered his head into his arms again and sobbed like a

child.

She screamed at him. "Get up. How can you just sit there like this? You're wasting time. Do something. You-"

"What do you want me to do?"

"I don't care. Anything. Just-"

"I've tried everything-"

"That's not good enough. If anything happens to him, I'll never forgive you. You'll be just as dead to me as mom is."

He looked like he'd been slapped.

"I'm sorry... I... I don't know what to-"

She slapped him across the face.

"You heartless, gutless-"

She swung again, but he caught her hand in mid-strike. He shoved it away.

"I deserve it. I deserve that and more. If we don't get him back. You won't have to worry. I'll take my own life."

"You won't have to worry daddy. If we don't get him back, I'll take it for you."

47

4:15 p.m.

Regan limped into the police station and found her way to the lab. She staggered around until she found who she was looking for.

"Jaxon. I need your help."

"My god Regan, you shouldn't be here. You should be-"

"I know. I know. I should be in bed, but this can't wait."

"Girl, what do you need? You've got this much tenacity, I'm not standing in your way."

"Don't make me laugh," she said, clutching her ribs. "I need you to have Max escorted from detox to the interrogation room. I also need your virtual tour set up in there."

"Give me a few minutes. I'll have it all ready for you… Now, you go sit down in the lounge. I'll come get you when it's done."

. . .

4:33 p.m.

Jessica walked into the room and looked at Max, who was handcuffed to a chair in the corner.

"Max, are you okay?"

"No, I'm not. My son is still missing. I'm in police custody. His life is in the hands of two men that I don't even know. If it were your kid, would you be okay?"

"No Max. I wouldn't. The window's closing, but there's still time. I need you to help me with a couple of things."

"Sure. I've nothing better to do."

"The voices Max. I think they've been brought on because your medication has been laced with a strong hallucinogenic drug. It's made you highly vulnerable to mental manipulation. It greatly heightens a person's susceptibleness to the power of suggestion. Is there anyone you can think of that has talked to you more than normal over the last few weeks? Perhaps been abnormally negative or suggestive about Carson being taken by spirits or any other entities? Anyone that has reinforced your belief in what you saw?"

He intently pondered her question. Finally, he nodded his head. "Sorry. I can't think of anyone."

"Anyone that you can remember messing with your

subconscious memory? Like relaxation techniques, massages, or meditation rituals?"

"No. I haven't done anything like that."

"Prayer or other forms of religious service?"

"No. Crisis pushes some people toward God. I guess I've sort of let Him down. I've moved away from faith."

"Then I'm not sure where these thoughts are coming from. Unless... Perhaps part of the drug puts you to sleep... then the memories come later. Maybe you're subjected to something in your sleep that you don't remember. Would you be willing to undergo hypnosis?"

"That's absurd. Take me back to detox-"

"Wait. I admit it's a long shot, but perhaps your subconscious remembers something you don't-"

"I was making just as much progress sitting there-"

"Max. A demon did not take your son. You are not dealing with reality. Think about how outlandish that sounds. The only reason you believe it, is because you think you remember it. Well those memories are false. This drug alters your memory and makes you believe certain things occurred that never did."

"I know what I saw-"

"Okay Max. Bad idea on my part. I thought you wanted to do whatever it took-"

"Don't question my commitment to finding my son. I'll help

any way I can, but there's no other reality. I saw a dark form throw my son over his shoulder and disappear. That wasn't a man. It was a demon. He took my son, and we'll never see him again."

"Okay… Next question then. You good for another?"

He reluctantly nodded. "I just hope it's more helpful than the last."

"Would you be willing to watch a video? It's actually pretty neat. I'm going to show you a recording, but you can't ask where it came from. I need you to see if you recognize anything or not."

"That sounds scary, but interesting-"

"So you'll do it?"

"Yes. If you think it'll help."

She pressed the play button and an image flashed in the center of the room. He studied it for a second.

"That's my house. How'd you get those ima-"

"You said you wouldn't ask."

He sheepishly shook his head. "Okay. What exactly am I looking for?"

"I don't know. Anything out of place. Anything that might be helpful. Anything that wasn't as you left it immediately after Carson was kidnapped."

"How am I supposed to do that," he answered, as he closely

examined the video.

"Just watch Max. See if anything jumps out at you."

The images flashed across the designated area. He scrutinized the various rooms across the house. He looked at the landscape outside and up and down the driveway. He examined the kitchen, bathrooms, and sitting area. The video flashed to Carson's room. Max immediately stood.

"I can't. You can't expect me to watch this."

He dropped his head and cradled them in his hands.

"Max. Please finish."

The images continued to roll forward. He peeked through his fingers, afraid to view it fully. After a few seconds, he appeared slightly more comfortable.

He abruptly stood again and animatedly moved toward the projection.

"Stop it. Can you stop the tape?"

"No Max. You need to look at it. We need anything."

"No. Stop the tape. I think I saw something. Play it back."

"What was it? What did you-"

"Just play the tape back."

Jaxon pressed the button and the tape rewound.

"There. Stop it there. Can you freeze it?"

Jaxon paused the image. Max stepped close, peering into the projection like he had just entered Carson's private area. He looked for several seconds, quietly gazing into the holographic bedroom. Finally, he turned to face her.

"His clothes. Some of his clothes are missing."

"How could you possibly know that Max?"

"Because I know how it looked. His closet. She kept his favorite outfits separated to the right. They aren't there."

"That's a stretch Max."

"You asked me to help. I am. And you aren't gonna believe me."

"Missing clothes Max; how do you know they weren't dirty?"

"Because there was an entire row of them. She had the clothes washed every other day. An entire row would not be at the cleaners."

She looked skeptical, so she continued with a different line of questioning. "Were you aware that your wife was having an affair?"

His head snapped toward her. His eyes held a sharp fury.

"You're lying. Why would you lie about that?"

"I'm not lying Max. We found her DNA in your bed with someone else's. Another males. She was playing house, and you weren't the daddy."

"No!" He slammed his fist into the wooden desk, cutting his knuckles on its edge. "Why?"

She had been harsh intentionally. She needed to know if he had been aware. If he had, it could have altered his mental acuity and added to the delusional effects of the drugs. It could also have been motive for his involvement.

She was certain that weren't the case. There's no way he could have faked that reaction. The pain was real. The shock wasn't feigned. The anger wasn't exaggerated. He exhibited the classic attributes of a man who'd been betrayed.

Earlier when he'd been questioned about the possibility of an affair, he'd been subdued. He wasn't surprised at all about the possibility. Now, he was highly disturbed by it. One thing was certain. Max Stanley was a man in conflict.

"I don't know Max. Honestly, I don't."

"I don't understand. I did everything for her."

"Sometimes that just isn't enough."

"It should be. I've got nothing else to give."

"I know it hurts, but this can't be our focus right now."

Max examined the image again. After a few intense moments he excitedly pointed.

"Wait! That's it. His travel bag. It's missing too. It was always on the top shelf. It's gone."

"Max, are you sure?"

He nodded his affirmation.

"It's never away from that spot unless he's gone. I know. I got it for him last Christmas. If he goes anywhere over night, he's got to have it."

Regan quickly reached for her phone. As he answered, she excitedly replied, "Arch. I'm with Max. He's looking at the tape of his home. I think we've been looking at this wrong. It's not a kidnapping."

48

4:57 p.m.

The water rushed into the jetties, spewing in every direction as it crashed into the rocks along the inlet. The rocks were three to four feet tall, with a foot or two between each one. They were staggered to create a barrier for the sandy shore against the daily beating of the tide.

Three boys cheerfully climbed the large boulders, jumping from one to the next. One of the boy's dads was fishing off a rock a few feet away.

"Don't go too far," he hollered over the deafening waves. "Be careful."

The boys only laughed, too young to be afraid of mere water on the solid surface of the rocks. He watched them for a few seconds, and then was distracted by a strong tug on his line.

He yanked back hard, convinced he'd hooked something massive. He pulled solidly, fearing his prize catch was going to get away. With each tug and reel, he realized his chances of completing the catch were increasing. He eagerly yelled for the boys to watch the battle.

They curiously gathered to see what beast he would pull from the fierce grasp of the ocean. The man urged one of them to grab the net, fearing that the catch would probably be too big for it. The line was rising to the surface.

Suddenly, it emerged, but it wasn't a fish.

A man's hand appeared beneath the ebbing flow. The white caps of the cascading waves made it barely visible. The boys scampered backward, afraid of what they'd seen. The man tugged again, and then fell to his knees and threw up into the water below.

Three feet down, still connected to his hook, was the body of a half-naked man. He'd been beaten so severely that his face was barely discernible as human. He'd been left to the elements for some time, as the water and its wildlife had eaten the flesh from several parts of his body. The man wedged his pole into a large crack in the rocks and ran to his truck for his phone.

"Don't go over there again," he called over his shoulder as he frantically put the phone to his ear.

Within minutes, emergency personnel arrived. The man was pulled from the water and pronounced dead on location.

There was no need to attempt life-saving protocols. It was painfully obvious that he'd been dead quite some time. They loaded his body into the closest ambulance and sped away.

Only, he didn't make it to the hospital. He didn't make it to the coroner's office. An FBI field agent confiscated the ambulance en route. He gave no explanation. Just pulled the emergency vehicle over, told the medical staff to get out, and left them on the side of the city street.

Twenty-five minutes later, Darryon's phone starting ringing. He picked up the private line.

"Agent Myles, whatcha got for me?"

"He's been found sir. There's a reason he hasn't checked in lately."

"He's dead?"

"Yes sir. Not pretty. Looks like he was beaten before they killed him. You think he talked?"

"No. Wasn't that kind of man. Woulda died first."

"That's what I figured. His badge, gun, and identification are missing. They knew he was an agent, and they killed him anyway. Brazen."

"We knew that going into this. We know the risks. Family been notified?"

"Not yet. Still compiling details... There's something else sir. I'm forwarding a photo to your phone. We're not sure what it means."

Darryon finished the conversation and hung up. He stared ahead, thoughtfully considering what he'd heard. Archer broke the silence.

"Everything alright?"

"Not really. Friend of mine. Fellow agent. Garrison Reed. We haven't heard from him in a minute. They found his body this morning. Washed up on shore around the Jetties."

Archer swore. "He was investigating heavy on this case. Max Stanley heard of him from a girl that turned up dead the next day. He wasn't covering his tracks too well. Not if Max turned something up on him. We've got to stop this Darryon."

"Arch, I'm gonna tell you something that's highly classified… We've been investigating Blanket Corp for a while-"

"Already know that-"

"What you don't know is that I've been personally leading the investigation. I wasn't on vacation when you called. My wife and I have been placed in the FBI's version of the Witness Protection Program. I'm out of hiding because I felt you were our best shot at finding anything to use against them. She'll never be safe until I end their reign. Eventually, they'll find us, because they've found everyone else that's ever worked their case-"

"I'm sorry Darryon. Now I wish I wouldn't have called… Wait, how'd you get my call."

"The number I gave you was a personal sat link given to me by the Bureau. It bounced off of plenty of relays and was forwarded from our encryption team before I answered it. A lot happens in a few short seconds."

Darryon's phone beeped, interrupting his discussion. He flipped open his leather case and opened the encrypted email. An image came into focus. It was crumpled paper. It was college lined and had been ripped from a spiral notebook. Small words were scrawled across the page in what appeared to be blood. Darryon read the words out loud.

Leaving this lonely life a stranger, yet receiving a hero's welcome after.

Home in the Elysian Fields, till their tired souls rapture.

By the light of the blood stained moon,

Heroes die, welcomed soon.

"What's that mean?" Archer muttered, concern written across his face.

"I'm not sure. It sounds vaguely familiar."

He exited the email and connected to his most recent call. "Hey. I've got you on speakerphone with Detective Archer Madsen. I'm assisting him on a connected case. Where'd the note come from?"

The coroner discovered it in an incision made in Agent Reed's left thigh. It was shoved in so deeply that she barely noticed it. If not for trying to determine the type of weapon used, she probably wouldn't have noticed it until much later… What do you think it means?"

"Not sure, but it sounds familiar. Have you run searches yet?"

"You know I have. Nothing so far in our databases. Expanding search parameters as we speak."

"I don't guess I need to tell you that we're running out of time?"

"I'm working as fast as I can."

Archer interrupted. "It's the Harvest Moon. The blood stained moon."

The voice on the other end of the line replied, "The Elysian Fields. It's Greek mythology. It's where the souls of heroes were sent as a reward for their good deeds on earth. It's the alternative to Hades, the place evildoers were sent."

Darryon almost screamed into the phone. "Pull up the location of the festival eight years ago. Indiana. It was in Indiana. What was the festival called?"

They both heard the rapid clicking of computer keys on the other end of the line. The clicks stopped a few seconds later.

Silence.

A deep breath.

"D. You aren't gonna believe this. The local festival at the time of the Harvest Moon was called The Festival of Souls."

"Were their any fields in the area?"

"D. Indiana is nothing but fields. You pretty much described the entire state."

"Just search the area. Any fields at the center of the main

events."

Silence again.

Clicks.

An exaggerated sigh.

"D. The main area of the Festival of Souls was located downtown. In a central park area of Indianapolis."

"Keep digging. That can't be it."

Archer interjected again, "Were their any places reserved for special groups? Blanket Corp enterprises?"

Again the clicking.

"I got a hit. Six in fact. There were six locations rented out to factions affiliated with Blanket Corp… One was a club downtown."

"Rule that one out. Next."

"Two were large hotel chain party floors. The fifth floor of the Hilton and the eighteenth floor of another one further downtown."

"No. Next."

"Two others were private hangers at the airport. Man, Blanket Corp knows how to throw a party. I'm working for the wrong company."

"The last one," Darryon said, ignoring the comment.

Clicking.

Silence.

More clicking.

"D. The last one was a large section of White River State Park. It doesn't appear that it can usually be rented like this. They must have paid a pretty decent sum to have the city close half the park down."

"Who was it rented to? What's the name on the deposit?"

"Doesn't say."

"That's it. Contact the Indianapolis Police Department. Tell them what they're looking for...

...Also, go back every eight years and find the same pattern. Contact those local authorities as well. Tell them we need this a priority. I don't care what they're working on. They can consider themselves on loan to the FBI...

...Contact headquarters. I want agents on sight ASAP. Do whatever it takes, but get our people in the field."

"Darryon, you think we might have-"

"I don't know. Just do it."

Darryon placed the phone in his sport's jacket pocket. He glanced at Archer, who was apprehensively observing.

"Arch, what are you thinking?"

"I'm thinking how risky what we're doing is. We could be wasting more time. Why would someone put a major clue in the body of a Federal agent they'd just murdered? Doesn't make sense. It doesn't feel right."

"I don't know, but it's something we have to investigate."

"You really think you'll find them? I would think they would've buried the evidence so deep we'd never find them. Unless, someone on the inside wants us to."

"Either that, or they're killing two birds with one stone-"

"What?"

"Save that thought, here comes Senator Wiggins. We've got some fraternizing to do."

49

6:23 p.m.

Three men in tuxedos walked toward them. The first extended his hand as he approached.

"Senator. I'll skip the pleasantries. I'm impressed to see you here, what with the recent scandal involving your son. I'd heard you were considering dropping out of the campaign."

The Senator shook hands with the man. "And miss the opportunity to see that smug look disappear when I told you personally that I wouldn't be conceding to your puppeteer candidate. Not a chance. Tell the governor it's gonna be tough sledding."

He let go of the man's hand. Archer stifled a laugh. The man's expression turned from condescending humor to looking like his wife had just caught him with a prostitute.

The second man slightly grimaced, but also seemed amused. He shook the Senator's hand as well.

"Glad you made it Senator Wiggins. While I don't share your political taste, I do admire your persistence. This country was built by men that advocated what they believed in despite overwhelming odds. It makes victory that much sweeter. Who are your friends?"

Senator Wiggins turned to them.

"This is Detective Archer Madsen and Special Agent Darryon Myles. They're actually the reason I'm here."

The first man spoke again, "And here we thought you'd come to offer your financial support for one of our many charities. As you know, it's great political maneuvering, and is also a good tax write-off."

The Senator pretended not to hear, blankly ignoring the man. The second man greeted both Darryon and Archer.

"What brings you fine officers to our humble conference? I'm sure you aren't here to learn about pharmacology."

Archer didn't wait for Darryon to take the lead. "You assume correctly sir. Do you have someplace a little more private that we can talk?"

"Certainly. Should I call our attorneys?"

"Are you guilty of anything-"

"Of course not," the Senator interrupted, giving Archer a stern look, "we're just wanting to have a friendly chat. That's all."

"Right this way then gentlemen," he said as he led them into a secluded wing of the building.

. . .

A few moments later, they walked into an executive lounge.

"Can we get you something to drink? A martini perhaps? Maybe you'd prefer something a little stronger?"

Darryon motioned away with his hand. "I'm afraid this is all business."

"It's okay to mix the two, Agent Myles. That's the secret to our success here at Blanket Corp. We encourage our employees to have a good time at work. It's a little known fact; companies who invest in their employees' level of satisfaction demonstrate the greatest amount of productivity."

That may be so, but I'm afraid a sharp mind and strong alcohol don't always equate for me."

"What a shame. I always think a little more clearly with the edge taken off."

The door opened and another man stepped into the room. He was older than the others, and immediately demanded respect. The atmosphere changed the moment he spoke. He wasn't just older; he was their superior. The others, who moments before had been jockeying for control, submitted to his authority like fledgling puppies.

"Welcome to Blanket Corp's Mega Conference. I've been expecting you."

Darryon and Archer eyed each other suspiciously. There

was something intimidating about him, something that made even the strongest man in the room want to turn away. He demanded respect. No, more than respect. They almost felt fearful.

Senator Wiggins walked toward him. "Hello sir. I'm-"

"Senator Wiggins. I know who you are. I know that you've decided to stay in the race after your son's... unfortunate situation. Others know that much, but what they don't know is that you've decided to run only after a little coaxing by Detective Madsen here. I'm just letting you see that I have extremely intimate details that others aren't privy too."

Archer interrupted, "How do you-"

"How doesn't matter son. Senator, I'd hate to see a failed campaign. So much wasted money for nothing. I have something for you, if you'd like to reconsider and drop from the race."

He produced an envelope and placed it in the Senator's hand. The Senator opened it. There were several forms, one of them a signed pardon from the executive branch of the United States government. The official seal of the president was watermarked in the stationary, and the president's signature was highlighted at the bottom of the page.

"What's this? How'd you-"

"It helps to know the right people Senator... I'm willing to offer your son's life in exchange for a commitment that you withdraw your name for good."

Darryon stepped forward. "You can't bribe a United States

Congressman in front of an FBI agent."

"Ah, the consistently arrogant Darryon Myles. For you, I have something else entirely. Enticing. Appealing. I'm sure that you'll not be able to refuse."

"I'm not stopping this investigation. If Blanket Corp is involved, I'm going to find out who is at the top, and they're gonna pay. You're not above the law."

He laughed. "Again, such arrogance. I must admit, I like that self-assuredness in people. It can carry you far."

He turned abruptly, his voice turning low and angry. "But it can also destroy you. You're rejecting my offer and you haven't even heard my deal yet Agent Myles."

"I don't need to, and it's Special Agent."

"Special indeed," he replied, removing a second envelope and handing it to Darryon. "Just look at what I'm willing to give you."

Darryon opened it. His mouth fell open. He clutched the envelop tightly in his left hand.

"As you can see. I know the location of your beautiful wife-"

"Are you threatening me?"

"Not at all… Agent... Sorry, Special Agent Myles. On the contrary, I'm offering you something no one else can."

"Oh yeah, what's that?"

"Peace of mind. If I could find her so easily, you can rest

assure that others will be able to. I can offer you protection of sorts. Make sure she's never bothered. I have the power to call of the dogs. Make them all go away. Forever."

"In exchange for what?"

"Nothing. You owe me nothing. You just simply walk away from this and forget it happened."

"You know I can't do that."

"Then let's just say a team of assassins had been sent to make sure the young and happening Gabe Myles doesn't make it through the day… I'm afraid there'd be nothing I could do."

Darryon moved toward the man, but the others intervened, cutting off his path. The man flashed a sardonic smile.

"You wouldn't want to do that anyway. I'm afraid my connections run extremely deep. You touch me, and you'd be a dead man. Your career would be over. And it has such promise. The sky's the limit with you. It's your choice."

The man turned toward Archer.

"And you Detective. I haven't forgotten about you."

"There's nothing you could give me that would be of consequence. So let's just end the charade."

"I'm afraid it's not that easy. If it were, anyone could be me. Think son. There's something your afraid of."

"What's that?"

"The truth."

Archer flashed a half-smirk. "I'm afraid I don't follow."

"About that night… You know… The night you found those men."

He opened the envelope and removed two pieces of paper and shoved them toward Archer.

"Look familiar? They should."

Archer looked stunned. The two men who had taken the girl so many years ago were lying in their own blood.

"Recognize your handiwork detective? Could you have done anything different? Was it revenge? You've blacked it out haven't you? You don't even know the truth anymore…

…It's only because you don't want to know. You've been afraid for so long that you've forgotten. How convenient…

…I can help you. I have proof… It will either exonerate or convict you. Or, it could just all go away. No one ever has to know… But for you Archer Madsen, I'm not quite done-"

"What else could I want?"

"A chance to keep a promise."

Archer keenly eyed him. The intensity burned with a passion as close to hatred as possible without crossing the line. Who was this man standing before them pretending to be God?

"What promise do I want to keep?"

"A promise to dying father."

"Max? He isn't dying."

The man returned his gaze.

"And I'm not talking about Max… It always bothered you didn't it… The fact you let that first one get away. The two men paid for their crimes, but the girl was never discovered. How long ago was that? One of your first cases wasn't it? What, I'd say about sixteen years?"

The comprehension of the man's words hit Archer like a bus. He felt sick. His breath suddenly became ragged. He gasped, taking in large gulps to try and level it again. The sudden pain in his side would not resolve. He struggled for composure. Every eight years. The children were taken every eight years.

"Do you think it's an accident that Blanket Corp chose your city for our reunion? You're tied to this detective. You've already been involved."

"What do you know about that?"

"I know you haven't been able to live with yourself. I know you've wished a million times over that you would have done something different. You've second-guessed every decision about that case more than any in your life. It's the reason you never had children. I can't imagine the guilt."

"Stop it. Enough."

"No wonder you hunted them down. I can't say I blame you."

"No. I didn't-"

"The truth is here Archer. Whether you killed them in cold

blood or not, it's yours for the taking. Personally, I wouldn't want to know. I'd rather just live with the knowledge, whether false or not, that I did the right thing."

"What about the promise?"

"You can bring her home. You can give a grieving father something to lay to rest. Maybe now he'll be able to bury the guilt and die in peace. You can finally give him closure."

"And what do you want from me in return?

"I want you to finish what you started. Find Carson Stanley and bring him home."

50

Darryon confusedly looked from Senator Wiggins to Archer. Senator Wiggins displayed no emotions. Archer looked stunned.

"I'm afraid I don't understand."

"It's quite simple. I want you all to continue your investigation into the missing child. Find Carson Stanley. Bring him home. Then, if you mention Blanket Corp, it will be in a positive light, thanking us for all of our support in making it possible. In exchange, I'm willing to grant each of you everything I just promised. I'm also willing to put the full weight of Blanket Corp at your disposal. We'll assist in the investigation."

"Why would you do-"

"Why doesn't matter detective. What matters is that this is

the only way you'll be able to ensure Carson's safe return, and you'll take the deal, because you know what losing him means. You've been there. It's hell."

Archer shook his head. "No. I'm sorry. It doesn't make sense. I'm not taking it."

"Senator Wiggins. Special Agent Myles. If I walk out of this room without an agreement, all of you stand to lose. Not to mention poor Carson, he stands to lose the most."

The Senator shifted uncomfortably. "Detective Madsen, we'd be foolish not to at least consider the offer."

"Don't you see what he's doing? He's putting us at odds. Divide and conquer. It's basic Sun Tzu. You can't be willing to hand him victory that easily?"

Senator Wiggins motioned toward Darryon, "Talk some sense into him. It's my son we're talking about. You're wife. This isn't a game. It's not about handing him victory. It's about ensuring what's best for our families."

"As opposed to what's best for our country? What's your price to not serve the best interests of the nation you've sworn to defend?"

Darryon looked conflicted. He looked at the photo again. Gabrielle was half in and half out of the pool. Her hair sparkled in the sunlight. Her sweet smile captured his heart. If anything ever happened to her-

"He's right Archer. I can't protect her. Someone was close enough to take this photo."

He suddenly felt a cool chill and almost lost his grip on the picture.

"Look closely Archer. Left breast. Red dot. We both know what that is."

A laser scope's red light was barely visible through the sunlight. The cameraman had caught it brilliantly.

"You know what that means. They could have killed her. Just like that, and she'd be gone. I can't live like that. Sorry Archer. I have integrity and virtues just like the rest of you, but I've got to look out for what's mine too. I can't let anything happen to her."

Archer nodded. "I get it. In your shoes, both of yours, I'd feel the same."

He turned back to the man in the suit. "Just answer one question. Why are you doing this? What's in this for you?"

"We get to lay an old nemesis to rest."

"I don't follow."

"There's a rebellion in Blanket Corp that needs to be put down. A faction of followers has lost its way, and is attempting to profit from our value system. In so doing, they've threatened our way of life. They've undermined the very virtues that have made Blanket Corp the respected entity it is. We can't allow that...

...Normally, we prefer to handle our own problems. However, this faction has broken the law, including kidnapping and murder, which we will not tolerate... I'm just sorry it's taken us so long to get to the bottom of this. It's been years in the making, but we've discovered how this faction operates and where they're going to be tonight. We can give you everything you need to end this madness, bring Carson Stanley, and nine other children home."

"And if we refuse the offer, you're willing to allow this faction to continue its dealings, sacrificing innocent children to fulfill your own agenda?"

"No. I'm afraid you misunderstand me. If you don't handle the situation, we shall. On our terms. I'm just afraid that our men don't have the same training as your Federally trained employees. Anyone could get hurt in the crossfire. I don't want this to turn into another Waco. Surely you understand that."

Archer nodded. "I understand all to clearly."

"Then you can see there's no other way. You must agree to our terms and put this behind us."

Senator Wiggins tugged Archer by the arm and pulled him close to Darryon, forming a semi-huddle.

"He's got us, and he knows it. Sometimes it's simply about choosing life. We've must survive to fight another day. Today's just not ours Archer. We don't have enough, and he's holding all the power."

Archer reluctantly agreed. Darryon patted him on the shoulder. "Let's do the right thing, for each other. That doesn't mean this is over."

Archer stepped forward. "It's my investigation. My decision.

I want some answers, then I'll give it to you."

The man smiled, "You have no position on which to stand, but so you can save face, I'll humor you. What do you wish to know?"

"This faction, what's their endgame?"

"It's simple really, but I don't know if you'll buy it… Are you a believer Detective Madsen?"

"A believer?"

"In the divine. Miracles. Christ. The Supernatural. The Greek Gods. Black Magic. Karma. The devil. The Buddha's Enlightenment. Anything?"

"I believe there are powers out there that can't be explained."

The man laughed. "That's it? Powers we can't explain."

He looked toward Darryon, confidently lowering his eyes. "No need to ask you Special Agent Myles. I've done my homework. You've become a believer over the last two years haven't you? That last case convinced you didn't it. Nothing like South Louisiana voodoo to open one's eyes."

Darryon neither confirmed nor denied. His eyes remained fixed on the man. Hatred intensely burning.

"And you Senator Wiggins, I don't need to ask you either. You better be a believer with all the conservative Christian followers you've amassed, or is that just a ploy to steal Republican votes."

Archer moved toward him, the men again blocking his path. He held his hands up in a non-threatening manner.

"I'm afraid I fail to see what my belief system has to do with what's happening here. I-"

"It has everything to do with what's happening," the man snapped. "It's as simple as a crisis of faith. Some people have it, others don't, and still others are fanatical."

"And that's how you explain this faction," Darryon asked. "Fanatics?"

"If there were a stronger word, I'd use it. They're believers in our cause at Blanket Corp, but they've gone astray. They have been for many years. We've just learned why…

…Believe me, it's alarming that we didn't catch this sooner. I like to contain things as early as possible. Keeps them from getting messy. I'm afraid in this case I've failed."

"What's this faction concerned with?"

"Blanket Corp's mission has always been to design the best drugs at the lowest prices. We believe the common man has just as much right to the best medical treatment as the wealthy. One goal has been to equalize the playing field by reducing the number of competitive drugs on the market. By doing so, we could control the market. Most companies in that position then skyrocket the prices. Not us. If we could gain control, we plan to make it affordable to all. We've spent billions trying to find ways to eliminate the need for competition…

…We've had several groups working different theories for

the past few decades. No one would say it, but we've been responsible for many of the vaccines and treatments around the world. We're the reason HIV isn't nearly as deadly as it once was. We're the frontrunners on the development of the Flu vaccine. Our research has led the world into treatments ranging from the common cold to cancer."

Senator Wiggins shifted positions. "We're well aware of your credentials. Get to the part we need to know."

"I'm afraid I don't know much, but what I do know is astounding. We're still compiling the details…

…This rogue group was founded in the early 1980's. It is considered an offshoot of a group that has always been our most radical. Developed in the early 1900's, they affectionately call themselves *Electi Pauci*, The Chosen Few."

"Who leads this group?"

"I don't know. We're trying to find that out."

"Why do they kidnap children every eight years?"

"That's the part you have to have some sort of faith to believe… They believe they're about to uncover the one drug that could be used to medically cure anything."

"Anything?"

"Yes. Anything."

"How?"

"The Messiah. One death to save many."

"That makes no sense. I don't understand."

"They believe they've recovered an ancient relic that has the power to heal. If they can combine the power of that relic with human DNA, they believe it will in essence produce a formula for a vaccine and treatment that would radically replenish whatever ailments the body faces regardless of the sickness. In short, they believe they're about to unlock a miracle drug that would revolutionize the medical industry. As a result, they'd become extremely wealthy and hopelessly famous. Our desire at Blanket Corp has never been about individual promotion. Most of the time, our company doesn't even gain recognition for its accomplishments. We prefer to remain in the shadows. Let others take the credit, we prefer to make a difference."

"What's the relic?" Darryon asked.

"One of the beams from Golgotha's tree."

"What?" Senator Wiggins gasped. "They believe they've found an artifact from the most powerful Christian symbol that's ever existed. Do you realize how controversial that is?"

"That's why they've kept it hidden from us, and the public, all these years. They wanted to prove its power first, develop the drug, and then state its origin."

"That's absurd."

"We believe so too Senator, but perception is everything. They believe in what they're doing, and they'll stop at nothing to see it become reality."

"Where'd the relic come from?"

"One of them could have made it up for all we know."

Archer forced out the words, "Why eight years? Why children?"

"You ready for this? They believe the blood of the innocents is human DNA in its purest form. They pulled blood from the relic, believing it's the blood of Christ. You know the power that represents. It's the *vitualamen insons insontis*. The Sacrifice of the Innocent."

"Sure," the Senator replied, "the blood that takes away the sins of the world."

"Exactly. But more importantly. The sacred texts indicate that the blood also brings healing."

"By His stripes are we healed," Senator Wiggins quoted.

"Yes. Emotional, physical, and spiritual healing all flow from the blood of Christ. This sect thinks they've unlocked that DNA…

…Through years of genetic testing, they also believe that it takes eight years for the blood of deity to mingle with the blood of humanity."

The man removed a few papers from a desk beside him. "Check the reports. We've been able to isolate the one factor every one of the kidnapped children have in common. Over one hundred of them, and they all share one characteristic."

Darryon snatched the papers and quickly examined the list. He snapped his fingers and thoughtfully pointed forward.

"The NICU. They all spent three days in some form of

NICU at birth. Even before NICU became a common term, they were still housing sick babies at hospitals…

…That's what this sect is trying to do. They're trying to mix what they believe is the DNA of Christ with the pure blood of innocents. Eight years is their incubation period…

…They insert the external DNA into the child at birth and monitor him for three days to make sure his body accepts the transfer. After eight years, they kidnap the selected children and harvest the blood. This isn't about the children at all. They're merely carriers. It's about the blood. It's always been about the blood."

Archer shook his head. "That's sick. Where'd they get that twisted notion?"

The man in the suit sat on the edge of the desk. "Who knows where men get their misconceptions. Who knows where the evil they design is contrived. No one can discover the genesis or logic for the evil that men do."

"Why do they keep trying, if it's failed all these years?" Darryon asked.

"Some of them wanted to quit. They thought it was pointless, and they'd never discover the magical cure. However, a recent leadership shift has altered the direction of the group. They once again feel they could be close."

"What did this new leader do to convince them?"

"Compelled them to believe that it hadn't worked, only because they hadn't found the right child. In Biblical terms, many false prophets came before the real Christ and claimed to be the Messiah. Some men even grew large followings. These followings were all short-lived once it was discovered that the men had no special power. According to tradition, only the blood of the real Messiah changed the world."

"So they're trying to find a Messiah again?"

"I'm afraid so, and they won't stop until they do."

"If I find out Blanket Corp is behind this-"

"We aren't detective. Stop your witch-hunt. I've given you everything you need to get to the bottom of this. End it before the harvest moon casts its glow, or they'll all be killed."

"How do we find them? How will we know where to end it?"

"I've made it easy. They'll be where this all started for you. The secluded land."

"Max Stanley's house," Archer bellowed. "It's the perfect place, and the last place we would've suspected."

"Detective, they're already setting up. I don't know where the kids are located now. If you show a presence before the right time, they won't bring the kids, and you'll lose them forever."

"Thanks for doing your part. We'll do ours. I just need one more thing from you. I'll call you with the details in a couple hours. Please be ready to move fast."

Archer started walking toward the door. The man stopped him with a shout from behind.

"I'm afraid it's not that easy Detective Madsen."

Archer whirled to face him. He looked dead into Archer's eyes. No emotion. He moved toward Archer with the guile of a serpent.

"Do we have a deal?"

Archer looked from the Senator to Darryon, who were both nodding their heads in agreement. Reluctantly, he extended his hand. The two men shook.

"Good. The Elysian Fields then."

"What?" Archer asked.

"My deal to you. You can finally put her to rest."

51

8:30 p.m.

Archer placed the call to the man from Blanket Corp. He'd told him there was one more thing he needed done. He informed the man of his plan. The man had set preparations in motion, gravely agreeing to provide what was necessary to make the arrangements happen.

Archer sat down with Darryon, Senator Wiggins, Max, and Regan. Jaxon hurried into the room and sat at the far end of the table.

"I've heard back from half of them so far. Indianapolis police have uncovered a dumpsite at the park. So far, they've discovered eight bodies. All children...

...San Francisco police report they've found four bodies in the wooded area we described. That was sixteen years ago.

...From twenty-four years ago, New Orleans police have found a burial site on a private strip near the airport. Three bodies so far...

...Atlanta police and Seattle police have found six and four respectively. All children."

Max angrily pounded the table. "How long are we gonna sit here and wait?"

"Max, if we go in now, we'll lose him when we're so close. We can't blindly rush them. We have to make sure all the children are on sight. We don't want to lose any of them."

"I tried calling Jessica. She's not answering. Her voicemail is full. I can't even leave her a message. She needs to know we've almost found him."

"I'll try to run a trace on her phone. If not, I'll scour surveillance cameras and check with my contacts until we find her. I'll get her here as soon as possible Max." Jaxon said, as he steadily inserted information into his computer.

Archer leaned across the table. "Any word from Indianapolis about the bodies? Anything that confirms the claims made by Blanket Corp?"

Jaxon read a report and visibly shuttered. "The coroner states that the victims were drained alive. Their blood was siphoned while they were still breathing. It seems they were tied down and their blood and major organs were harvested."

"That supports his version of the truth. This group was involved for the profit. Those organs command a good deal of money on the black market," Darryon confirmed.

Senator Wiggins felt sick. "How could anyone be so cruel as to bind a child and drain the life from him? These people don't deserve to live. We have to find out who is at the top."

Jaxon nodded, "I'm working on it. I've got Indy P.D. looking into the name of the person who signed for the land rental at the festival eight years ago. They're supposed to let me know any time."

Courtney burst into the room, heavily panting from the slight run across the lab. She moved toward him. "Jaxon, that video you had me working on. I did it. I was able to isolate the feed. It's perfect."

"What video?" Archer asked.

Jaxon took the iPad from her hand and looked at it. He watched the scene unfold and smiled.

"Courtney, This is perfect."

"What video?" Archer repeated.

Jaxon pushed the iPad in his direction.

"The video from Tyler Wiggins alarm clock. Watch closely. The dark figures that took the girl, she's removed all the grain and clarified their reflections in the mirror on his dresser."

Archer watched closely, Max peering over his shoulder. As the first man entered, Max stuttered.

"That's him. That's the dark form that took Carson."

"Watch Max. It's not an evil spirit. He's a man."

Max watched the man walk into view. He swiftly rocked forward.

"That's Morgan's bodyguard. He… I can't…"

Regan studied the video closely. "That's the man who said he wanted to come back for me. Get a swab and compare it to that sample I took. I guarantee you it's a match. I recognize the eyes."

She hesitated, making her decision reluctantly. She didn't know why, but she felt he should know.

"Max, remember when I told you that we found DNA of another man in your bed?"

Max nodded. "I remember."

"It was his," she said, pointing at the muscular bodyguard on the screen.

Max shook his head and headed toward the door.

Jaxon's phone chimed, alerting him of a message. He opened it. He couldn't contain his excitement.

"Arch. I got word back from Indianapolis. They found out who rented the land eight years ago. There was one name on the rental receipt; LeDiv."

52

9:13 p.m.

The moon became visible over the skyline. He didn't know why, but staring into its abysmal surface gave him a harrowing chill. The aura was alive with a rigid intensity. Movement to his left startled him, but he couldn't take his eyes from the chilling, craterous moon rising into the darkening sky.

It was large, swelling to fullness. Childish fears of werewolves and vampires would normally be elicited by the bloodthirsty glow.

Not tonight.

Not him.

He didn't need to fear ghouls from the Crypt keeper's coffin. He was terrified enough of the men who had captured him and kept him about in a rabbit's cage.

He continually blinked, his eyes still rapidly trying to adjust to the dimness of the environment. The light wasn't great, only the glow of the few orbs that were situated on temporary street lamps lining the field. Shimmering moonbeams provided the remainder of his partial luminous surroundings.

However, the limited light seemed blinding to him. He' been wearing the blindfold for the past two days. They'd only removed it a few seconds ago. He was extremely frightened, not because they'd done something to him, but because of what he'd heard them discussing.

Nex per messis luna had meant nothing to him at first. It only took on a horrific life of its own once the slow one had asked the others what it meant. The leader had responded by saying it meant "death by the Harvest Moon."

He was too young too die. He just wanted to see his mother again. To sleep in her bed and feel protected because she was there, and she'd never let anything happen to him.

He wanted to play baseball with his father again. To catch the pop-ups his father would throw to him in the front yard.

He wanted them both. He missed the little things. Like eating supper around the small table, the one they seldom used but always talked about making a greater focus.

If he could go back, he wouldn't be so stubborn about brushing his teeth at night, getting up in the mornings, eating his vegetables, taking a bath, or going to bed on time. He'd do anything to just be able to go back home.

A few days ago he'd dreamed that she'd come for him. She'd taken him from the narrow cage and saved him from the limited space and horrific food. She'd held him closely for a long time, making him feel safe, warm, and loved. However, he'd grown uncontrollably sleepy and had passed on in her arms. He'd been disappointed to awaken soon after, only to discover it had all been a merciless moment of sleeping reverie.

He continued to stare into the moon's powerful radiance, until a soft voice from behind alerted him.

"Carson."

He apprehensively turned to face it. There was no one there.

Darkness.

Shadows cast in a violent paleness.

Hollow emptiness.

"Carson."

He turned in the other direction. "What? Who's calling me?"

He couldn't run. The chain around his ankle kept him from moving more than three feet in any direction. He wanted to scream, but that would only alert the guards, which created another problem all together.

"Please, I'm really scared."

A lone figure stepped from the shadowy tree line. The figure was only slightly imposing, but there was no familiarity there. He didn't recognize the build, gait, or voice.

The figure stood a few feet from him. It donned a rustic brown robe pulled tight around the collar. A large hood closed around the person's face, revealing eyes and nothing else. No features could be discerned from under the shrouded covering.

"I'm proud of you Carson. Of all the subjects, you've done best. I believe you're going to make your family proud tonight. You could be the one... Our Messiah."

Carson shuttered. Something in the voice was repulsive. The external appearance alone seemed non-threatening, but there was a malicious intent more discerned than visibly noticed. He tried to step away.

"You can't hide Carson. We both know the chain isn't long enough for you to go anywhere. Just relax and enjoy the night. It's all about you. Bask in your glory. Revel in your power. This is your crowning moment, the time your temporary life is immortalized for the ages. Don't run. You must embrace the moment."

The figure took a step toward him. He picked up a stone and hurled it toward the surging darkness. It easily avoided his throw.

"That's not nice Carson. That's not the way the Messiah would play. Hundreds are gathering to watch the chosen one ascend...

...We've waited so long for this. And it could be you. You're special Carson. I hope you can see that."

"Then let me go," he pleaded. "I just want to go home."

"I can't. Exceptional power demands extraordinary feats. It's time to fulfill your destiny. You were born for this."

"Please. I just want to see my parents."

"You will soon enough, for you carry the cure in your veins. Once harvested, you'll live again. You just have to believe. We're going to send you on the journey. Then, you'll wake up a new vessel, better than you were before. You'll come back immortal, having transcended death. Just like the Christ...

...His blood and yours, the perfect blend. You'll see Carson. We aren't here to hurt you. We're here to set you free."

Carson suddenly heard movement all around him. People had started chanting. Their words were unrecognizable. He started to cry.

The figure moved toward him and wiped his tears. He slapped the hand away. Surprisingly, it slapped him back, knocking him sprawling across the soft packed ground.

"I'm sad for you Carson. The whole earth rejoices, and you loathe the idea of becoming a legend. The world sings your praises. Stories will be told through the ages about your actions tonight. How do you want to be remembered? The whiner who cried his way into oblivion, or the champion who willingly traded his life to pay the price for depraved humanity?"

Carson ignored the question. He didn't even fully understand what it meant. He studied the noise unfolding around him. The people were cheering like rabid fans at a sporting event, as groundskeepers place nine more stakes in the ground around him. The metal poles were being screwed into a bottom frame that was already cemented four feet into the dirt. The chain looped to the pole that had been erected six feet into the air.

More people were flooding the area. Mothers marched children toward the commotion, cheerfully pulling them toward the show, as if they were attending the circus. Young teens ran from post to post, slapping against them, testing their strength.

One man was passing out t-shirts. The logo's background was a rugged, shining cross. The subscript read *From ten comes one. From one to eternity. Festival of Souls.*

Carson was squeamish. A few older children meandered toward him, staring intently into his soft blue eyes. A young woman stopped beside him and ran her fingers through his wavy hair.

"He's just a boy. How will he save us?"

She was interrupted by the screeching sound of tires sliding on pavement. The white van skidded to a stop a few yards from the standing poles. The back doors swung open and three men jumped from the back of the van, waving their arms in the air in a fantastical celebration. A fourth man shoved a young girl from the truck. She landed hard on her knees and struggled to regain her balance. She failed, and her face was buried in the soft mud beneath her.

The crowd roared with applause.

Shed her blood.

Shed her blood.

Shed her blood.

Carson lunged forward, trying to help her stand to her feet. Sometimes the greatest strength comes from feeling needed. He temporarily forgot his own fear and struggled against his chains to reach her. She was sobbing uncontrollably. She was just a small girl.

Afraid.

Alone.

Broken.

One by one, kids were herded from the van. They were sportingly tied to the metallic stakes placed directly in front of the audience. They were cast as trophies for the onlookers to mock, intimidate, and interact with. Their last moments on earth were fearfully orchestrated.

Carson looked upward. The moon was cresting, growing ever larger. It's amber light forced the shadows from the ravenous crowd to dance like murderous stick figures. A huge bonfire erupted twenty feet away. The captive children could feel its warmth permeating their skin, removing the chill of the twilight air.

Twelve people moved forward from the outskirts. They wore various animal costumes, each conjuring images of unworthy sacrifices for a jealous deity. Each was symbolic that no animal would be needed, for today the deity demanded a more perfect bloodline.

The crowd chattered with excitement as the twelve unidentifiable figures marched single file and took their places in seats chosen and carefully constructed specifically for this occasion. The chairs sat high above the crowd, allowing the twelve to spectate without being disturbed by the zealous disciples.

A lone figure emerged, as if appearing from thin air. It wore a thick, white fleece robe. This costume had no hood concealing the identity, as did the others. Instead, there was a horned goat's head pulled down completely over the figures head. The powerful magnificence of the ram caused the masses to surge with approval.

The person walked to the head of the group and faced the throng standing before the children. It lifted both arms into the air, and the crowd roared.

The costumed figure slammed its hand toward the ground. The ambiance was filled with a shattering silence. No one breathed.

The horde's exuberant gaiety instantly calmed to a hushed tranquility. Everyone stared, mesmerized by their leader. Only observed once every eight years, this was a welcomed sight.

Carson recognized the rough voice as the one that had whispered to him earlier. It screamed, "Let the festival begin," and threw the hands back up in joyous celebration. Each person in the crowd placed an ornamented mask around their head. Each face was completely hidden in the obscurity of the evening.

The party started again. A private free-for-all. The only rule was there were no rules. Have fun. Fulfill the night. Take pleasure in the beauty and merriment of others, and never take off your mask.

Dancing. Promiscuity An evanescent glory.

And just a few feet removed, among ten children-

Panic.

Anxiety

Tears.

53

10:43 p.m.

"Where's Max?" Archer gruffly demanded. "Our contact from Blanket Corp came through."

"I shouldn't have told him about the affair. I thought it might snap him into the realization that LeDiv is probably responsible, regardless of the line that Blanket Corp is feeding us. With the control he's exhibited over his daughter, I doubt Max can persuade her to leave Morgan's side. She won't be able to accept his role in this."

"Anyone located her yet?" Darryon asked. "If Max contacts her, it could get dangerous. Doesn't she already feel he's delusional?"

"She does," Archer replied. "She took a restraining order out on him a couple of days ago. She'll call if he contacts her.

Anyway, we can't wait for him. We've got to move now."

"I don't think we'll find her," Regan interjected. "I think she's part of this."

"What makes you say that?"

"Something she said to me when I first interviewed her. She said her brother's bones were still rotting in a field somewhere. I took it as mere objective opinion then. Looking back, and with the new evidence we've gathered from the past, I think she knows something about her brother's death. I think she knows where he was buried."

"We'll keep our eyes out. She could be at the center of this, although I don't see it. She seems to care for her son way too deeply to be involved."

"Let me go with you. I want to help," Regan pleaded.

"Not this time," Archer firmly replied. "We don't know what's gonna happen out there tonight. Besides, we need you here. Keep trying to reach Max and Jessica."

He touched her hand with his. Their eyes met, and they both nervously smiled.

"Come back," she said, and waved as the small group made their way through the door.

11:17 p.m.

The small group drove off the road and stopped on the outskirts of Max's land. A limo in the distance flashed its lights, breaking the fragile obscurity of the midnight hour. Archer pulled his car close to the stretched vehicle, and they got out.

The man from Blanket Corp motioned for them to get in with him. They each pulled themselves into the narrow doorway and sat down.

"Put these on," he stated, as he handed them each a small pin. "It's a universal pass. Everyone that sees it will consider you a distinguished guest, here with express permission of the highest authority in Blanket Corp. You won't have trouble once you get past the gates."

"Once we get through? You expecting trouble there?"

"No, because I'm escorting you in, but once inside, you're on your own."

He motioned for his driver to move the car forward. He removed masks from a paper bag by his side and handed them to the entourage.

"Without these, you'll be too easily recognized. They aren't foolish. They know you've been closing in…

…Live the festival gentlemen. Breathe it. Be who you're not. Just be who you're not."

11:33 p.m.

Max slowly moved toward the group. He'd crawled up the creek bed, making his way through the field toward the crowd. He'd been listening to their music and laughing long enough, and it repulsed him. If he had his way, he'd tie every one of them up and throw them in that stupid fire they'd built too close to the children. The cries of the eight year olds forced to watch the party in their honor had long since been drowned out by the incessant reveling.

He was almost to a grove of trees when someone moved a few feet away. He lay perfectly still, praying he wouldn't be noticed. They were laughing. Romantic happiness, the kind that people share when their thoughts are carnally indulged.

They came into view, moving quickly to the grove of trees he'd been moving toward. Her blouse was already half unbuttoned. The young man wasn't wasting time. He hurriedly picked her up and carried her toward the taller grass. He pushed her toward the soft earth and fell down, half on top and half beside her. He kissed her passionately, moving his lips toward her neck.

Opportunity seldom aligns for long. Max had learned to take advantage of every chance when it's presented. That rule is only magnified the more that's at stake. The couple was occupied, and Max wasn't going to miss this one.

Seventeen feet. That's the distance that can be closed before the average person can physically register a threat and respond. Max was closer to ten.

He searched and disappointedly couldn't find anything to use as a weapon. Finally, his hand ran over a large stone. It was smooth around the edges, probably having been dragged up from the creek during a flood. It was slightly larger than his hand, and it was relatively heavy.

He didn't want to, but there was no other choice. There was no line he wouldn't cross to save his son. He clutched the rock firmly in his hand and lunged forward. The rock made contact with the back of the young man's head. He toppled forward and landed hard on the ground. There was no movement. Max was unsure if he was dead or not, but he knew for certain that he was unconscious. He removed him from the girl and quickly covered her mouth with his hand.

"If you scream, I'll kill you. You understand?"

"Please. I don't want to die. I'll do anything you want. Just don't kill me."

Max sat her up slowly and moved behind her. She fearfully turned her head, trying to discern his intentions. He pulled her toward him, the back of her head falling firmly against his chest. She cried, afraid of what was coming.

Only, it wasn't what she expected. He wrapped his hands around her neck and tightly squeezed. She struggled against his grip, but he was much too strong. Her body thrashed for a few seconds, and then she went limp. He let her go, and she slid down beside her lover.

Max stooped beside them onto his knees. He didn't know why, but he was crying. Not a passionate, uncontrollable wail, but a gentle shamefulness. He wished there could have been another way. There wasn't. He was running out of time.

He placed two fingers on the girl's throat. There was a faint pulse. A few seconds later he identified the boy's pulse as well. They'd be out for a while, but they'd both live. He removed the boy's mask and robe, put them on, and moved into the crowd, blending into their intense festivities. He painstakingly pretended to be joyful, slowly making his way toward the place of the sacrifices. In the center of the ten metal rods someone had erected a stone altar.

54

11:48 p.m.

Archer watched the commotion with intense hatred. He wanted to pull his gun from the thick-skinned robe and empty both clips into the contemptible crowd.

However, the ten armed men hiding in the crowd made him reconsider. They were low profile. No one knew they were there. They blended with the other revelers, except for the semi-automatic weapons Archer could see outlined underneath. They were part of the group, but not part of the festivities. The Chosen Few had made sure they were protected.

Senator Wiggins was right beside him. Darryon moved closer. Lieutenant Bradley Smith, Regan's uncle, stood between the two. Archer stepped about a foot from them.

"I don't have a plan. The chance of getting those kids out of here without starting a war is impossible. I've counted at least ten armed guards, and there's probably more that I didn't notice."

The Lieutenant nodded. "Was thinking the same thing. This is suicide... Did you notice the two hanging back toward the rear of the altar?"

Archer casually moved his body in that direction. "I didn't, but I got them now."

He repositioned his earpiece, shoving it further into his ear. "Regan, please tell me you've got some good news."

"Sorta, SWAT is on location. They're positioned two miles away. It will take them about three minutes to ram the gates and be with you the field. Do you realistically think you can hold them away from the kids for three minutes?"

"Not a chance," Bradley replied. "We won't last thirty seconds against their firepower, and these people are fanatics. No telling what they'll do once the fireworks start."

Archer sighed. The Lieutenant was right. As bad as they wanted to get the kids out, they were outnumbered and outgunned.

Archer picked up his head. "Regan. I'm gonna follow my gut-"

"But Arch, you said that always gets you in trouble when you're trying to protect others-"

"And you said it wouldn't."

He could hear her smile through the radio. "And you choose now to test my theory."

"It's all we've got… Just get ready to send SWAT in hot. I'm going to try and buy us some time. When I start, get SWAT rolling. If they're late, we're all dead."

12:00 a.m.

A trumpet sounded, bursting through the night air. All the extracurricular activity died, as the carousers stopped what they were doing and hurriedly gathered, pressing in as close to the altar as possible. The moment had arrived; the reason for their eight-year meeting was finally coming to fruition.

The leader in the fleece robe moved toward the front, standing behind a makeshift podium constructed from the same stones as the sacrificial bed. Both hands raised into the air.

"*Permaneo vitualamen mos patefacio ianua.* The last sacrifice will open the door…

…We've waited over a century. This power hasn't been witnessed in two millennia. Since the death of Christ the world has waited for another savior. Tonight, we find him."

The crowd surged. Regan shouted through Archer's earpiece, but the crowd roared so fervently that it interfered with the transmission. Archer clutched his earpiece tightly, covering it with his left hand. He still couldn't make out the garble coming through.

The leader stood with raised hands again. The raucous roars fell silent on cue. Like the might of the ocean's tide cascading against the earth's rocky restraints, the crowd swelled to boisterous highs, only to retract like lonely waters driven back into the sea.

"Bring the first child."

Two men moved forward and grabbed one of the girls, pulling her hard against her chains. Finally breaking her free, they forced her forward toward the rocky altar.

"No. Stop. Help me! Please! Help me!"

"Are you not worthy of a warrior's death," the leader screamed. "Make it slow with her. Painful. Make her earn the right to be heard."

Again the noise of the cheering onlookers echoed across the plains.

"Wait," someone yelled from the skyward poles. "Leave her alone."

The leader sulked forward. Silence. "Who spoke out of turn?"

No one blinked. Air was sucked from the atmosphere. No one breathed. Every one feared that any action might be mistaken as a confession. The onlookers searched to find who had interrupted.

"If no one screamed, then continue, take her."

Chains rattled against one of the furthest poles.

"Let her go."

The leader stepped amongst the children, the ram's horns threateningly pointing like an accusatory scepter. Eight year-old Carson Stanley stood to his feet, making himself as tall as he could. The high priest smiled, barely visible through the horned mask.

"You honor us with your courage, but is your blood worthy to be mingled with the Christ?"

The leader turned back, stopping at the altar to sprinkle a crimson fluid onto the center. As the blood stained the rocks, the voice was heard from behind the heavy veil.

"It's time. Put her back. Honor the noble hero's request. Leave her alone. His life shall not be forcibly taken. He's offered to freely give his life for hers. Like the Christ, he must be our Messiah."

The men rushed the girl back to her restraints. Two others picked Carson from his bands and pushed him toward the stones. He crashed to the ground, as he was thrown at the leader's feet.

Carson looked up from the dust. He slightly discerned a smile beneath the shadows of the ram's head. The figure extended a hand to him. He reluctantly accepted and was robustly yanked to his feet.

"The Chosen One."

The crowd roared.

Laughter.

Happiness.

Clapping.

Shouting.

"We've finally found the one for which we've waited. Generations have passed, and one is now finally worthy. Since I was a child, I've been a part of this crowd. Like all of you, I've watched, celebrated, and waited for the One to prove worthiness…"

Tears glistened in the moon's radiant glow. They escaped onto the fleece covering. Carson felt them drip onto his arm from the leader's face. Their warmth was a drastic contrast to the coolness of the midnight air.

The leader sniffled, and the dialogue continued, "I'm certain we've found him… our Savior… Carson Morgan Stanley."

Max pushed his way through the frenzied crowd. He was fifteen feet from Carson. He couldn't just grab him and run. There was no chance they'd be able to escape. He needed a diversion. Yet, as desperately as he searched, there was nothing helpful. He was alone. He was unarmed, and his only child was about to be executed on an altar of stone.

The people quieted, as the voice rang out again. "Let us honor a few people who greatly deserve it. They've sacrificed everything in an effort to preserve humanity and keep the sustaining tradition of the Festival. Their sacrifice allows all of us the privilege of a better life…"

The cheerfulness in the raspy voice was easily discernible. "Please. You know who you are. Step forward and take your places among the worthy. Now, behold as we make history. God has smiled upon us."

Several people moved forward, as the rest of the crowd backed away to give them room. Cheering erupted again as fifteen people ceremoniously separated from the crowd. The small group gathered by the altar, as the leader moved to them. Again the deafening silence. The only sound was the distant howl of a coyote singing its lonely song to sickly moon.

The leader extended a scepter over the group. "May God grant you all the strength to finish the journey. In our personal Gethsemane, we'd rather that this cup pass. Grant us the audacity to stare at death and release our earthly possessions. From dust. To dust. We've received. Now, we give."

The leader motioned for them to move, "Take your place next to the offering you willingly bestow."

The group dispersed, as each member moved to stand beside one of the children. Three children had two representatives stand beside them. One child had three masked figures hover over her. The remaining five children had one representative each. One figure remained near the leader, before turning and walking toward Carson. The figure grasped Carson's legs, and helped as two men lifted him onto the altar.

Carson kicked against the restraints, but it was no use. The figure firmly held him; as the two men strapped him down so tightly that he could barely breathe.

Max's heart pounded urgently in his chest. He noticed the design of the altar for the first time. A narrow crevice had been routed through the sides of the stone, running into a deep vat at the bottom. A slight bowl had been formed underneath where Carson was tied.

The blueprint was obvious. The children were going to be murdered, probably cut in a major artery. The blood would then pool into the bowl on the altar. As the bowl filled, the liquid would channel through the crevice, ultimately ending in the vat at the bottom. The designers would have their collection. The bodies would then be disposed of, thrown in the large bonfire. The merry onlookers would eventually return to their normal lives. Their friends, neighbors, relatives, and co-workers would be forever unaware that they walk among psychopaths.

The leader stepped toward the altar. "Uncover yourselves. Let God see the depth of your sacrifice. Allow others to bear witness to your extreme willingness to yield to God's plan. It's okay to cry; there's no shame in pain."

· · ·

Archer's radio cracked again as the crowd jumped and shouted. He looked at the two men beside him and demonstrated his lack of understanding. Both shook their heads. They couldn't make out Regan's excited chatter either.

The children's representatives removed their masks. It was obvious, the people standing in pairs were proud parents; parents willingly ready to sacrifice their own kids. The group with the three representatives consisted of a mother, father, and grandmother; two generations of blind ignorance. The remaining groups were mothers standing next to their child.

Tears fell. There's nothing as sickening as a parent betraying the fragile innocence of a child. The confused children bawled, agonizingly pleading to be rescued by the people they thought loved them most. Parents trembled, waging a hellish war of indecision. Every instinct urged them to save their own flesh and blood from the pain, but something powerful kept them there.

Blind Faith.

Sincerity. Severely misplaced.

Compassion. Extremely misguided.

Sacrifice. The beauty of martyrdom.

Max gasped as the mask was removed from the last representative standing over Max at the altar. He now knew why he hadn't been able to locate her. The removal of the mask revealed the tear-streaked face of Jessica LeDiv.

55

Max leapt forward, his screams penetrated the solemn commotion, causing an abrupt hush. All eyes turned on him. Murderous expressions were exhibited on almost face, as the people wondered what intruder would dare hinder their sacred tradition.

Two armed guards easily restrained him, pulling him to the ground. He forcibly tried to get up but was unable to move under their weight.

"Jessica, he's our son. How could you give him to this? Don't let them take his life."

She smiled. Tears soiled her face. Her mascara stained her white robe. She appeared a peculiar blend of serenity and anxiety.

"Max, It's already done. He's proven to be the one. I

couldn't be more proud of him. You should join me Max. This is his defining moment, his baptism into a better world."

She touched Carson's chin and rubbed her hand to pinch his cheek. The damn opened, as the emotion he'd tried to hold burst out. The fear and desire to live ebbed from his eyelids and spilled down his tiny face.

"Momma. Please. Help me. Daddy, help."

She patted his head. "Don't let your father's weakness corrupt your resolve. He just doesn't understand like we do Carson. It's okay to be afraid. Even Jesus prayed that he wouldn't have to carry his cross. But he still did, and now the world's a better place."

"Jessica. Please. You're a sick woman. Let me get you some help. Don't lose Carson like you did your brother… We love you Jessica… You don't have to destroy our family. We want to be a happy family again."

She shook her head in disbelief. "I don't know how you found out about my brother, but you'd never understand. I stood right where you are now. I watched my mother and her father tie him down. They let me join them. I held his tiny hands as they trembled when the blood began to run down the stones. I watched the life drain from his baby blue eyes. And I understood. I got it. It's about giving yourself for others. I was proud then…"

She looked into the crowd still standing in awkward silence. "And… I have never been more proud… Until tonight… My son… Willing to save us all."

The crowd that had been subdued and partially confused filled the meadow with a sickening roar. The leader's hands again extended, bringing sudden silence.

Max yelled, "If he's so willing, why don't you untie him. You shouldn't need the restraints."

The leader ignored Max's cries, addressing the crowd instead, "Please. He is an unwilling participant, but let's welcome Max Stanley, Carson's father. He'll come around in time. He'll look back on this and recognize the beauty that lived in the chaos."

Max thrashed against the men holding him. "Morgan. You coward. I know it's you. Why don't you take off your mask and show yourself? Why are you the only one still concealed? Let Carson see you encourage the crowd to take his life."

The leader laughed, a revoltingly hideous cackle that was more an expression of finding pleasure in other's pain than a display of humor.

"Morgan. You think Morgan has the fortitude to lead something this powerful. Morgan LeDiv wouldn't have become anything without me. He's nothing more than a weasel in an expensive suit. He's too weak of mind to understand and too sentimental to give up his grandson."

Max appeared stunned. "Who... Who-"

The figure removed the mask. Max's head fell. Regan had been right. Someone had fed into his delusion, keeping him holding on to what he believed was real. The drugs had been wearing off, but he'd still erroneously held to the belief that a supernatural force had been prevalent. He'd been reluctant to let that belief die, because she'd reinforced it with a similar story of her own.

It was clear. They'd played him perfectly.

The restraints.

The locked door with the alarm.

The "warden."

Murdering the man that had helped him.

Her disappearance when he'd returned with Conrad. That move had been brilliant. It had further caused the detectives to think he was insane, while further proving to him that the conspiracy was alive.

He'd been played. Like mother like daughter. They'd planned this from the beginning. For eight years he'd lived a lie. For eight years their only son had been an experimental scapegoat to be offered as a sacrifice under the Harvest Moon.

"Sandra. Please. You've lost so much already. You don't-"

"Lost. I've lost nothing. I've given. Freely I received, I've freely given it back. I've no regrets."

Max buried his face in the grass. Bitter tears fell. Sandra placed her mask back on and removed a twelve-inch dagger from a rustic scabbard. She held it high into the air, clutching it tightly against the glare of the bloodthirsty moon.

"Ex nex adveho salus. Deus creatio ex nihilo."

She continued to hold the knife high, the moonlight sparkling off of its sharp blade.

Archer leaned in, "What's she saying?"

The Senator replied, "My Latin is rusty, and she doesn't speak it fluently, but she said that God created the world from nothing. She also said that life for many will come by the death of the One."

The radio cackled again. "Archer, did you copy?" Regan pleaded.

The crowd soared as she placed the dagger near the child's throat. The radio cracked again. Her voice was audible, but indistinct.

"Regan, it's too loud. Tell them to move in now. I've got to stop this."

He removed the earpiece from his ear and tossed it to the ground. He couldn't hear her anyway.

Regan screamed back, only they never heard her through the noise.

"Archer, there's a problem with SWAT. I've lost contact. If I can't re-establish, they won't be coming. I need a few minutes. Archer. Senator. Uncle Bradley. Confirm please. There's no SWAT. I repeat; there is no SWAT."

56

Archer stepped forward, removing his robe, and brandishing the Blanket Corp pin. He authoritatively hollered through the thin mask still covering his face.

"By order of the Blanket Corp counsel, I order you to stop."

Armed guards drew their weapons and trained them directly at him. Senator Wiggins and Bradley stayed slightly behind, still blending with the crowd. It didn't matter; Archer preferred it that way.

"As you can see," he said, pointing to the emblem on his shirt, "I'm here representing the counsel."

Sandra LeDiv lowered the knife, momentarily placing it back in the scabbard. "This is my Trust. Over the decades, we've amassed a broad following. Everything we're doing has been sanctioned by Blanket Corp. I'm sure you're aware that we're acting under their purview."

Archer faced the crowd. "Are you all certain of that. You've been following a renegade. She no longer possesses the board's approval. Are you willing to risk your lives following the lunacy of a rebel? I've been sent here to investigate."

He scanned the assembly, sensing their nervousness. "I have to give my report in the morning, and I don't like what I'm seeing. This isn't what Blanket Corp stands for. It won't be tolerated…

…Each of you has a choice; you can leave now and live, or you can stay here and face judgment with this rebel faction. Blanket Corp will have an eradication team here within the hour."

"That's absurd," Sandra screamed. "The Concilium would never send an outsider. It's against policy. They'd never violate procedure."

The people murmured, most obviously agreeing with her. Archer shifted uncomfortably. He'd been in dangerous situations before, but he'd never had so many guns pointed toward him at once. His mind raced for a way out.

"Who says I'm an outsider. That's what you'd like them to believe-"

"You carry the pin, the mark of a guest. You don't belong here."

"I belong here just as much as you. I've given my share. I'm not a member of the Concilium. I clean up corporate messes, and that's exactly what you've made of this Trust."

He turned and studied the hillsides. There was no movement. Where were they? They should have been there by now?

"What?" Sandra mocked. "Your eradication team isn't coming?"

She looked at the men. "Kill him."

"I wouldn't do that," Archer cautioned. "She's just the rebellious leader of a lowly Trust. Blanket Corp is who you work for. It's the largest privately owned and funded cooperation in the world. It can create a lot of hell in your already messed up world. Unless you want that, I'd stand down."

"Don't listen to him. He isn't one of us. He has no authority here. He's lying."

He studied the crowd again. "Please. Go home. None of you need to get hurt."

"You're a liar. The Concilium would never stop us short of finding the cure."

"It's over Sandra."

"Show yourself then," she demanded. "Prove it to us. Show who you are."

"You know the rules of the Festival. Everyone remains anonymous unless we so choose to break the tradition. I'm invoking my right to secrecy."

He didn't know if his idea was true, but most of the crowd wouldn't either. He only needed to convince a few of them to leave. If a small segment would, most of the others would follow. The pack always needs a leader, someone to start the ball rolling. Then, without fail, the rest will follow.

"For my own safety, I choose to remain anonymous."

"If you're so high and mighty at the top of the pyramid, you have nothing to worry about. Take off the mask."

Where was SWAT? Something was terribly wrong. They should have been swarming in five minutes ago. He was losing the crowd; he could feel the shift. They were gaining confidence with her every rebuttal.

Darryon caught on to Archer's attempts. He also noticed the emotional retraction of the crowd. He suddenly threw his hands forward in disgust.

"This doesn't feel right. I'm going home. Nobody would sneak in here without the Counsel's approval. He's obviously consulted with them. He knows too much."

He walked away from the group, pushing his way toward the back. Bradley did the same.

"I'm leaving too, at least until we get their approval again. I'm not going against them."

Senator Wiggins turned and followed them. A low murmur started in the crowd and grew to a ferocious buzz. Many members turned and walked toward the cars parked further up the field.

Suddenly, headlights lined the sky. The maddening sound of approaching vehicles overrode the chaos from the crowd.

SWAT trucks rolled onto the grounds, herding the people moving toward their cars into small groups. The groups were lined up in the field and forced to their knees.

Other vehicles continued to roll closer toward the remaining horde still surrounding the altar. The armed guards fled, distracted by the army of SWAT members closing in. Max leapt to his feet, as the two men released him and ran.

Sandra screamed. Not out of panic or fear, but out of disgust. Her carefully laid plans were destroyed, and she'd given everything to build this empire. She couldn't just watch it crumble around her.

Archer immediately recognized the sound, as she swiftly moved near Carson. The unmistakable scrap of cold steel across soft leather filled the air. She raised the blade again and swiftly brought it down toward her squirming grandson. Max screamed, darting forward and reaching out with both arms.

Archer shot her. Her head rocked backward, and the dagger clanged off the slab of stone. Jessica scooped it up and clutched it in her left hand.

"Why Max? It was almost done. His legacy. It was almost complete."

"Don't do it," Archer yelled, but it was too late. She was at Carson's side before he finished the sentence. His gun leapt the second time, as Jessica was slammed backward. She landed right next to her mother.

Archer heard screaming from further up the hillside. He turned to see SWAT still lining the people into small groups.

The black BDUs and masked uniforms had never looked so welcomed.

More SWAT members ran toward the group clustered near him. Max reached Carson and removed his restraints. He held his son close as they both cried. Archer clasped the back of Max's shirt collar.

"It's over Max. Let's get him to a hospital."

He called out to one of the SWAT members, displaying his badge. He jumped when gunfire erupted from one of the groups further up the field.

He couldn't believe what he was seeing. SWAT had opened fire on unarmed civilians. They had been placed on their knees and were now being systematically executed.

The group of bystanders nearest him panicked and immediately scattered in various directions.

Archer turned for Max again, but he was gone. He was running away from the group, clutching Carson in his arms. "Max. Stay with me. Max."

It was no use; Max couldn't hear his screams over the gunfire and tormented cries of the fleeing people. Archer turned to run after him. An explosion erupted further up the field near the vehicles. He whirled in that direction.

Senator Wiggins and the Lieutenant pulled up beside him. "What's going on?" the Senator questioned.

"I don't know, but we'd better leave."

Another explosion rocked the earth a few feet away. Dirt

flew, splattering them with a heated intensity. The small huddle was broken, each man being rocked backward by the ferocity of the blast. Senator Wiggins landed a few feet away.

Archer couldn't find Lieutenant Bradley. He rolled over onto his back and struggled to move. He saw his earpiece lying in the dirt near him and placed it into his ear.

"Regan. Come in. Regan."

Like him, it was spent. He looked into the sky. It loomed directly overhead. It's ghastly radiance cast a delicate, fiery shadow on the field. The words played through his mind.

Death by the harvest moon.

Leaving this lonely life a stranger, receiving a hero's welcome after.

Home in the Elysian Fields, till their tired souls rapture.

By the light of the blood stained moon,

   Heroes die, to be welcomed soon.

57

Archer lay in a stretcher at the rear of the ambulance. Emergency personnel had helped him only minutes earlier. He was still woozy from his second blast in three days, but he was coherent. The Senator had already been taken away in an ambulance. He was pretty banged up but in stable condition.

Darryon walked up to him. "I got lucky. They missed me in the commotion."

Archer grimly looked up, his face blank. "It was a massacre."

"I know. The man in charge of the tactical unit has no explanation. He claims that none of his men opened fire. He's interviewed them one by one."

"I know what I saw Darryon. They killed people in cold blood. They lined them up and executed them. It was a bloodbath."

"I saw it too Arch." He reluctantly looked away. "We better keep this between us until we figure out exactly what's going on. The Senator agrees."

"How many were killed D?"

Darryon shook his head. He tugged at his lower lip with his top teeth.

"D. How many?"

"All of them."

Archer closed his eyes and pressed his head against the stretcher. "You mean me, you, the Senator, and the Lieutenant. We're the only ones that made it out of that field alive?"

Darryon clinched his teeth together. His cheeks tightening. He mumbled something under his breath. "I'm afraid so Arch. They were all killed. And… The Lieutenant didn't make it."

Archer sat up. A lone tear gently made its way down his cheek.

"Max?"

Darryon removed his phone from the clip at his side. "Knew you'd have to see it."

He handed Archer the phone. Max was lying in the field, blankly peering into the starry sky. Carson was cradled in his arms. A father protecting the only thing he had left that mattered.

More tears slipped from his eyes. He closed them, quickly wiping the evidence away.

Darryon understood. There weren't any winners. The rogue group had been revealed, but evil had ultimately triumphed. The battle never stops.

Archer angrily muttered, "How can the United States government get away with the murder of over one hundred civilians? That team needs to be held accountable."

Darryon placed his hand on Archer's shoulder. "Relax Arch, There's nothing we can do about it now. Let's live to fight another day. This is far from over."

Darryon grasped the top of the stretcher as the EMT came to place Archer in the back of the ambulance. Darryon lifted the top and stepped in. As the stretcher was placed, he sat down beside Archer. Neither spoke. The ambulance doors closed, and the moon's bloodstained rays disappeared behind them.

EPILOGUE

The man in the suit was escorted into the lavishly decorated room. His superior was waiting for him. The Superior handed the man a drink as he moved beside the open window. The view was breathtaking. They were thirty floors up, peering over the ocean on one side and the city on the other.

A news reporter yapped on a large television. The two men listened to the unfolding story.

The memorial service will be held tomorrow evening at Bryson's Cathedral downtown. It's for family only. Lieutenant Smith was killed in the line of duty attempting to stop an armed robbery at a convenience store.

In other news, it's been two days since the high body count found in the field belonging to highly respected lawyer, Morgan LeDiv. In a shocking twist, it's been discovered that he was the leader of a secret cult responsible for systematically murdering children every eight years.

Details are still being revealed, as bodies of missing children are being recovered from various mass graves in many of our nation's largest cities. This crime spree is estimated to have existed for several decades, and has possibly spanned three generations of LeDivs.

One hundred and thirty-four people were found dead in the field around the LeDiv home two days ago, including the bodies of his daughter, son-in-law, and grandson. FBI forensic scientists and special investigators claim that this is the most tragic case of mass suicide in our nation's history. In the tradition of Jim Jones now infamous Flavor Aid, the followers of this cult took their own lives in pursuit of a Utopian dream. Men, women, and children swallowed cyanide pills at the request of Mr. LeDiv.

Morgan LeDiv wasn't among the victims in the field, but he was found dead in his office the following morning. Investigators believe that he couldn't follow through with his own suicide, but then he couldn't live with the guilt of so many deaths. He died at approximately 8 a.m. yesterday morning from a self-inflicted gunshot wound. I'll be with you all day, as more of this heartbreaking story unfolds. I'm-"

The Superior muted the television and raised his glass into the air. The two men clanked them together.

"You did great work. Pulling that off was nothing short of a miracle. Inserting our field agents with their SWAT team was brilliant. Our agents disappeared after the sacrifice of the innocents."

"Thank you sir. Selling out that Trust was the right decision. They took the fall, and it removed all suspicion from Blanket Corp. The Feds will never know the Trust wasn't the rebel unit we made them out to be."

The Superior nodded, "You've earned much respect. You're cementing your position on the Concilium. Soon, you'll be accepted."

"Yes sir. I'm just sorry we lost her. Sandra was irreplaceable."

"A necessary sacrifice. It went even better than we'd hoped. She was a rising star, but you know what they say, those burn out just was quickly as they come in."

"It's just sad, everything she went through to get here, bypassing her husband to move up the ranks without his awareness. He had no idea that he was always passed over because his reclusive wife had replaced him."

"Sometimes life isn't fair. You'll learn that soon enough."

The man in the suit smiled. "I guess I will… It's a shame he wasn't willing to sacrifice the boy."

"Yes, if he'd have gone with the plan we offered eight years ago, we would never have had to approach her when the boy was born. You can't gain approval from the Concilium without paying the ultimate price."

The man in the suit was thoughtful. "Do you think they'll be a problem? The Senator? Darryon Myles? Archer Madsen?"

"No. I don't. We've made sure of that."

"Why'd you elect to let them live? I could have had them killed as well. It would have been easy."

"Too many questions would have been asked. Now, there's no one to ask those questions. A detective, a United States

Senator, and an FBI agent were all there. If they ask questions, they must betray the government they've sworn to protect. They won't do that. Besides, they've each got too much to lose by pressing harder. They know what we're capable of now."

"The government won't investigate?"

"No. They're too busy covering their own tracks. They've no idea of our involvement. You heard the news. They've already passed it off as another Jonestown. Our name hasn't even been mentioned, nor has a massacre.

The man in the suit peered out of the high window. "Did you recover the artifact?"

The Superior removed a painting from the wall and flipped a switch that was hidden behind it. A row of books slid sideways from his bookshelf. Behind the missing row was a safe. He unlocked the safe and removed a box ten inches wide and twelve inches long. He broke the seal, and gingerly held the ornamented relic for the man in the suit to view.

He peered over the side.

A large fragment of wood. Stained in blood.

"Cruor of crux cruces."

The Superior nodded, "Blood of the cross."

He slipped the lid closed and replaced it. "Another Trust has already committed to continue their research.

The man in the suit smiled. "One of many, we are one of many."

Dear Reader,

I would like to personally thank you for taking the time to read this book. If you enjoyed the book, please feel free to let me know. I love hearing from fans. I have also written other fiction and nonfiction Christian books that I'm sure you would enjoy as well. Thanks again for reading.

Sincerely,

jonathan r walton

Email me: jonathan@jrwbooks.com

Please learn more at www.jrwbooks.com

For inside information please join my book club at www.jrwbooks.com/insider

Follow me: Twitter @jrwbooks
www.facebook.com/jonathanwaltonauthor
www.goodreads.com/jonathanrwalton

www.ingramcontent.com/pod-product-compliance
Lightning Source LLC
Chambersburg PA
CBHW070135100426
42743CB00013B/2705